Teaching and Learning with ICT in the Primary School

This new edition of *Teaching and Learning with ICT in the Primary School* introduces practising and student teachers to the range of ways in which ICT can be used to support and extend teaching and learning opportunities in their classrooms. In an increasingly technological world, it offers teachers a toolset to help children develop openness to learning about new technologies and awareness of how to use them effectively for a wide range of purposes throughout their lives.

Fully updated and expanded, with new chapters reflecting the abundant changes in the field, this timely and engaging book offers practical guidance underpinned by the latest research and teaching. It is illustrated throughout with case studies and examples, and focuses on how technology-based practices can support the teaching of individual subjects, as well as a range of teaching and learning styles. Key topics covered include:

- ICT to enhance the teaching of literacy and numeracy
- effective technologies for teaching and learning science
- understanding visual literacy
- computer programming in the classroom
- developing assessment with technologies
- e-safety
- ICT in Modern Foreign Language teaching
- nurturing developing musicians through technology
- special educational needs and technology
- ICT in the Early Years
- using mobile technologies for authentic learning
- multi-play digital games and online virtual worlds.

Written for training primary teachers, as well as more experienced teachers and ICT co-ordinators looking for guidance on the latest innovative practice, *Teaching and Learning with ICT in the Primary School* offers advice and ideas for creative, engaging and successful teaching and learning.

Sarah Younie is MA Programme Leader and Principal Lecturer in Education Studies at De Montfort University, UK.

Marilyn Leask is Professor of Educational Knowledge Management at the University of Bedfordshire, UK.

Kevin Burden is Course Leader for the Advanced Certificate in Sustained Professional Development at the University of Hull, UK.

201460622

Teaching and Learning with ICT in the Primary School

Second edition

Edited by
**Sarah Younie, Marilyn Leask
and Kevin Burden**

Routledge
Taylor & Francis Group

LONDON AND NEW YORK

Second edition published 2015
by Routledge
2 Park Square, Milton Park, Abingdon, Oxon OX14 4RN

and by Routledge
711 Third Avenue, New York, NY 10017

Routledge is an imprint of the Taylor & Francis Group, an informa business

First edition published 2000 by Routledge

British Library Cataloguing in Publication Data
A catalogue record for this book is available from the British Library

Library of Congress Cataloging in Publication Data
Teaching and learning with ICT in the primary school/edited by Sarah
    Younie, Marilyn Leask, Kevin Burden. – 2nd edition.
    pages cm
    Previous edition edited by Marilyn Leask and John Meadows.
    Includes bibliographical references and index.
    1. Education, Elementary – Great Britain – Computer-assisted
    instruction. 2. Internet in education – Great Britain.
    3. Telecommunication in education – Great Britain. I. Younie, Sarah,
    1967– II. Leask, Marilyn, 1950– III. Burden, Kevin.
    LB1028.5.T382 2015
    372.133'40941 – dc23
    2014012535

ISBN: 978-1-138-78314-0 (hbk)
ISBN: 978-1-138-78315-7 (pbk)
ISBN: 978-1-315-76882-3 (ebk)

Typeset in Galliard and Helvetica Neue
by Florence Production Ltd, Stoodleigh, De

Printed and bound by CPI Group (UK) Ltd, Croydon, CR0 4YY

Contents

Illustrations

Figures

Tables

Tasks

Case studies

Notes on contributors

Jon Audain is a Senior Lecturer in Primary ICT and Music at the University of Winchester. Jon previously worked as a primary school teacher and as a county-based Advanced Skills Teacher. He also works as a freelance musician, Apple Distinguished Educator and conductor and has worked for both Hampshire and Portsmouth Music Services.

Daniel Ayres is a Senior Lecturer in Initial Teacher Education at the University of East London. Before joining UEL he taught children across the primary age range, at schools in the London Boroughs of Tower Hamlets, Newham and Redbridge.

Gary Beauchamp is a Professor of Education and Associate Dean (Research) in the School of Education at Cardiff Metropolitan University. He worked for many years as a primary school teacher, before moving into higher education where he has led undergraduate and postgraduate courses in education. His research interests focus on ICT in education, particularly the use of interactive technologies in learning and teaching.

Jeff Beaudry is an Associate Professor in the Department of Professional Education at the University of Southern Maine, USA. He teaches courses online and in blended media formats with webinars and video networks and has produced numerous Web 2.0 multimedia, such as podcasts and interactive videos, for the University of Southern Maine. His research interests include exploring issues relating to visual learning.

Gina Blackberry is a Research Fellow at the Australian Catholic University in Brisbane, Queensland. Prior to completing her doctorate, she worked as a high school teacher and journalist. Her research interests include teachers' professional learning, ICT integration and pupils' disengagement from reading.

Helen Boulton is a Reader in Technology Enhanced Learning and Teaching at Nottingham Trent University and a National Teaching Fellow. Helen's work is published nationally and internationally and she is Vice-Chair of the Association for Information Technology in Teacher Education.

Kevin Burden is a Senior Lecturer and Researcher in Augmented and Mobile Technologies at the University of Hull, where he is the Director for postgraduate teaching across the Faculty of Education. He was previously a school teacher and has worked in the higher education sector for fifteen years. Kevin is on the editorial board for MESH guides on ICT (see www.MESHguides.org).

Helen Caldwell is a Senior Lecturer in Teacher Education at the University of Northampton, where she is curriculum leader for Computing. Prior to this, she was an assistive technology adviser for Milton Keynes Council, a regional manager for the Open University Vital programme and an ICT coordinator across the 5–16 age range.

Patrick Carroll is an ICT Coordinator and British Council Ambassador at Shaw Wood Academy, Doncaster. Patrick has taught in Key Stage 2 for the last ten years and is continuing his research into the uses of augmented reality within education.

Nic Crowe is the Programme Leader for Contemporary Education at Brunel University. He is an experienced Education Practitioner with a background in technology and cultural studies. His research considers the educational opportunities offered by digital games.

Sara Flynn is a teacher undertaking a PhD at Brunel University with a focus on digital technologies and learning.

Marian Henry is a teacher, with a Doctorate in Education, a Masters in Media Studies and a Bachelor of Education, who has taught at all levels of education in Dublin, Ireland. She is committed to informing her classroom practice with relevant theory and research and is particularly interested in fostering children's critical literacy, learning and citizenship in the Digital Age.

Andrea Holloway is a Senior Lecturer at the University of Worcester, teaching maths and computing on both the undergraduate and postgraduate programmes at Worcester. She was also a Sandwell Leading Maths Teacher and Dudley Maths Coach, supporting colleagues in delivering the primary maths curriculum.

Gareth Honeyford is the Strategic Lead for Initial Teacher Training (Primary) for Essex Teacher Training. Previously he ran the PGCE Programme at the University of Northampton where he was also a teaching fellow and subject lead for ICT in Education. He has taught pupils from reception to post 16, worked for Becta and various governement-funded initiatives, including Excellence in Cities, City Learning Centres and Education Action Zones. He has written and researched many aspects of ICT including Web 2.0 and digital video.

Paul Hopkins has taught in a number of schools and universities in a range of roles. He now works at the University of Hull, leading the primary science PGCE programme. His research interests are around technology enhanced learning.

Christina Kuegel is a Senior Lecturer and Course Co-ordinator for Education Studies at the University of Bedfordshire, UK. She originally trained to be a teacher in the USA and then worked in the UK at a special school for children with severe learning difficulties before moving into higher education. Her research interests include technology to support children with severe learning difficulties and development of play skills for pupils with autism.

Marilyn Leask is a Professor in Educational Knowledge Management at the University of Bedfordshire, UK following a career as a teacher, assistant headteacher, local authority officer/public servant responsible for developing online communities of practice for local government and online resources for teacher training. Her research interests are in harnessing the power of digital technologies to support professional development (see for example MESH on www.MESHguides.org).

Aisling Leavy lectures in mathematics education. She has an interest in technology and mathematics, statistical thinking and reasoning, pre-service teachers' teacher education and children's mathematical thinking.

Damian Maher is a Lecturer in the School of Education at the University of Technology, Sydney (UTS) Australia. Damian teaches in the primary undergraduate programme with one of the subjects focusing on ICT in schools. He also conducts research in schools exploring how technologies can support learning.

Michael James Malone is a primary school teacher in Clarecastle National School and works as an adviser with the Professional Development Service for Teachers, Ireland. His research interests are the use of ICT for teaching and learning and e-learning environments.

Rory McGann lectures in ICT/Digital Learning at Mary Immaculate College, Limerick. Particular interests include ICT-related policy in education, programming in the primary classroom, online applications, digital content creation and ICT leadership.

David Morris is a Senior Lecturer in Initial Teacher Education at the University of East London. As a specialist ICT teacher, he has taught pupils in every year group from nursery through to Year 11.

John O'Shea worked as a primary school teacher prior to his appointment as Lecturer in Educational Methodology in Mary Immaculate College. His research interests are mathematical problem-solving, mathematics teacher education and teaching methodologies that support student understanding from a constructivist perspective.

Monika Pazio is currently reading for a PhD in Education at the University of Bedfordshire, specialising in technology application in early language learning. She also works as a Lecturer in Education Technology at the University of Greenwich. Prior to that she had taught languages across the different age groups and levels.

Mandy Peace is a Senior Lecturer at the University of Wales, Trinity Saint David, Swansea. Mandy initially taught in the primary sector, and later in university on a range of undergraduate and postgraduate programmes, with the emphasis on technology enhanced learning. Research interests include the effect innovative technologies have on learning and teaching.

Tim Pinto is the e-Safety Manager for Yorkshire and Humber Grid for Learning (YHGfL). He was previously a Head of RE in Cottingham School, near Hull and has worked extensively supporting the CPD of teachers in the use of IT, with particular reference to e-safety.

Christina Preston is a Professor of Education Innovation at the University of Bedfordshire. She founded the MirandaNet Fellowship in 1992, a professional organisation where educators share their knowledge and experience about the value of digital technologies in learning.

Marion Scott Baker has forty years' experience in Foundation Stage and Key Stage One in both the private and public sector, including twenty-four years in headship positions. Building on this experience and her qualifications in the field of Specific Learning Difficulties she has managed projects and delivered consultancy across the UK, USA and India. She now works as a freelance Educational Consultant in Berkshire.

Sharon Tonner is a Lecturer in Education at the University of Dundee where she teaches ICT to primary and secondary student teachers. Her research interests are the use of mobile technology in learning environments as well as the use of technology to enhance teaching and learning. Sharon is also an eTwinning ambassador for the British Council due to her extensive work in connecting schools around the world through the use of technology.

Gurmit Uppal is a part-time Senior Lecturer at the University of East London. She leads the primary computing and ICT element of the Primary PGCE Programme and has conducted research into the impact of PGCE ICT programmes in relation to trainee competence when using technology in the classroom.

Deb Woods is an Australian primary school teacher who has a demonstrated and recognised passion and commitment to using ICT to enhance learning and to improve the educational experiences and outcomes for students of all ages. Deb was the recipient of the 2013 Queensland College of Teachers' Excellence in Teaching Award.

Sarah Younie is a Principal Lecturer at De Montfort University and Programme Leader for the MA in Education Practice. Sarah is also a Senior Research Fellow at the University of Bedfordshire. She has experience of leading international and national research projects with ICT. She was Chair of the Association for Information Technology in Teacher Education and is the Lead Editor for MESH guides on ICT, see www.MESHguides.org.

Preface

> If we teach today as we taught yesterday,
> we rob our children of tomorrow
>   (Dewey, 1944, p. 167)*

You will be teaching young people, many of whom can expect to be alive in the twenty-second century. The changes they will face in their lifetime are unimaginable so it is essential that pupils are prepared to be resilient and adaptable. An openness to learning about new technologies and an awareness of how to use technologies effectively for a wide range of purposes are part of the toolset they will need to be effective citizens, family members and employees over their lifetime.

We would like to thank Paul Hopkins and Mandy Peace, authors in this book, who drew our attention to the saying above. During your career you can expect to find that education attracts a lot of attention from politicians and in some countries, there are no checks and balances to protect educators from politicians keen to create a headline by imposing change, but who have no long-term responsibility for educational outcomes in the way that educators do.

So depending on the context in which you work you may find you have to accommodate political objectives in your professional practice, which may be contrary to the professional values and knowledge about effective teaching outlined in this book.

There is, however, a worldwide collaboration of educators building an evidence base for practice that we are part of and which we hope will provide you with evidence-informed professional support during your teaching career – see MESH Guides on www.MESHguides.org. These guides will in due course present research that outlines the value to learners of the technology tools that are mentioned in this book. If you register to receive the MESH Guides newsletter you will be kept abreast of new developments.

We would like to thank all the authors who have shared their research and their ideas through this book. We hope you find the ideas stimulating and that your pupils learn more than they would do otherwise from your implementation of at least some of the suggestions outlined.

Marilyn Leask, Sarah Younie and Kevin Burden
March 2014

* Dewey, J. (1944) *Democracy and education.* New York: The Macmillan Company.

1 Learning in the Digital Age
Developing critical, creative and collaborative skills

Marian Henry

Introduction

There are many compelling reasons to use ICT in our classrooms, from motivating students and enhancing the learning experience to facilitating planning and the organisational elements of education. All of these are significant but the focus of this chapter is broader and deals with the complex relationship between education, changes in society and children's lives. It is inspired by doctoral research that asked: 'Is learning changing in the Digital Age?' where I looked at how society and children's lives were changing outside of school and how education was responding to this. The chapter is in four parts. The first is an overview of literature and research relating to the concept of the Digital Age and education. We will then look at how children are understood within the Digital Age, their informal engagement with ICT outside of school and how this relates to ICT use in school. The third section presents some of the key findings from the empirical research that I conducted with education stakeholders and children. One of the most prominent findings was the importance of fostering children's critical, creative and collaborative abilities, as these are seen as crucial in ensuring that children can flourish in the Digital Age. The final section explores how you can do this in your teaching.

At the end of this chapter, you will be able to:

- critically reflect on literature and research relating to the Digital Age, technology and education;
- think in a deeper way about the digital generation and how we understand their existing ICT skills;
- recognise the importance of fostering children's critical, creative and collaborative skills;
- develop strategies for putting this knowledge into practice in your classroom.

The Digital Age, technology and education

The term 'Digital Age' describes how society, culture, politics and economics are increasingly suffused with digital technologies. In this way, the term is closely linked to other popular concepts such as the 'Information Society' or 'Knowledge Society'. What these titles have in common is that they place information at the heart of contemporary life. In *Theories of the Information Society* (2006) Frank Webster highlights that 'information' has become a distinguishing feature in discussions of the modern world over the past thirty years. He points out that while theorists and scholars take many different views on how our world is changing and developing, there is some level of consensus about the salience of 'information' in contemporary society. The centrality of information is closely linked to the continuing development of digital technologies. It is against this backdrop of the growing significance of information, and the tools that promote and sustain it, that twenty-first century education finds itself.

Education and society have a dynamic and interactive relationship. This means that they influence each other. What happens in education has an impact on how society, the economy, culture and politics develop. The reverse is also true because changes in society, culture and politics have a bearing on what is expected of education. ICT in education is a clear example of this interactive relationship. The significant investment in, and promotion of, technology in education is not limited to particular schools, or districts or countries. At present, nearly every country in the world, regardless of geopolitical, economic or social circumstance, has implemented an educational technology strategy (Selwyn, 2011). Towards the late 1990s in many Western countries, the industry around information and communication was seen to have taken over from the more traditional manufacture of goods (Webster, 2006; Selwyn, 2011). This shift was perpetuated by the development of digital technologies and the use of these technologies in education was important in developing the information economy within a country. What is common among these policies is a close interlinking of education with employability, productivity and the wealth of the nation. Investing in ICT use in education is a core element in investing in the future of the national economy (Ball, 1999). This is especially important in a global competitive economy.

Not surprisingly, the attitudes to ICT in education policies tend to be enthusiastic. In Ireland, the promotion of ICT is enthused about and described as 'a pivotal force' in changing learning (DES, 2008a). However, to say that ICT changes or revolutionises learning is technological determinism – meaning that we see technology as causing change. ICT may play a role in change, but technologies can't have an impact without people to use them and to appropriate them into their lives. It is easy to get swept up in the idea that technology will or has changed learning, but this attitude is ultimately disempowering to teachers. As was found in a recent NESTA report 'Technology has no impact on its own – it all depends how we use it' (Stokes, 2012: 8). Technology is part of the story, but in order for ICT to have a positive impact on learning, we need teachers to be informed users of it in the classroom.

Children in the Digital Age

Good pedagogy builds from what children already know and understand. When it comes to the children we are now teaching do we see them as digital natives or digital novices? The concept of the 'digital native' was introduced by Marc Prensky to describe children who have spent their 'entire lives' surrounded by ICT. He claims that due to their interaction with ICT they 'think and process information fundamentally differently from their predecessors' – digital immigrants (2001: 1–2). While digital immigrants may learn and use new technologies they tend to retain their 'accent'. The problem for education then, according to Prensky, is that digital immigrant teachers are trying to teach digital natives in an outdated language. According to Prensky, these students are wired differently and learn differently, and therefore both the methodology and the content of our teaching need to change.

Don Tapscott writes about the 'digital generation' (1998). He distinguishes between how different technologies enable different forms of engagement – contrasting the 'television generation' with the 'net generation'. Television is a push medium where 'a relatively select band of producers (broadcasters) decide what content is to be created, create it and then *push* it down analogue or digital channels at audiences, which are assumed to consist of essentially passive recipients' (Naughton, 2012: 142). The net, on the other hand, is a pull medium where the consumer can actively choose what information they want to access and 'pull' it down to their computer, television, smartphone or tablet. This encourages more active, open and democratic engagement. Where television could be seen to dumb down its users, use of the net could be seen to raise their intelligence. What both Prensky and Tapscott do is equate technological change with enabling children to think, learn and engage with society in new and better ways. The job of education is to catch up with the children and use ICT more. While their assertions are popular, there are elements to their claims that are problematic.

Digital divides

The 'digital native' argument assumes that *all* children grow up surrounded by technologies, but to what extent can we be sure this is the case? Children have different levels of access to, and use of, ICT depending on their socioeconomic status, their parents' attitudes to the use of technology (Livingstone and Boville, 2001) and their own preferences (Livingstone and Helsper, 2007a). This gap between children's use of ICT is referred to as the 'digital divide' and giving children access to ICT in schools and libraries is presented as an answer to bridging the divide. This assumes that access to technology solves the problem, but research has shown that there are very few children who do not use the Internet, in contrast to adult populations, undermining an understanding of a clear divide between users and non-users. The digital divide in relation to children is less about *if* they use the ICT and more about *how* they use it. Livingstone and Helsper (2007b) argue that there is a 'continuum of digital inclusion'. This describes children's use of ICT from basic activities such as information-seeking to more sophisticated uses such as interactive and creative activities. They point out that there is not one digital divide but a number of divides that are based on gradations of inclusion. There can be divides between children of different age groups, genders and socioeconomic classes, and these divides are evolving over time (Tsatsou, 2011). Furthermore, research shows that children with access to computers and the Internet at home gain more from their experiences of ICT when they are in school and so instead of ameliorating a divide, schools may exacerbate it (Suss, 2001; Meneses and Mominó, 2010). Rather than assuming that all children are digital natives and 'wired differently', we need to think more rationally about the range of skills that children come to school with and how we can help each child develop and build on their existing skills.

Digital natives or digital novices?

Discussions of children engaging with media have long been polarised into those who champion it and those who are concerned about it, and this was the case long before digital technologies. David Buckingham (2000) writes that the media have frequently been blamed for provoking indiscipline and aggressive behaviour, for inflaming precocious sexuality and for destroying healthy social bonds. The online environment serves to reignite and add to the list of concerns that parents, adults and policymakers may have in relation to children (Buckingham, 2011). Technological prowess can be seen as bringing young people into the adult world and 'threatening the still powerful construction of childhood as a space of innocence and imagination' (Facer and Furlong, 2001: 452). There are many books that present childhood as being under attack from advertisers and marketers (Mayo and Nairn, 2009), online bullies and predators, and that the use of ICT encourages sedentary lifestyles, withdrawal, isolation, reduced attention spans, increased anxiety and pressure (Palmer, 2006). On the other hand, in recent years there has been a move towards seeing children as heterogeneous, non-passive, autonomous, diverse and versatile agents actively appropriating the Internet in meaningful contexts of their everyday lives (Meneses and Mominó, 2010). Buckingham argues that children are presented in oppositional ways depending on who is making the point and what they wish to gain from it on behalf of children. 'The campaigners who purport to be speaking on behalf of children and defending their interests tend to present them as powerless while the marketers, who might be seen as attempting to manipulate them, present them as powerful' (2011: 21). Within education the digital environment presents a number of challenges in relation to protecting children from inappropriate content, sharing of personal information, online bullying and predators. The reaction to this might be to encourage children to avoid the digital world or to be cynical of it. However, recent research found that in the context of young people's online activities opportunities and risks are related (Livingstone and Brake, 2010). This means that the more skilled users experience both more opportunities *and* more risks. Also risk does not necessarily lead to harm. Therefore, policies that seek to limit children's risk may also limit their opportunities. While we may wish to protect children from harm, the emphasis may be better placed on preparation – giving children the tools with which to navigate the digital realm safely, responsibly and in ways that are rewarding and enriching.

How we in education can prepare children to participate in a Digital Age was one of the main areas I explored through interviews with stakeholders in the education process and the findings of this are presented below. I also wanted to hear from children about their attitudes, opinions and experiences with digital media both at home and in school to see how this might inform how we can make meaningful changes in learning in the Digital Age.

Research findings

Stakeholders

The stakeholders in education who contributed to this discussion ranged from third level lecturers and an IBM executive to teachers and a parent. The stakeholders were asked questions about their view of the Digital Age and how education is and should be responding to it. They were enthusiastic about the opportunities that ICT could afford education, but also saw a number of challenges to how we use ICT in schools. While technical skills and the use of ICT were seen as important, a key element that emerged from the interviews was the bigger question of educating children to live and learn in a digital world both as children now and also as future workers and citizens. I have summarized three of the relevant findings and the suggested implications for education in the table below.

Table 1.1 Findings from interviews with stakeholders

Finding	*Implication for education*
The Digital Age is a time of information abundance but information is not the same as knowledge.	Children need to develop critical skills to access, analyse and evaluate digital texts so that they are informed and competent communicators.
The Digital Age represents opportunities to engage with and participate in society and culture in new ways.	Children need to develop their creative skills in relation to the full range of media so that they can find their voice and express themselves in the digital environment.
In the Digital Age, there is a great emphasis on the 'collective' both in relation to working with people in different geographic locations and pursuing interests and friendships.	Children need to learn to work collaboratively – sharing with, and learning from, others.

Children

When I spoke to children, it was clear that their engagement with ICT outside school is about more than an interaction with a machine. It was a prominent element of their interactions with their family, friends and the wider world. Children spoke fondly of family time spent watching movies or playing imaginative games with friends based on their favourite TV shows. Their taste in content was a significant motivator for ICT use and 'transmedia consumption'. This means that they follow content across media; if they like a TV show they will look up the website. It is this pursuit of interests that motivates children to broaden their ICT use and experience new media rather than a desire to improve their technical skills. Their taste was also central in asserting their identities. For example, to show how grown up they are, they might declare that a particular website was for babies. In this way, children using technology outside of school is not so much about technology – it is about culture (Buckingham, 2007).

There is a tendency in policies to acknowledge children's use of technology outside of school and see education improvement as being based on incorporating this into formal learning. For example, in Ireland one report stated that children engage in information learning in 'ingenious and impressive ways' and that we need to 'incorporate these new skills' (DES, 2008b) into the formal learning environment. This may not be as easy at it first appears, however. In my own research with children, they saw ICT in school as being different to at home. Home use was characterised by fun, freedom and autonomy while in school they spoke of using the Internet to look up information but only being allowed some freedom when their "work" was done. In the Irish context, these findings were verified by both the PISA 2009 (Cosgrove *et al.*, 2011) and EU Kidsonline (O'Neill *et al.*, 2011) reports that showed very little overlap between children's use of ICT in school and at home. Furthermore, studies such as Livingstone *et al.* (2005) indicate that children's everyday interactions with technology are not necessarily ingenious and innovative; rather they are relatively banal and focused mostly on information retrieval, communicating with friends and general entertainment.

The combination of the conclusions of the literature and research and the findings from the stakeholders and children indicate that the world outside of school is changing, both with respect to children's lives now and also in relation to their employment and social participation in the future. ICT represents ways to enhance our existing pedagogies and it also represents new lessons for children to learn. Rather than hoping that their home skills will seamlessly transition to the school environment, we should begin from children's existing knowledge and skills and where possible interests. The stakeholders felt that using technology to enhance curricular areas and develop technical skills was important but not enough. Children also need to be taught to be critical, creative and collaborative learners in order to be prepared to participate in the Digital Age. The final section explores each of these skills and outlines some tips for how you can foster them with the children in your classroom.

Fostering critical, creative and collaborative skills

Critical skills

ICT is often presented as a 'tool' for learning – a technology. What we have to remember is that these are *information* and *communication* technologies. These technologies shape how we access and share information and how we communicate. As such, they are more than simply tools; they are *media*. As David Buckingham writes, media do not ". . . offer a transparent window on the world. . . . media *intervene*: they provide us with selective versions of the world, rather than direct access to it" (2003: 3). When we interact with media – from websites and YouTube to newspapers and books – we are not looking through a transparent lens; the information has been selected and edited. The information has been *mediated*. As children navigate the World Wide Web they are interacting with 'digital texts'. Enabling them to interpret and create meaning in relation to these digital texts is closely related to the teaching of literacy and the following sections essentially are about how we can apply the deep engagement with text that you are encouraged to have in relation to books and print and to apply it to the full range of digital media.

Children need to learn with and through technology, but they also need learn *about* ICT. This enables them to develop the critical, higher-order thinking skills to engage with the full range of media they encounter both in school and at home. The extent to which they are encouraged to develop these critical skills through using media as a teaching aid – i.e., using a website about animals in a science lesson – is questionable. This is because when media are an aid to learning, the focus is on the animal content as opposed to developing the child's understanding of who made the website, who funds its development, how certain animals or issues are presented, etc. Learning about digital media develops critical skills because children are encouraged to question and make judgements about the quality and trustworthiness of the information they are accessing. In this way they are learning how to be discerning and judicious digital media users. While children may come to school with confidence and competence in using technologies, they do not necessarily come with fully developed analytic and evaluative skills. In an era where there is an abundance of information, one of the most important things we can do in education is develop these critical skills.

A good way for children to learn to be critical is through small group interaction with a teacher guiding the process. Reflecting on her own experiences of fostering critical literacy in primary school pupils, Swain reflects 'I would argue that in order for pupils to adopt critical perspectives independently, they first need opportunities to explore this with an experienced reader, so that they can understand the principles involved.' (2010: 135). In relation to still images, moving images, sounds and websites children can be asked to discuss the authorial intent, to develop an alternative perspective, or to read against the given interpretation. The discussion should be open-ended and while the teacher can lead the discussion, it is best if the children discuss the topic without feeling that the teacher has an ultimate 'right answer' in mind. The teacher's questioning style is therefore very important. Questions should be open and begin with statements such as 'I wonder why the author said . . .' Space needs to be made for deliberation and discussion. The challenge for you as a teacher is that you have to have some sense of where the discussion may go, but at the same time, if you steer it in that direction, you are stopping the children from having their own authentic reactions. Through critical discussion, children learn to listen to their own interpretations and they also learn to listen to others.

Content creation

We would never teach children to read but not to write. Teaching children to 'write' across a range of digital media, is an integral part of helping them to learn in a Digital Age. It is important for a number of reasons. First, creating their own content enables them to see themselves as creators of content and not just consumers. Creating content in the form of a digital video, a photograph with a caption or contributing to a class wiki is empowering for children as it lets them be in control of the production process. It gives them a sense of agency also as they can represent their views, experiences, concerns and interests. In essence, giving children the opportunity to create content is about encouraging them to find their voice in the Digital Age. I have worked with children creating short movies and there is a tendency for groups of boys to want to make extended fight scenes with zombies and ninjas. My role as their educator is not to pass judgement on their taste or interests, rather I can help them define the narrative and tell the story in a way that makes sense to the audience.

How do I enable children to learn critically and creatively?

When you want to foster children's critical and creative abilities in relation to their use of ICT there are two key things to remember. The first is that critical and creative activities are closely related. As children analyse digital texts, it helps them understand the choices they make when creating their own digital texts. Similarly, when children are creating content, they learn about how to communicate with their audience and about the vast range of choices made by producers of content they enjoy. Second, developing critical and creative abilities is not about having a body of information you want children to learn. Nor is it about a list of skills or tasks you want them to complete. It is about developing their undertanding. We want children to understand the digital world, how it works and how they can engage with it in ways that are rewarding and fulfilling for them. For this, you want them to develop understanding of four key concepts – production, language, representation and audience (Buckingham, 2003). Each of these concepts is described below and strategies that you can use are outlined.

Task 1.1 Creating a class blog (see also Chapter 3)

Creating a class blog is a large-scale and ongoing task. It will develop as you and the children learn more and add and take from the content they present. The emphasis here is on the process of working critically, creatively and collaboratively. Encouraging the children to reflect on their work and to improve it is an important part of the process. Over time, you want to ensure that you are addressing each of the four concepts. Also the critical and creative processes do not need to be limited to the class blog or Internet, they can also be developed in relation to other curricular areas such as visual arts, music and civic and ethical education.

Production

Studying production with children involves helping them to understand that there are many interests at stake in media production such as understanding the role of public service broadcasters, private companies, the use of advertising and media regulation.

Critical

- Look at other class blogs or children's websites and ask the children 'Who made this?', 'Why did they make it?', 'What information do they want the reader to gain?', 'Have they left out any information?', 'Why would they do that?'
- You can also get the children to see if there are any advertisements. They could discuss why this is and how the ads are chosen for the medium or content.

Creative

- When you begin to create a class blog with the children, encourage them to think about what their key message(s) are, how much information they want to communicate and what the best way is to communicate it. As children discuss their choices and reasons for these, you can ancourage them to reflect on the choices made by other producers of media. Children should also have plenty of time to edit and rework their ideas over time.

Language

Different media and different genres use different forms of language. Each language has its own codes and conventions. For example, a television programme makes use of certain conventions in relation to the opening credits, the types of camera shots, or music used. A soap opera will have slightly different codes and conventions to a sitcom or current affairs programme.

Critical

- In the case of a class blog, the languages we have are print, sound, still images and moving images. Children can decide what is best for the information they want to impart.

- Encourage the children to look carefully at other blogs and at the images or text used.

Creative

- Children also need to decide if they want the content to be funny, serious, emotive, etc., and how different modes of communication may help this.
- They can choose fonts and colours and discuss their choices.

Representation

Media products invite us to see the world in particular ways and not others. Studying representation may prompt questions about postive or negative images, bias, stereotyping and realism. The children could be asked how a blog depicts the topics that are shown. How are the female/male, young/old, good/bad characters portrayed?

Critical

- Compare two versions of the same story.

Creative

- When children have some experience of creating digital content, you can ask them to represent it for two different audiences. This helps them to think about how different people have different perspectives. Media content is not a 'transparent window on the world'.
- Ask children to tell a well-known fairy tale from the perspective of another character.

Audiences

Studying audiences means looking at how audiences are targeted and addressed.

Critical

- Children can discuss what they think the target audiences for different websites are. Would they choose to look at this website? What do they think of the content and who it is aimed at? Advertising is also relevant for discussion in relation to audiences.
- Considering audience also involves reflecting on one's own media use, habits and patterns of use in everyday life. What or who influences their choice of media? What do they really enjoy, or not enjoy? How do they find out about new content – websites, films, television shows?

Creative

- Creating content for two different audiences (as above).

Collaborative learning

The critical and creative ideas above require that children work well together. It is important as teachers that we don't assume that children can collaborate. Group work, even for adults, can be challenging. Therefore, as part of your planning, you will need to have some strategies to help the children to work together, such as assigning clear roles. Learning to collaborate is about more than just working with others: it is about seeing others as a source of knowledge, as people we can learn from and also as the sum of the parts being greater than each individual (Poore, 2011).

One of the key elements of Web 2.0 is the idea of many people working together to create something. A good example of this is Wikipedia. Children need to be taught and guided through content creation using digital tools. Creating a class wiki, or engaging with social media through a service such as Edmodo, can give the opportunity to discuss and discover the advantages and disadvantages of communicating through these media. In this way children learn how to share information in a responsible way. It may also be upsetting for children if someone edits or changes what they have written on a class wiki but this provides an opportunity to introduce the idea that even experienced authors produce many drafts before their work is ready for publication. Working on collaborative projects can be challenging, but these are important lessons for children to learn as they are relevant to the Digital Age. Teaching and reflecting on these challenges with children is valuable in enabling them to participate in the digital environment.

Summary and key points

The overall aim of this chapter was to broaden your understanding of learning with and about ICT. It is important to teach children about, with and through ICT not simply because it 'enchants the disenchanted' child or because it makes learning 'more fun' (even though these are important), but because the children we teach live in an age where ICT is a core element of how we learn, work, play and connect with and contribute to society. The sections above challenge some of the 'common sense' attitudes to the use of ICT in education. The aim is not to undermine the use of ICT or to say that it is not necessary or relevant. My aim is to inspire a deeper and more critical perspective on the role of ICT within our society and how we can enable children to use ICT within their learning.

In the empirical research with stakeholders in education it was felt that developing children's technical skills is not enough for education to do; we must also prepare children to flourish in this new information and communication environment. This means giving them the opportunity to develop critical, creative and collaborative skills. I outlined why and how these skills can be fostered in the primary classroom, and hope that you will be inspired to incorporate these suggestions into your teaching.

If you are a student teacher check which requirements for your course you have addressed through this chapter.

Further reading

Bazalgette, C. (ed.) (2010) *Teaching media in primary schools.* London: Sage.
 This is a great book about how to teach children about media in primary schools. It has chapters relating to research and lesson plans.

Buckingham, D. (2007) *Beyond technology: Children's learning in the age of digital culture.* Cambridge: Polity.
> This book is a good critical reading of the use of ICT in education and how it relates to children's lives.

Selwyn, N. (2011) *Schools and schooling in the Digital Age: A critical analysis.* Oxon: Routledge.
> This book explores in a deep way the use of technology in education.

Webster, F. (2006) *Theories of the Information Society* (3rd edn). Oxon: Routledge.
> Webster gives a great insight into the most prominent theories of the Information Society. It is a great way of learning about some of the main theories.

Additional resources and websites

EU Kidsonline official website. This study is across Europe and is about enhancing our knowledge of European children's use, risk and safety online.
www2.lse.ac.uk/media@lse/research/EUKidsOnline/Home.aspx
BBC. Report on Internet literacy by the BBC in 2012:
http://downloads.bbc.co.uk/learning/learningoverview/bbcmedialiteracy_26072012.pdf

References

Ball, S.J. (1999) 'Learning and the Economy: A "policy sociology" perspective'. *Cambridge Journal of Education*, 29(2): 195–206.

Buckingham, D. (2000) *After the death of childhood: Growing up in the age of electronic media.* Cambridge: Polity.

Buckingham, D. (2003) *Media education: Literacy, learning and contemporary culture.* Cambridge: Polity.

Buckingham, D. (2007) *Beyond technology: Children's learning in the age of digital culture.* Cambridge: Polity.

Buckingham, D. (2011) *The material child: Growing up in consumer culture.* Cambridge: Polity.

Cosgrove, J., Perkins, R., Moran, G. and Shiel, G. (2011) *Digital reading literacy in the OECD Programme for International Student Assessment (PISA 2009): Summary of results for Ireland.* Educational Research Centre, St Patrick's College. Available online at: www.erc.ie/documents/p09digital_reading_literacy_summary.pdf. Accessed on 15 August 2011.

Department of Education and Science (2008a) *Investing effectively in information and communications technology in schools 2008–2013: The report of the Minister's Strategy Group.* Dublin: Stationery Office.

Department of Education and Science (2008b) *ICT in schools: Inspectorate evaluation studies.* Dublin: Stationery Office.

Facer, K. and Furlong, R. (2001) 'Beyond the myth of the "Cyberkid": Young people at the margins of the Information Revolution'. *Journal of Youth Studies*, 4(4): 451–69.

Livingstone, S., Bober, M. and Helsper, E. (2005) 'Active participation or just more information?' *Information, Communication & Society*, 8(3): 287–314.

Livingstone, S. and Boville, M. (eds) (2001) *Children and their changing media environment: A European comparative study.* London: LEA.

Livingstone, S. and Brake, D.R. (2010) 'On the rapid rise of social networking sites: New findings and policy implications'. *Children & Society*, 24: 75–83.

Livingstone, S. and Helsper, E.J. (2007a) 'Taking risks when communicating on the Internet: The role of offline social-psychological factors in young people's vulnerability to online risks'. *Information, Communication and Society*, 10(5): 619–44.

Livingstone, S. and Helsper, E.J. (2007b) 'Gradations in digital inclusion: Children, young people and the digital divide'. *New Media and Society*, 9(4): 671–96.

Mayo, E. and Nairn, A. (2009) *Consumer kids: How big business is grooming our children for profit.* London: Constable.

Meneses, J. and Mominó, J.M. (2010) 'Putting digital literacy in practice: How schools contribute to digital inclusion in the network society'. *The Information Society*, 26: 197–208.

Naughton, J. (2012) *From Gutenberg to Zuckerberg: What you really need to know about the Internet.* London: Quercus.

O'Neill, B., Grehan, S. and Ólafsson, K. (2011) *Risks and safety for children on the internet: The Ireland report.* LSE, London: EU Kids Online.

Palmer, S. (2006) *Toxic childhood: How the modern world is damaging our children and what we can do about it.* London: Orion.

Poore, M. (2011) 'Digital literacy: Human flourishing and collective intelligence in a knowledge society'. *Literacy Learning: The Middle Years*, 19(2): 20–6.

Prensky, M. (2001) 'Digital Natives, Digital Immigrants'. *On the Horizon*, 9(5). Available online at www.marcprensky.com/writing. Accessed on 18 May 2013.

Selwyn, N. (2011) *Schools and schooling in the Digital Age: A critical analysis.* Oxon: Routledge.

Stokes, K. (2012) 'Decoding learning: The proof, promise and potential of digital education'. *Education Journal*, 149: 8–12.

Suss, D. (2001) 'Computers and the Internet in school: Closing the knowledge gap?'. In S. Livingstone and M. Bovill (eds) *Children and their changing media environment: A European comparative study.* London: LEA.

Swain, C. (2010) '"It looked like one thing but when we went in more depth, it turned out to be completely different": Reflections on the discourse of guided reading and its role in fostering critical response to magazines'. *Literacy*, 44(3): 131–6.

Tapscott, D. (1998) *Growing up digital: The rise of the net generation.* New York: McGraw Hill.

Tsatsou, P. (2011) 'Digital divides revisited: What is new about divides and their research?' *Media, Culture & Society*, 33(2): 317–31.

Webster, F. (2006) *Theories of the Information Society* (3rd edn). Oxon: Routledge.

2 Digital story telling

Helen Boulton

Introduction

Story telling is an important aspect of our lives, whether it is informal among family and friends, bringing a sense of coherence to our lives, fiction or non-fiction, or formal within our school curriculum and our working lives. Developing the creativity of children is an essential aspect of both formal and informal development. Barrett (2006) aligns digital story telling with student-centred learning strategies: student engagement, reflection for deep learning, project-based learning, and the effective integration of technology into learning, while Robin (2008) focuses on active learning.

With respect to terminology, Ohler (2007, viii) argues that story telling comes first, digital second and supports a change in terminology to 'story digitalising'; an argument many primary teachers would support. Sadik (2008: 480) describes digital story telling as 'a simple but powerful method to help students to make sense of the complex and unordered world of experience by crafting story lines', and Skinner and Hagood (2008: 12) as 'an opportunity for children and adolescents to design multimodal narratives that represent and reflect upon their lives and interests'. As a teacher it is therefore essential you plan for the development of story telling with your pupils and then consider which technologies might support your pupils. Try not to let the technology distract from the story.

This chapter focuses on digital story telling through the lens of the teacher facilitating their pupils to create digital stories. However, you may also want to consider creating your own digital stories to use in class to help to explain difficult concepts, facilitate discussion and engage pupils in the content. This chapter will start by examining how we can teach story telling in the primary classroom and then examines the range of technology that might be utilised to enhance the telling of the story. Case study examples of how teachers have incorporated digital story telling into their classrooms at two primary schools are shared. We will now look at the objectives for this chapter.

Objectives

At the end of this chapter you should be able to:

- state what digital story telling means in the primary classroom;
- plan for digital story telling in your classroom, drawing on appropriate pedagogy;
- explain a range of technologies associated with digital story telling;
- consider how you might assess digital story telling.

What does story mean in the primary classroom?

'A story has a beginning, a middle, and a cleanly wrapped-up ending' (Alexander and Levine, 2008: 20), but with new technologies stories may not follow this formula, indeed new technologies enable the primary classroom to facilitate digital story telling including hyperlinks, different media, different paths to follow in the story and may include the participation of others from across the globe in writing the story.

In creating a digital story pupils will develop a range of skills in researching, using technologies and developing storyboards to organise and construct their story or narrative (Banaszewski, 2005). You might also want to extend the activity to include self or peer assessment, thus providing opportunities for your pupils to critique their own work or the work of others.

Robin (2008) introduces three distinct types of stories: 'personal narratives', 'stories that inform or instruct' and 'stories that examine historical events', while Sadik (2008: 287) focuses on 'authentic learning tasks using digital storytelling'. Ohler (2008) talks of pupils being encouraged to engage emotionally and give their viewpoint, possibly through a news report of a day at school, or a field trip.

Digital story telling links to the school curriculum through 'speaking and listening'. Robin (2008: 220) describes digital story telling as 'a powerful teaching and learning tool that engages both teachers and their students'.

Task 2.1 Introducing digital story telling into your classroom

Having had an introduction to story telling, consider the key aspects of pedagogy you will need to consider when preparing to introduce digital story telling to your classroom. Write down the key aspects of pedagogy and then consider how these will need to be considered in relation to digital story telling. Think about the changes you may need to make to the arrangement of your classroom and what you will need to consider about the children in your class. Then think about the technology aspect of digital story telling. Consider what you have access to in terms of technology, what technologies your class know how to use, or could learn to use through their digital stories. Make a list of the technologies alongside your pedagogy. Keep these in front of you while you read the rest of this chapter and add your reflections to them as you develop your knowledge and understanding of digital story telling and how you could use it in your classroom.

Pedagogy

Story telling can engage reluctant learners and those who might find story telling using their own drawings or handwriting challenging. The BBC (www.bbc.co.uk) defines digital story telling as 250 words, a dozen or so pictures and two minutes in length. They align the need for definition to that of poetry, requiring constraints to define the form, for example a haiku is a poem written using 17 syllables, and the 14 lines of a sonnet are written in iambic pentameter. However, there are no specific rules for story telling so you can create your own – you may want to create rules with your class through a 'brain storming' activity.

You will need to start by identifying the learning outcomes for the project. You should refer to Bloom *et al.*'s (1956) Taxonomy when writing learning outcomes. You will also want to consider the elements of literacy that you are going to develop and include a learning outcome relating to the development of the use of technology. An excellent example of integrating literacy can be seen in the Eureka School case study later in this chapter. You will need to set clear goals for your pupils to achieve. You might want to link the goals to timings to ensure the project completes on time, and you may want to link each goal to assessment criteria. Remember to build in formative assessment. If this is going to be a project over several lessons you may want to devise a checklist to help your pupils to see how they are moving forward and so that you can ensure deadlines are met. Remember to build in sufficient time for the end phase of the digital story; adding titles, music and transitions develops creativity in the classroom but needs careful time management. At this planning stage consider your pupils and how they learn. Digital story telling can be a good way to encompass learning styles. When you are planning your digital story telling project try to consider how you might incorporate Gardner's Multiple Intelligences (1999) such as kinaesthetic, interpersonal, intrapersonal, linguistic, visual-spatial, naturalistic and rhythmic.

Digital stories can be made in groups or individually; therefore you will need to decide whether your class will work as a group or individually. When groups are working together to construct a story you are facilitating them in constructing knowledge in a social context, known as a constructivist approach to learning, as well as fostering active learning (Sadik, 2008). Working as a group can enhance pupils' experience of writing the story and can help to develop literacy skills to a higher level. Désilets and Paquet (2005) discuss a collaborative group story telling project using a wiki, setting out the experience in sessions in order that other teachers can follow the same process. Their findings indicate that allowing groups to self-organise can be more beneficial. Within groups the more computer literate are able to help those who are less literate.

The next stage will be how to introduce digital story telling into the classroom (Weis *et al.*, 2002). How you do this will depend on how much story telling your class has already completed and their ability to use associated hardware and software. You might want groups to brainstorm possible stories if they are going to be working in groups; you might want to invite in a professional story teller to share some stories to help individuals to explore their own creativity in story writing (an example can be seen in the Whitemoor Academy (Case study 2.2 below)); or you may have finished a curriculum topic and want the stories to reflect an element of the topic.

You will need to decide early on what type of 'digital' story you want your pupils to complete. This may be based on their age or knowledge of using technologies; for example, you may want to start with an audio digital story using digital voice-recording hardware, or appropriate software such as audacity (www.audacity.com) pre-installed on class computers, or tablet recording apps, before moving them to video cameras, etc. Whatever you decide to use, you will need to check that it is working and plan for charging time so that you don't run out of power at a crucial stage. You will find more information on hardware and software later in this chapter.

An example of how digital stories can be introduced into the classroom is given in Case study 2.1.

Case study 2.1 Digital story telling at Eureka Primary School with Years 4 and 5

This case study focuses on one of many stimulating ways digital story telling is utilised at Eureka Primary School, Midway, Derbyshire (see Figure 2.1). This is a smaller than average primary school with a larger then average number of children with special needs, disabilities and English as a second language. The school has been using digital story telling in various ways to develop literacy and phonics for a number of years. Various software is used to enhance digital stories such as Flip Flaps for creating storyboards, animation software, KerPoof, Scratch and the school's virtual learning platform. Teachers encourage the pupils to choose which technologies to use in their digital story telling and when needed the teachers show pupils how to use the different technologies, gradually building computing skills. In this case study the use of Myst, a graphic adventure video game, provides a focus for digital story telling. Myst puts the player in the role of a 'stranger' who uses a special book to travel to the island of Myst; as images unfold on the screen pupils are encouraged by their teacher to explore their imaginations and develop creativity while writing their stories. At the start of the project, which lasts several weeks, the pupils are encouraged to create a character profile of their stranger, including aspects such as appearance, behaviour, thoughts, what others think of their character and their likes and dislikes.

At the start of the lesson the teacher displays Myst on a whiteboard with a mixed group of Years 4 and 5 and facilitates the class, who take it in turns to say which way the stranger should go. Next to the whiteboard is a flipchart with key literacy terms that are being developed through the project: nouns, adjectives, verbs, adverbs, similes, metaphors, personification, alliteration and onomatopoeia. These are referred to through-out the activities. The teacher initially leads each session to review what has happened previously in the digital story, drawing out key literacy terms that the pupils have learned and encouraging them to use them in their digital stories. The teacher encourages the pupils to engage with the video game through using their senses to think how the stranger feels in different areas of the island and asking them to write their feelings in their books using specific aspects of literacy that are being learned. Each segment of film lasts only a couple of minutes and is then paused while the pupils use this stimuli to write more on their own digital story, applying different aspects of literacy. Pupils are then encouraged to share what they have written both in pairs and with the whole group, receiving praise and encouragement throughout by their teacher, thus receiving formative feedback to develop their sentences further.

Each lesson moves the pupils further forward in their development of key literacy terms and also moves them forward in discovering different aspects of Myst Island, through which they are developing their own digital stories. The engagement, enjoyment, development of literacy and development of creativity through stimulating imaginations make it exciting for pupils and impacts on their developing stories and engagement in the lessons. Differentiation is observed through the development of their stories and ways in which pupils are able to share progress with each other, supporting peers through feedback and thus developing their self-esteem and confidence.

Generally storyboards are introduced early into the process; how much time is given to this process will depend on your class's previous experience. A storyboard can consist

Figure 2.1 Pupils from Eureka Primary School developing their digital story.

of a piece of paper split into boxes; pupils organise ideas into a coherent story then write into each box the order of the story. With digital story telling you would also ask pupils to include information on which technologies they will be using, etc. You may need to explain how to use different hardware or software, although most pupils will have developed knowledge of a range of these informally at home and more formally through school. You may want to brainstorm a range of appropriate technologies and software and identify 'champions' for each one that other pupils can go to for help during the project. An example of a storyboard from the Whitemoor Academy case study can be seen in Figure 2.2.

As your pupils develop their digital story they will need to solve many problems, including those experienced when using technologies. This will develop your pupils' computational thinking and digital wisdom skills.

Task 2.2 e-Safety

e-Safety is an aspect of every teacher's role that has to be learned and embedded into practice. Take some time now to familiarise yourself with your school's policy. Find out whether you will need to send letters home to parents, and if so how early you will need to do this in relation to the start of the digital story telling activity. Research any sites you will use from the Internet for digital story telling. Look at the CEOP site (www.ceop.police.net) – what else can you learn from this site that will help you in preparing for the digital story telling activity?

Put this evidence in your PDP (Professional Development Portfolio) to show awareness of e-safety.

If you are going to use software that may expose your pupils to the Internet, or have plans to upload stories to YouTube or other social networks you will need to consider e-safety access and rules. In your planning ensure you are familiar with your school's e-safety policy; for further information, a good starting point is the Child Exploitation and Online Protection Centre (CEOP) (www.ceop.police.net) and its ThinkUKnow (www.thinkuknow.co.uk) site, or the e-safety resources produced by the Association of Information Technology in Teacher Education (www.itte.org.uk). (See also Chapter 19.)

You will also need to consider health and safety. For example how will the class be working, in groups or individually; how will you organise the classroom? You will need to consider trailing wires and the space the pupils will be working in. If you're going to be on a field trip when the digital story telling is going to take place you will need to ensure you have met all health and safety requirements for the trip, and consider how you will charge equipment, how it will be used on the trip and how you will back up any copies.

At this point consider the whole process of the activity and what additional preparation you will need to do such as creating a folder for the work to be stored, searching for appropriate images and sounds for your pupils to access, and ensuring there are sufficient microphones. Decide on the range of technologies your pupils will have access to; will they need any helpsheets, or video clips on how to use some of the technologies? (TeacherTube and YouTube have short video clips on many technologies that you might be able to utilise); remember to check access to video clips through your school's firewall.

Part of the preparation needs to focus on how you will assess. As with any task that is going to be assessed you need to have criteria that you must share with your pupils. You may want to award marks for different aspects such as the story elements of literacy, planning, artefacts created such as the storyboard, literacy skills, use of technology and overall presentation of content. Your consideration of literacy may include various literacies such as written, oral, cultural, information and visual. You will also want to make clear links to the curriculum the school follows and identify which aspects will be assessed. If the story has been developed by a group you may want to assess how each pupil worked within the team. Nicol and Macfarlane-Dick (2006) discuss the importance of formative assessment and its impact on development, progression and motivation. You may want to build in some peer and self-assessment formative feedback to help individuals/groups to develop their digital story at planned times during the project, such as during the development of the storyboard.

Finally, consider how pupils will share their final digital stories and with whom. For example, in the Eureka case study the digital stories were shared within the class and at Whitemoor Academy they were shared with a wider community of parents and other schools. Sharing stories will provide a sense of achievement and celebration.

You may want your pupils to use a blog (see Chapter 3) so they can reflect regularly on the development of their digital story, such as problems solved and new skills and knowledge developed, thus developing skills in criticality. Their blog could include how they would improve their digital story and what they will do next time they have this opportunity. You can use this information to plan future lessons, ensuring opportunities for your pupils to develop any identified weaknesses. You may want to give parents access to the blogs so they can provide support at home and share the experience.

What technology can I use?

There is a whole range of technology available to support digital story telling, some of which has already been mentioned, such as digital voice recorders and video cameras. It is not the intention to provide a definitive list of technologies because what you use will depend on your pupils and availability, and new technologies have become available since the publication of this book. There are websites that will provide suggestions for technology such as www.whiteboardblog.co.uk/2011/06/10-tools-for-digital-storytelling-in-class/.

When considering your pupils think about what they would benefit from using or what they have used before that would enhance the story. Remember to encourage your pupils to incorporate the technology they plan to use into the storyboard.

Technologies you may want to consider are: computer or tablet; scanner, camera or mobile technology such as phone or tablet with camera facility for creating images; microphone (this doesn't need to be expensive and your computer/tablet may have one built in); speakers/sound (again most computers/tablets have speakers built in); webcams; digital recorders; Flip cameras; Green Screen (these can be expensive, but you may well be able to borrow one locally); printer; tripods; range of software such as Audacity, video-editing software, Adobe and PowerPoint. Remember to consider pupils' level of digital literacy, which will impact on this activity – for example, can they create folders, manipulate text and images, upload files from flip cameras, edit to add titles, voice and sounds? Build in time to let pupils experiment and learn new technologies from each other. You might want to ask pupils to create simple clips of how to use key equipment and upload to your school Virtual Learning Environment (VLE) for others to follow, or reuse TeacherTube clips that explain the different technologies.

Web 2.0 technologies may also be used in digital story telling. For example, you may want to utilise a blog space as suggested above to tell a powerful story of their experience. If you have permissions, you may decide to upload the video stories your class have made to YouTube for wider sharing. Désilets and Paquet (2005: 1) found that being able to write and share stories with the general public can be a 'powerful incentive' to write; some primary schools use Twitter for pupils to tell a story with each pupil adding a 'tweet' and taking the story in different directions. You might also want to use an image-sharing website such as Flickr as a resource of images for your class to access, or to upload specific images that your class then uses as the basis for the story. Alternatively you may want to utilise a wiki, such as www.pbworks.co.uk or http://docs.google.com for groups to develop a story collaboratively (Désilets and Paquet, 2005), or KerPoof referred to earlier. You might also encourage your class to use Voicethread (www.voicethread.com) to create image slides then add audio to each slide; with this software others can add to the story so it has multiple voices.

If you feel overwhelmed with ideas of different technologies a useful place to start is with InAnimateAlice (www.inanimatealice.com). This site has an interactive story about Alice, that you can use as a starting point, and comes with a free-to-download education pack including links to the Primary National Curriculum, a starter activities booklet, resources and information for parents. Equally, you may want your class to create an audio story then upload this to your school's VLE or other Internet site to share their story as a podcast.

Finally, you will want to think about how your pupils will present their digital stories. Is this going to be a presentation just to you and their class, or more widely such as in Case study 2.2?

Task 2.3 Digital story telling – considering technologies

Consider how you might approach the range of Web 2.0 technologies outlined above with your class in their next story telling project. In starting this task you might want to reflect back on a story telling project you have either taught yourself or observed being taught. Think about whether this activity could have been enhanced through the use of Web 2.0 technologies, such as prompts or a starting point using Flickr with all of the children starting at the same point, then developing their own middle and ending. You might want to consider making a story of the children writing their stories using a Flip camera, or your mobile phone, and upload it to the school's VLE, school website, or YouTube so the class can show their family and friends.

Put your reflections on how you would approach digital story telling in your PDP folder to evidence developing practice.

Case study 2.2 Whitemoor Academy's use of digital story telling in the classroom

This case study focuses on a project with Year 5 pupils. Whitemoor Academy is a larger-than-average sized primary school with above average numbers of pupils from minority ethnic groups and who speak English as an additional language. Through a successful bid for external funding the school was able to buy in a project co-ordinator for their digital story project who had worked for the Broadway Cinema in Nottingham. The project, which was a week-long project on story telling, started with pupils watching a long sequence from the film 'War of the Worlds'. This was followed by various activities to stimulate creativity and story telling. For example, the pupils all thought about someone they might have lost during the 'war', either a fictional character or someone they knew, and were encouraged to bring in photos from home and create a 'missing person' poster. Each pupil wrote a diary event imagining they had lived through the first day of the war shown in the film sequence. In the next activity pupils were split into two groups – one group spent the day working on a short film with help from the co-ordinator with no talking and music chosen by the teacher. They then recorded their voices and were shown how to add this to the film they were making. In the film pupils were encouraged to use their imagination and act out what they thought might happen next in the 'War of the Worlds' film. The second group spent a day making a news story in groups of four: a reporter, an eyewitness to an event, an anchorman and a weather person. The group wrote the story, filmed it, then used green screen technology to film a weather forecast. The project co-ordinator again supported this activity, bringing in professional lighting and film cameras. The pupils then went through a similar project using the film 'I am Legend', which developed their creativity in describing landscapes, etc. Each pupil wrote a digital story using a storyboard (see Figure 2.2, for example) and incorporating specific aspects of literacy such as personification, first person and onomatopoeia. One pupil said it was their best literacy lesson ever and made learning literacy fun.

The films the pupils made were initially shown to the group, then the school. The films are also to be shown to parents at a special film event and the pupils have been

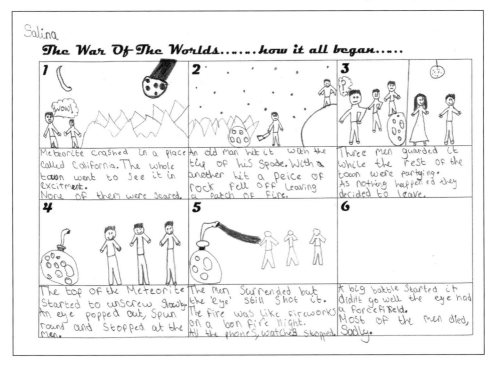

Salina

The War Of The Worlds.......how it all began.....

1 [wow!] Meteorite crashed in a place called California. The whole town went to see it in excitment. None of them were scared.

2 An old man hit it with the tip of his spade. With a another hit a peice of rock fell off leaving a patch of fire.

3 Three men guarded it while the rest of the town were partying. As nothing happened they decided to leave.

4 The top of the Meteorite started to unscrew slowly. An eye popped out, spun round and stopped at the men.

5 The men surrended but the 'eye' still shot it. The fire was like fireworks on a bon fire night. All the phones, watches stopped.

6 A big battle started it didit go well the eye had a force field. Most of the men died, Sadly.

Figure 2.2 Storyboard developed by a pupil at Whitemoor Primary School.

invited to broadway cinema, along with pupils from other schools involved in similar projects, to see their films on the big screen.

Task 2.4 Using film to stimulate digital story telling

Reflect on a film you have seen that you could utilise in teaching your pupils digital story telling. Think about the section of the film you might show to pupils and where you might end it to encourage your pupils to think creatively about the next part of the film. Consider the planning stages you will need to work through to turn this into a live project; what are the challenges you face? What artefacts will you need to create for your project?: think about a storyboard, poster, mind map, list of key literacy words, film observation sheet. Next consider which technologies and software are available for you to use for this project. Now plan the project in more detail, including a session plan with aims, objectives, differentiation and assessment criteria.

Put this evidence in your PDP to show how you will use literacy to develop a digital story using a range of technologies. If you are a student teacher, talk to your mentor about putting this project into practice.

Summary and key points

In this chapter we have explored what digital story telling means in the primary classroom and how you might use this in your professional practice. The digital aspect of story telling will change as new technologies are introduced. You have learned that the story can be the main element through which you introduce your class to new technologies, creative writing and literacy elements of the National Curriculum.

However you decide to teach digital story telling, remember to plan it carefully, consider the pedagogy, development of knowledge and technology effectively and creatively, then consider which tools will be the most appropriate, thus developing pupils' digital wisdom (Prensky, 2010).

If you are a student teacher check which requirements for your course you have addressed through this chapter.

Further reading

Ohler, J. (2007) *Digital storytelling in the classroom: New media pathways to literacy, learning, and creativity.* Newbury Park, CA: Corwin Press.

Additional resources and websites

www.cyanworlds.com/products/index.php. Myst, referred to in the Eureka Primary School case study, can be downloaded from this site.

www.dsaweb.org is the Center for Digital Storytelling and has further advice and support materials. Accessed on 8 April 2013.

www.iste.org/learn/computational-thinking is a useful site for continuing research into computational thinking introduced in this chapter.

www.kerpoof.com is owned and operated by Walt Disney and provides a 'place' for children in primary education to create digital stories and explore creativity.

www.teachmeet.org.uk explains the concept of Teachmeets and helps you to find your local Teachmeet organiser.

www.tes.co.uk/teaching-resource/Digital-Storytelling-tools-online-6176830/ includes a short video resource hosted by *Times Educational Supplement* showing a selection of great free resources that can be used in digital story telling – aimed at KS1 and 2. It includes information on sites that allow the creation of animation, comic strips or enhance story writing in some other way.

www.whiteboardblog.co.uk supports technology in the classroom. There is a section on technologies to support digital story telling that you may find of interest.

References

Alexander, B. and Levine, A. (2008) 'Web 2.0 storytelling: Emergence of a new genre'. *EDUCAUSE Review*, 43(6), 40–56.

Banaszewski, T.M. (2005) 'Digital storytelling: Supporting digital literacy in Grades 4–12'. Dissertation. Georgia Institute of Technology.

Barrett, H. (2006) 'Researching and evaluating digital storytelling as a deep learning tool'. In *Society for Information Technology & Teacher Education International Conference*, pp. 647–54.

Bloom, B.S., Engelhart, M.D., Frost, E.J., Hill, W.H. and Krathwohl, D.R. (1956). *Taxonomy of educational objectives: Handbook I, Cognitive domain*. New York: David McKay.

Désilets, A. and Paquet, S. (2005) *Wiki as a tool for web-based collaborative story telling in primary school: A case study.* EdMedia 2005, World Conference on Educational Multimedia, Hypermedia and Telecommunications. Montréal, Québec, Canada. 27 June–2 July 2005. NRC 48234.

Gardner, H. (1999) *Intelligence reframed: Multiple intelligences for the 21st century.* Basic Books (AZ).

Nicol, D.J. and Macfarlane-Dick, D. (2006) 'Formative assessment and self-regulated learning: A model and seven principles of good feedback practice'. *Studies in Higher Education*, 31(2): 199–218.

Ohler, J. (2008) *Digital storytelling in the classroom: New media pathways to literacy, learning, and creativity.* Newbury Park, CA: Corwin Press.

Prensky, M. (2010) *Teaching digital natives: Partnering for real learning.* Newbury Park, CA: Corwin Press.

Robin, B.R. (2008) 'Digital storytelling: A powerful technology tool for the 21st century classroom'. *Theory into Practice*, 47(3): 220–8.

Sadik, A. (2008) 'Digital storytelling: A meaningful technology-integrated approach for engaged student learning'. *Educational Technology Research and Development*, 56(4): 487–506.

Skinner, E. and Hagood, M.C. (2008) 'Developing literate identities with English language learners through digital storytelling'. *The Reading Matrix: An International Online Journal*, 8(2).

Weis, T.M., Benmayor, R., O'Leary, C. and Eynon, B. (2002) 'Digital technologies and pedagogies'. *Social Justice*, 29(4): 153–67.

3 Blogging to support digital literacy in schools and universities

Helen Caldwell and Gareth Honeyford

Being literate in a real-world sense means being able to read and write using the media forms of the day, whatever they may be . . . (and) literacy now requires being conversant with new forms of media as well as text, including sound, graphics, and moving images. In addition, it demands the ability to integrate these new media forms into a single narrative, or 'media collage', such as a web page, blog, or digital story.

(Jason Ohler, 2009)

Introduction

Literacy skills have always been important in schools and universities, but increasingly it is 'digital literacy' that is seen as vital to support the capability of our students to engage with, and have an impact on, our changing world. Collaborative forms of expression such as blogs and wikis, the proliferation of easy-to-use web and coding tools, and the growth of social networking are altering the way we interact with information and with each other, placing the emphasis on active dialogue and construction. If we are to help our students gain fluency in digital literacy, we need to harness these technologies and nurture the emergent learning communities they foster. This poses a challenge for educators (Feiertag and Berge, 2008; Churchill, 2009).

Blogs are a particularly powerful format in an educational context as they allow learners to define their own spaces and to populate them with words and media of their choosing. According to Freeman and Brett (2012), 'Blogging is characterized by an individual exploration of ideas of personal interest through frequent online posts, documenting ideas as they emerge over time.' Yet blogs can go even further than this by fostering ideas-sharing and enabling students to actively learn from their peers as well as from their teacher (Halic *et al.*, 2010). This combination adds a hugely valuable dimension, as Steve Wheeler suggests: 'Collaborative learning does not undermine or contradict personalised learning. It simply amplifies it.' (2013).

This chapter looks at using blogs to document learning from these two perspectives, the personal and the collaborative, drawing examples from student teachers at Northampton University and from primary pupils in Northamptonshire schools. In both settings, the role of blogs in supporting the cycle of sharing, implementing and evaluating practice is explored and discussed so that teachers can replicate and build on the emerging themes.

Objectives

By the end of this chapter you should be able to:

• identify some of the advantages of blogging for student teachers and for primary pupils;
• compare the blogging medium with other methods of recording progress;
• explore the use of a personal blog as a reflective journal;
• introduce a class blog in your primary school or organisation.

Blogging at Northampton University

Background

Mainstream initial teacher education at the University of Northampton offers routes to qualified teacher status (QTS) for Primary and Early Years at both undergraduate and postgraduate levels through a three-year BA QTS course and a one-year PGCE. Students are offered a balanced curriculum encompassing pedagogical and subject knowledge across a range of subjects, including computing and technology enhanced learning.

The ICT element of both the undergraduate and postgraduate routes has for several years been assessed via an ePortfolio of ideas based on a series of PowerPoint slides with links to related resources. In 2012, however, the e-portfolio was replaced with an online blogfolio in the belief that creating a blog not only provided good evidence of students' understanding and ability to use ICT, but developed a transferable skill that would enhance their digital presence when applying for jobs and when in post. We also thought it would give them a first-hand taste of the powerful motivation that can stem from writing about personally relevant topics for a live and responsive audience, rather than simply preparing work to submit to a tutor, and hoped it would inspire them to celebrate their future pupils' learning in a similar way.

In adopting the blog format, we were aware that digital literacy these days means being able to combine media across platforms and draw upon a range of tools to create digital artefacts of various kinds. The blogs offered our students the chance to embed such things as games, slideshows, photostories, online walls, comic strips, computing projects and videos, and reflect upon them in situ through a series of posts over time. In this way, the blogs grew into highly visual and interactive reflective journals.

The blogs also gave our students the option to share their work with an audience and to control their privacy settings. Some chose to keep their work private until it was finished; others shared ongoing work with a selected peer group. Most, however, went public from the start, allowing people to interact with the material and add comments as the blogs evolved. A key difference between the e-portfolios and the blogfolios, then, was the opportunity to view a range of work in progress, with both the student blogs and the tutors' own blogs modelling the medium's potential.

Precedents

Evidence of the efficacy of using blogs in an educational setting is plentiful and many researchers put forward compelling arguments for ways in which blogging can provide new learning opportunities in the higher education environment (Williams and Jacobs,

2004; Wheeler, 2010). They suggest that blogging can help build learning communities (Yang, 2009), encourage students to create and share content (Farmer, 2006), promote active collaboration and reflection (Fessakis, Tatsis, and Dimitracopoulou, 2008; Reupert and Dalgarno, 2011), increase ownership of learning (Farmer, Yeu and Brooks, 2008) and enable students to learn from reading each other's work (Ellison and Wu, 2008; Churchill, 2009). In post-secondary settings, Freeman and Brett (2012) found that key factors in harnessing a blog's potential as a communicative tool were frequency of writing, topic resonance with students' own interests and timeliness of entries. Working with foreign language students, Ducate and Lornicka (2008) also noted the positive impact of students being able to express themselves on self-selected topics. In the context of primary teacher education, students at Plymouth University reported that their writing skills improved as a result of their desire to write accurate and relevant content to a collaborative wiki (Wheeler & Wheeler, 2009), and Deng and Yuen's study of blogging for shared reflection by student teachers on placement concludes that they function well as reflective devices (2011). We were therefore confident that our blogging initiative for student teachers at the University of Northampton would reveal a number of benefits.

Introduction to blogging

Blogfolios were first introduced to Year 3 students, potentially the most challenging group as they were well used to the routine for the e-portfolio, and, as predicted, they were initially very reticent. In order to ease the transition, the similarities between the two approaches were highlighted, focusing particularly on the elements of commentary and reflection. The next group to be introduced to blogfolios were PGCE students, typically very busy and often mature, but with the benefit of not having a prior expectation of assessment items. Finally, the blogs were introduced to first and second year undergraduates. All students used their free university subscription to the Edublogs Pro tool. Naturally, there was a range of social networking expertise within each student cohort: a group of around twenty-five students would typically include one or two experienced bloggers, around half maintained an online presence through Twitter, and the majority were regular users of Facebook. It has been suggested that interaction between blogging software and other social media software can result in an enhanced communication environment (Kim, 2008), and it was certainly the case that many of our students found that tweeting and blogging went hand in hand.

A staged approach was taken to the introduction of the blogs, with some teaching time spent during the first session explaining the features of the Edublogs tool. The students were supported in setting up their blogs and writing a welcome post. There was an option to keep the blog private but students were encouraged to make them public so as to join in with the growing online community. ICT sessions over the following weeks covered themes such as programming, mobile technologies, control, data, information literacy and animation, with the weekly directed task being a related blogpost. A typical post would describe a student's personal exploration of a digital tool, reflect upon issues to consider when using it with pupils, suggest links to relevant sites and give examples of classroom resources. Additional blogging skills such as using widgets, creating a blogroll and embedding media were introduced gradually over the course of the module.

Additional support was provided by the class blog, which linked to all the student blogs, and by the tutors' personal blogs. The class blog served as a model, as a homepage with signposted resources, and as an advance organiser outlining the content and links for each week. Static pages on the class blog included blogging how-tos, tutors' screencasts and assignment guidance, all of which helped to scaffold students' learning beyond the face-to-face sessions.

Perhaps the most important feature of the class blog was the wiki page of links to the student blogs that enabled easy access for commenting by all and, ultimately, for marking by tutors. This changed the learning dynamics within the groups by giving students opportunities to see each other's work in progress and allow ongoing comments from tutors and students. There were many pingbacks to the tutor blogs, as the students referenced them in their own reflections, and between the student blogs as they used them as a medium for sharing teaching resources produced collaboratively in the sessions.

The blogs were graded using a marking rubric covering four main areas: 'context', 'coverage', 'content' and 'resources'. We'll use these themes to describe the student blogs.

Context

'Context' looked at students' choice of blog theme and layout, how effectively they used media, tools and features, the organisation and categorisation of posts and the management of comments. The Edublogs tool offers a choice of 137 themes, each with customisation options such as the chance to add header or background images and arrange a choice of widgets in the sidebar. Students were drawn to the ease with which images and media could be inserted and embedded, and many gave their blog a personal ambience through their choice of images, title and tagline, and by populating the sidebar with features such as their Twitter feed, an animated tag cloud or a visitor map. Within posts, they learned to upload images, video and documents, to add hyperlinks, and to embed an array of online tools such as Scratch games, Wordles, mind maps, animated slideshows, infographics and interactive message walls. These visual features combined to give individual blogs their own distinctive look and feel (see Figure 3.1).

Coverage

'Coverage' referred to each of the taught session topics and sought evidence of the twin themes of documenting the development of personal ICT skills and exploring ways of embedding ICT in the Primary Curriculum. We also looked for evidence of students' further browsing and reading through posts containing relevant discussion, links and related resources. Finding methods of capturing and sharing content created in the sessions by uploading to YouTube or Flickr, creating screencasts and snipping images became an integral part of the sessions, and it was clear that the act of publishing was itself a source of motivation. According to one student, 'There was more of a purpose for writing the blog as others can read it . . . we are able to share them and learn from each other's experiences.' Students began to bring work from other university modules into their blogs such as music compositions and digital science posters. Conversely, it was satisfying to see them apply their growing repertoire of ICT skills in other subjects, by using iPad comic-style apps to introduce a location in geography or a face-morphing app to create a Viking character in history, for example. As another student explains, 'It is beneficial to share resources with each other, and as student teachers, supporting each other is important . . . the best thing about blogging is the end result!'

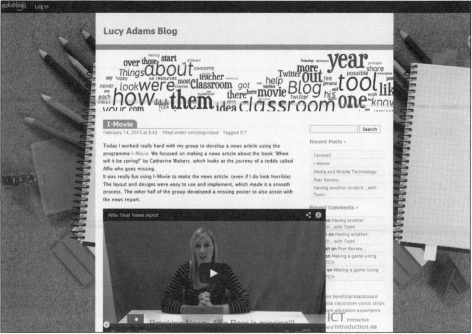

Figure 3.1 Examples of student teachers' blogs.

3.1a Rosie's Blog: PGCE Primary ICT http://mypad.northampton.ac.uk/12403257/
3.1b Lucy Adams' Blog http://mypad.northampton.ac.uk/12409084/2013/02/14/i-movie/

Content

Within the marking rubric, the theme of 'content' looked for a fluent commentary with evidence of original ideas. In a 'good' set of posts description of personal skills development was threaded with lively discussion around such issues as pedagogy, differentiation, classroom organisation, assessment and e-safety. Students learned through experience that blog writing is a genre with its own conventions and techniques; concise, clear writing is more important than the ability to sustain a long argument in an essay. Some were initially uncertain of what tone and voice to adopt, but became bolder over time through reading each other's posts, and a strong vein of individual expression began to emerge, with many finding the medium a satisfying channel of honest expression,

> the best aspect of blogging was being able to personalise your site and write freely, rather than in a formal manner . . . I feel that the blog allows you to express yourself more than you would in a usual assignment because they are less formal and you are encouraged to write in your own voice.

This resulted in a range of approaches, from short, pithy posts about students' own ICT experiences to much longer vision statements for the use of computers in schools: 'The blog is more flexible to use. Posts can be as long or short as you like, and this felt more natural.' And many found the freedom motivating, as the immediacy of composing a running account replaced some of the drudgery of extended essay writing; 'I can blog any time of night and day, and I enjoy it!'

Resources

This final assessment strand considered how well students worked together in pairs and groups to create 'classroom-ready' resources during creative curriculum planning sessions around the module themes. A repository of these resources was created via the class blog for students to draw upon for teaching placements. This activity also served as a

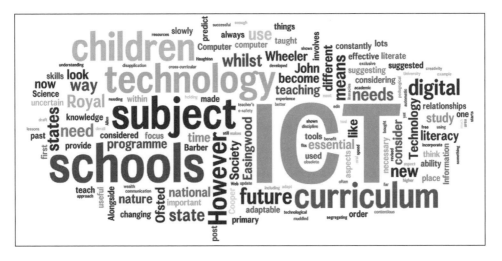

Figure 3.2 Example of a vision statement post.

starting point for considering other avenues for professional sharing such as Twitter, webinars, online TeachTweets, face-to-face TeachMeets and social bookmarking through sites such as Delicious and Pinterest. It became apparent that the value of online sharing was being taken on board when, in one session, several students began to blog and tweet breaking news about the National Curriculum without prompting. One student sums up the value of the collaborative approach, 'The impact of teamwork is invaluable . . . it allowed us to come up with more ideas and bounce off each other . . . through these sessions I produced resources I would not have been able to on my own.'

Student feedback

Having blogged in the autumn term (2012) with our cohort of over 100 Primary Education Year 3 students, we gathered evidence from seventy-eight students via an online survey and filmed a number of face-to-face discussions. This revealed a number of indications of potentially exciting outcomes from the use of the medium, including:

- the positive effects of peer-to-peer feedback and support;
- improved quality and volume of assessment evidence;
- enhanced motivation and engagement;
- enhanced sense of identity as insightful and skilful professionals.

Table 3.1 gives a flavour of the survey responses.

It is clear that the presence of a commenting audience and an opportunity for dialogue provided an incentive to write and facilitated informal peer-to-peer learning:

> I feel that other students on the course provided me with effective feedback that helped me to improve . . . I liked that people could comment; it made me more aware of my audience . . . being able to see what other people think can be very thought provoking.

It was also interesting to watch an online community emerge as our bloggers linked across blogs and as a number of blogs received hits from outside the university by local teachers, on Twitter, via comments from authors cited, and from as far afield as the Massachusetts Institute of Technology through their Scratch website. The visitor maps on the blogs provided visual evidence of the way these connections were expanding and reinforced the idea that the use of social media can dissolve boundaries of time and place. As one student said, 'It was very inspiring to receive comments about our projects from all around the world. I can see blogging would be a great way to develop networks with other teachers.'

From the tutors' perspective, the option to tap into student blogs in progress provided a potent source of teaching feedback, giving us a chance to adjust and review content as we went along, as well as offering new opportunities to track progress. We were more able to spot those who needed help and encouragement, and identify those who were falling behind. Towards the end of the module, students were given a more formal opportunity to peer assess each others' work using a checklist and a copy of the marking rubric in preparation for submission.

Table 3.1 Blogging – selected questionnaire items completed by 78 Year 3 students

	Agree (%)	Unsure (%)	Disagree (%)
1 Before the course I was a confident user of ICT in everyday life	92	6	1
2 I had previous experience of writing a blog	14	3	83
3 Once I got used to it the blogging tool was easy to use	76	18	6
4 My blogfolio is a good representation of what I learned on the course	86	8	6
5 The blog helped me to express my own voice and opinions	92	4	4
6 The addition of media to the blog helped capture my ICT work	89	5	5
7 I was satisfied with the standard of my blog writing	77	17	0
8 The blog helped me reflect on ICT use in schools	81	14	5
9 Getting comments from my peers helped me	51	38	10
10 Blogging improved my access to feedback	58	31	9
11 I was happy to share my blog	85	3	12
12 Writing for an audience motivated me to produce a higher standard of work	70	14	15
13 Blogging helped me feel part of a larger community of practitioners	53	26	22
14 The blogging process helped me keep up with my ICT work	74	6	19
15 Blogging has helped me engage with my ICT work	82	9	9
16 The class blog helped me prepare for the sessions	68	13	21
17 Being able to see other students' blogs helped me	86	6	8
18 Collaborating in teams has encouraged me to try new things	92	6	4
19 I will use some of the resources in my teaching	81	12	7
20 I would like to blog with my pupils	69	22	9

For tutors and students alike then, in a university setting, blogs provided greater scope for learning together and sharing resources and ideas, but at the same time allowed students to create online spaces reflecting their own personalities, in which they felt at home and able to record thoughts in an individual way: 'I have certainly become more engaged in ICT, and blogging has provided me with a communication link to my colleagues' ideas and thoughts . . . I was always on task, which is rare for me!'

Task 3.1 Which widget is which?

Look at the blog screenshot shown in Figure 3.3, an example from Mark Fairley Group 3. Can you:

- define a tag cloud, a visitor map and a wiki?
- explain why some tags are larger than others?
- identify three ways to navigate the blog?
- find a link to a related site, a previous post and to posts on the same topic?
- explain options for sharing the post?
- think of three ways of improving the blog?

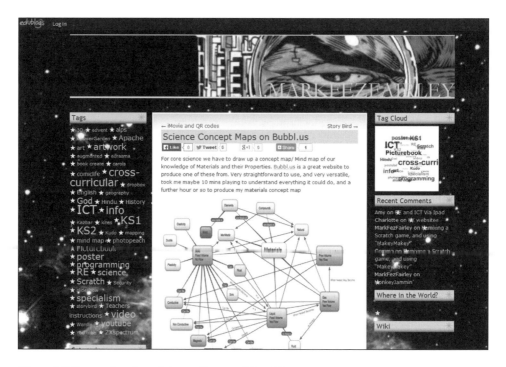

Figure 3.3 Screen shot from Science Concept Maps blog.

Blogging in Northamptonshire schools

Background

Northamptonshire has developed a strong legacy of primary school blogging built over the last seven years, supported by the grassroots Better Learning Through Technology (BLT) network. Over twenty schools have joined in with a multi-site blogging BLT initiative, which has supported them in establishing sets of school blogs.

One of the keys to success, they say, is to integrate blogging into school practice so that it has a genuine place in school policy and routines, rather than being an add-on, thereby avoiding a drop-off of activity once the initial flush of excitement wears off. Another is to make the use of class blogs optional for staff and encourage them to tailor their use to their class learning goals, so as to establish a range of blogs for different purposes across the age ranges.

Reflecting on their experiences, BLT members think that blogging has promoted school engagement beyond the classroom. They have seen an improvement in pupils' motivation to write, and they would like to think that blogging has also had a positive impact on writing quality. Over time, the emphasis in the blogs has moved from simply showcasing work and taking pride in audience numbers, to focusing on how best to use the blogging medium for genuine learning dialogues within school and further afield. By sharing and celebrating their pupils' learning in a wider community and welcoming contributions from all, they have encouraged parents and children alike to adopt a more active relationship with learning so that it becomes something that everyone does.

We've chosen four sample blogging projects to illustrate these ideas.

Blogging to develop a framework for learning

'Dull and Boring Project': Northampton Primary Academy Trust (NPAT)

Pupils across five local schools arrived one morning to find that two villains, 'Dull' and 'Boring', had removed all the excitement from their learning environments (see Figure 3.4). School websites were censored, displays covered, playtime cancelled, libraries closed and desks rearranged in rows. Staff immersed themselves in role as victims and helped a storyline take shape through a series of emergency assemblies and secret meetings. Adding tension to the plot was a password-protected blog with a victory meter, enabling pupils to plan their counter-attack by inventing their own superheroes and undertaking joint missions. By the end of the week the blog had received over 21,000 hits and 1,900 comments, and had slowly filled with colour as pupils planned an epic day of fun learning to celebrate their victory. The overall aim was to help pupils gain insight into what makes effective learning and to use this to provide a springboard for future collaboration between the schools.

'Friendly Frogs Project': Bridgewater Primary School

A whole-school writing immersion week was inspired by the wordless picture book, 'Tuesday' by David Wiesner (1991) on the theme of an invasion of frogs. It began with the discovery of slime around the school pond, backed up with virtual slime on the school blogs. Although they couldn't see them, pupils discovered that they could communicate with the frogs via secret video messages and Twitter. Through these exchanges the frogs gave the pupils the informational titbits they needed for their class science and writing challenges, and asked their own questions about humans. Staff noted an immediate impact on motivation to write, with pupils choosing to create letters and thank you notes to the frogs alongside their class compositions. Since the project took place, the habit of visiting and writing for the blogs has become embedded within the daily classroom routines. A positive outcome of this has been a progression from using

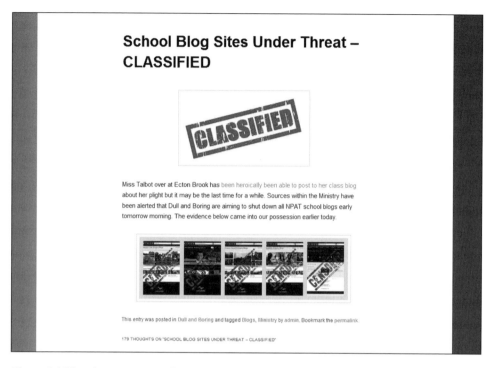

Figure 3.4 Blogging to promote learning dialogues.

blogs to inform parents, to using them to provide a context for engaging in real discussions about class projects: two local schools collaborated on a science project and gave each other feedback on their instructional writing, for example.

Blogging to facilitate wider engagement

'Virtual Field Trip': Kingswood Primary Academy

A five-week Year 1 humanities project was based around the topic of London. The culmination of this work was a virtual field trip in which small groups of pupils used green screen techniques to film themselves talking about their chosen London landmarks and then edited the film to add the appropriate background images. Visitors to the classroom could view these films by holding mobile devices up to an interactive display that made use of an augmented reality app. They could also follow the progress of the pupils' research on the class blog, which prompted a good deal of off-site engagement by children and parents during the project as well as providing a home for the finished products. In addition, the work was shared with schools in the USA and New Zealand as part of a quadblogging initiative, with each school in the group taking turns to give feedback over four weeks, and the resulting commentary gave the class an insight into contrasting localities.

Blogging for personalised and differentiated learning

'Our World My Future Talks': Simon de Senlis Primary School

Pupils developed 'TED-style' talks over several weeks on topics of their own choosing and delivered them to a packed lecture theatre at the University of Northampton. During the process they became immersed in their themes, with ideas ranging from 'chocolate' to 'computers' to 'comedy'. They used ICT to capture interviews, surveys, visits, cooking and creative work, and then weaved the results into media-rich presentations that supported their individual talks. What made the presentations even more special is that the pupils all had statements of SEN for moderate learning difficulties and speech and language. Being able to revisit their evolving ideas each day as they added to their presentations and share them on the class blog meant that they could take them forward at their own pace, and follow personal routes of inquiry with a real sense of ownership. The blog also provided a space for celebrating and reflecting on their remarkable achievement, enhancing its impact on their speaking and writing confidence.

Task 3.2 Pros and cons of blogging

Blogs can be an effective tool for teachers and learners across educational settings. Compare the blog format with your current format for capturing your own ICT work and for recording pupils' work in school. Use the grid below to gather pros and cons. Consider factors such as assessment, differentiation, use of media, purpose, reflection, ease of use and e-safety.

Table 3.2 Pros and cons of blogging

	My ICT	*Pupils' ICT*
B		
L		
O		
G		
S		
O		
T		
H		
E		
R		

What these four examples have in common is that blogging sits firmly in the midst of a host of related activities such as practical work, talk, drawing, writing and filming. The blogs are a way of tethering pupils' ideas and outputs, allowing them to be shared and reviewed, and often moved forward as new connections are made in response to dialogues taking place in real or virtual spaces. Used in this way, the blogs have a powerful role to play as an embedded part of the learning process.

Conclusion

What can we learn from the stories and examples provided above? What stands out for us is the way in which blogging can add new dimensions to already excellent teaching and learning, and can open up a host of possibilities and opportunities at all levels. In schools, pupils and teachers benefitted through a collaborative culture and a more active approach to learning, so that it became something that everyone did together, in a community, rather than something done in isolation or just in the classroom. The medium of blogging expanded each school's learning goals across a wider sphere, as well as capturing individual learning journeys, turning pupils into positive contributors.

In universities too, we found that blogs can combine both the personal and the public perspectives of effective learning. They allow for reciprocal exchanges within a community of practice and provide media-rich familiar spaces for students to document their own development. This has resonance with the idea that interaction between individual and collective experience leads to deeper learning – learning which is more reflective and transferrable (McCluskey, 2011; Turvey, 2006). This style of learning needs to be part of our student teachers' toolkit if they are to equip their pupils with the flexible responses they will need for an emerging future in which change is endemic.

What also stands out is the role of the teacher. As our university students and our school pupils learned to express their ideas using these digital literacies, they continued to need help to integrate traditional literacies. In this more public arena, it is even more necessary to be able to construct a coherent narrative and our role as teachers in enabling them to achieve this is more important than ever. Students and pupils alike need to be able to evaluate the quality of their work, help their peers do likewise, and learn to express themselves clearly, tapping into wider learning communities so that they can make, share and find with discernment, and with a better understanding of their own achievements and capabilities.

At both ends of the educational spectrum, then, we have seen blogging raise the level of engagement way beyond expectations, with many learners going far beyond the requirements to produce blogs that were professional looking and collaborative and, in doing so, learning far more than we had imagined possible.

Summary and key points

Whether used in primary schools or universities, blogs have the potential to capture creativity and reflection, to foster a sense of community, to encourage collaboration between peers, and, ultimately, to enhance learning in a powerful and engaging way.

Lessons learned

Universities:

- Allow time for blogging to catch on.
- Give students control over privacy settings.
- Promote commenting and comment as a tutor.
- Teach the basics and provide simple 'how-tos'.
- Respond to requests for help.
- Use online bulletin boards for FAQs.
- Draw parallels with schools blogging.
- Show how blogs can help students' careers.
- Use RSS to subscribe to student blogs.
- Support students to make timely posts.
- Consider whether to make blogging compulsory at first.
- Model good practice via a tutor's blog.

Schools:

- Have clear safety guidelines and an Acceptable Use policy.
- Emphasise the benefits to parents.
- Provide opportunities for pupils to develop ownership.
- Allow pupils to take responsibility for cascading skills.
- Promote sharing and commenting.
- Consider a ground-up approach rather than a compulsory rollout to staff.
- Give teachers choice and control over the content and direction of their class blogs.
- Put the vision before the technology and have a clear idea about the aims.
- Use blogs for different purposes depending on the age of the pupils.
- Model good practice via a Head's blog.

If you are a student teacher check which requirements for your course you have addressed through this chapter.

Further reading and relevant websites

Northampton Primary Academy Trust (NPAT) ('Dull and Boring' project) http://y1.kpsblogs.net/tag/virtuallondontrip/

Andrew Evans Year 1 Blog at Kingswood Primary ('Virtual Trip to London' project) http://y1.kpsblogs.net/tag/virtuallondontrip/

Simon de Senlis School blogs ('Our World My Future' project) http://simondesenlisblogs.org/

Bridgewater Primary Blogs ('Friendly Frogs' project) http://bridgewaterblogs.net/

Mr Mitchell's Blog (2012) http://mrmitchell.heathfieldcps.net/

Clark, D. (2012) 'Blogs: Vastly underused teaching and learning tool'. Available online at: http://donaldclarkplanb.blogspot.co.uk/search?q=Blogs. Accessed on 29 May 2013.

Davis, E. (2006) 'Characterizing productive reflection among preservice elementary teachers: Seeing what matters'. *Teaching and Teacher Education: An International Journal of Research and Studies*, 22(3): 281–301.

De Andrés Martínez, C. (2012) 'Developing metacognition at a distance: Sharing students' learning strategies on a reflective blog'. *Computer Assisted Language Learning*, 25(2): 199–212.

References

Churchill, D. (2009) 'Educational applications of Web 2.0: Using blogs to support teaching and learning'. *British Journal of Educational Technology*, 40(1): 179–83.

Ellison, N.B. and Wu, Y. (2008) 'Blogging in the classroom: A preliminary exploration of student attitudes and impact on comprehension'. *Journal of Educational Multimedia and Hypermedia*, 17(1): 99–122.

Deng, L. and Yuen, A.H. (2011) 'Towards a framework for educational affordances of blogs'. *Computers and Education*, 56(2): 441–51.

Ducate, L.C. and Lornicka, L.L. (2008) 'Adventures in the blogosphere: From blog readers to blog writers'. *Computer Assisted Language Learning*, 21(1): 9–28.

Ellison, N. and Wu, Y. (2008) 'Blogging in the classroom: A preliminary exploration of student attitudes and impact on comprehension'. *Journal of Educational Multimedia and Hypermedia*, 17(1): 99–122.

Farmer, J. (2006) 'Blogging to basics: How blogs are bringing online education back from the brink'. In A. Bruns and J. Jacobs (eds) *Uses of blogs*, pp. 91–103. New York: Peter Lang Publishing Inc.

Farmer, B., Yue, A. and Brooks, C. (2008) 'Using blogging for higher order learning in large cohort university teaching: A case study'. *Australasian Journal of Educational Technology*, 24(2): 123–36.

Feiertag, J. and Berge, Z.L. (2008) 'Training Generation N: How educators should approach the Net Generation'. *Education and Training*, 50(6): 457–64.

Fessakis, G., Tatsis, K. and Dimitracopoulou, A. (2008) 'Supporting "learning by design" activities using group blogs'. *Educational Technology and Society*, 11(4): 199–212.

Freeman, W. and Brett, C. (2012) 'Prompting authentic blogging practice in an online graduate course'. *Computers and Education*, 59(3): 1032–41.

Halic, O., Lee, D., Paulus, T. and Spence, M. (2010) 'To blog or not to blog: Student perceptions of blog effectiveness for learning in a college-level course'. *Internet and Higher Education*, 13: 206–13.

Kim, H.N. (2008) 'The phenomenon of blogs and theoretical model of blog use in educational contexts'. *Computers and Education*, 51(3): 1342–52.

McCluskey, A. (2011) 'Learning in dissolving boundaries'. Available online at: www.connected.org/learn/dissolving-boundaries.html. Accessed on 29 May 2013.

Ohler, J. (2009) 'New-media literacies'. Available online at: www.aaup.org/article/new-media-literacies#.UaWybWR9dlp. Accessed on 29 May 2013.

Reupert, A. and Dalgarno, B. (2011) 'Using online blogs to develop student teachers' behaviour management approaches'. *Australian Journal of Teacher Education*, 36(5): 5.

Turvey, K. (2006) 'Towards deeper learning through creativity within online communities in primary education'. *Computers and Education*, 46(3): 309–21.

Weisner, D. (1991) *Tuesday*. New York: Houghton Mifflin.

Wheeler, S. (2010) 'Open content, open learning 2.0: Using wikis and blogs in Higher Education'. In *Changing cultures in higher education*, pp. 103–14. Springer-Verlag Berlin Heidelberg.

Wheeler, S. and Wheeler, D. (2009) 'Using wikis to promote quality learning in teacher training'. *Learning, Media and Technology*, 34(1): 1–10.

Wheeler, S. (2013) 'False Frontiers'. Available online at: http://steve-wheeler.blogspot.co.uk/2013/03/false-frontiers.html. Accessed on 29 May 2013.

Williams, J.B. and Jacobs, J. (2004) 'Exploring the use of blogs as learning spaces in the higher education sector'. *Australasian Journal of Educational Technology*, 20(2): 232–47.

Yang, S.H. (2009) 'Using blogs to enhance critical reflection and community of practice'. *Educational Technology and Society*, 12(2): 11–21.

4 Being creative with technology

Using ICT to enhance the teaching of literacy and numeracy

David Morris, Gurmit Uppal and Daniel Ayres

Introduction

Your ability to be creative with ICT is very much down to your confidence to use these technologies, and your understanding of their pedagogical value in the classroom. This chapter draws upon research (www.uel.ac.uk/ks2ictproject) that explores the ways in which technology-based practices can enhance the teaching and learning of literacy and numeracy in the primary classroom. Examples of leading-edge practice in primary classrooms are presented and a range of e-tools is considered, including mobile devices, video collaboration and Web 2.0 technologies, as well as Quick Response [QR] codes. This chapter will provide you with practical guidance on planning and organising new technologies to support teaching and learning in the core subjects. As ICT resource settings in schools vary considerably, this chapter also identifies ways for you to overcome a lack of provision, which may be a barrier to learning.

Objectives

By the end of this chapter you should be able to:

- Use a range of online resources and tools to enhance your teaching of literacy and numeracy.
- Incorporate technologies into your lessons, to support creativity.
- Overcome situations where a lack of ICT resources may present barriers to learning.

Background

Although much classroom-based practice relies on teacher exposition and instruction, good teaching and learning is characterised by the provision of opportunities for pupils to learn independently. Previously, opportunities for pupils to make decisions about the use of ICT in their learning – required by the English National Curriculum – involved pupils being taught how to think creatively (DfEE and QCA, 1999). More recently, the revised English National Curriculum for computing also expresses the need for pupils to be 'competent, confident and creative users of information and communication technology' (DfE, 2013, p. 178).

In England, the ICT curriculum is shifting towards a model that places greater emphasis on computing and programming as opposed to developing pupils' ICT skills

(Royal Society, 2012). However, providing creative learning opportunities in the primary curriculum is important because of the perceived motivational impact on learning (DfEE, 1997). A key aspect of this lies in applying a dialogical approach to ICT, whereby meaningful interactions with technology are characterised by purposeful collaboration and underpinned by pupil involvement (Tanner and Davies, 2011). After all, it is important to understand that the dialogic pedagogy that takes place between pupils and between the teacher and pupils is just as significant as the subsequent interaction with the technology itself. For example, a teacher–pupil discussion concerning the literary processes involved in storyboarding an animated movie is critical in ensuring deep rather than superficial learning takes place.

It should not be assumed that the use of technology in itself, for example online resources such as timers and games, leads to a creative learning environment: it is, rather, the interactive nature of ICT that is important. In order for pupils to engage with ICT in a purposeful and creative way, careful planning and preparation are vital. Apart from teaching pupils how to use the technology, you will also need to encourage them to work collaboratively and develop their own approaches (Hargreaves *et al.*, 2003, p. 224). This may be achieved, for example, by getting pupils to work in small groups to create a movie that relates to a topic or theme. ICT can also have a positive impact on pupils who may find conventional classrooom settings challenging, and who may therefore benefit from 'peripheral or incidental learning' whereby they may learn new 'manipulation skills' while engaging with technologies (Wheeler *et al.*, 2002, p. 378), which supports the notion of the link between the motivational aspect of ICT and attainment.

Many pupils arrive at school with the skills and confidence to interact with their peers, utilising new and emerging technologies. However, teachers must be aware of the difference between pupils' familiarity with technological advances and their ability to apply technology in creative and innovative ways for learning. So, how do you facilitate the creative use of ICT for learning? Opportunities may not always happen as a direct result of your classroom teaching, but may derive, for example, from extra-curricular activities; see the examples in this chapter.

Creativity

Ofsted (2009) and Becta (2010) recognise the link between effective practice and creative teaching, yet they fail to define the term 'creativity'. The National Advisory Committee on Creative and Cultural Education (NACCCE), however, defines creativity as 'imaginative activity fashioned so as to produce outcomes that are both original and of value' (NACCCE, 1999, p. 30). Futurelab (Williamson and Payton, 2009), on the other hand, discuss creativity in terms of pupil independence and pupil-directed learning. However, Green's (2012, p.147) skills framework separates creative skills from information, media and technology skills and considers that creativity:

- is concerned with making connections;
- is focused on problem solving and higher-order thinking;
- involves an element of risk-taking;
- encourages exploration;
- involves collaboration.

The notion of collaboration, however, is also supported by the model developed by Wheeler *et al.* (2002, p. 370) in which social interaction constitutes an 'activity mode' that is vital to the creative process. In this way, shared project work, and the processes involved, can be recorded in order to document the journey that culminates in a final piece of collaborative work.

Case study 4.1 Extra-curricular example (1)

Year 2 pupils at an after-school ICT club were given opportunities to extend and apply their skills in creating digital images. This derived from their work based upon the theme of space, which involved them creating their own images of the solar system. After completing some scientific writing, they independently suggested compiling their work into a presentation, which they designed and produced applying the digital artwork skills they had been developing in their club.

Designing a creative curriculum that employs the use of technologies may be achieved through your own technological preferences, insights and approaches to teaching, although teaching your pupils about creativity as a concept and how to be creative is equally important (Edwards, 2012, p. 114). When deployed effectively, technologies can provide an ideal vehicle for the promotion of creativity, although you will also need to consider the additional skills of, for example, risk-taking, exploration and collaboration, which can be developed through the use of online collaborative real-time writing tools such as Popplet, PrimaryPad or Padlet in English, while learning platforms, such as Mathletics, can be employed to encourage healthy challenges through a personalised learning approach.

The following case study provides more detailed examples.

Case study 4.2 Using ICT to promote creativity in the core subjects in Key Stage 2: a joint project with Havering School Improvement Services (HSIS) and the University of East London (UEL)

Overview

As part of the UK government's ICT Grants Bid 2012, UEL was successful in securing funding to undertake a school-based case study with our partnership schools in order to:

- develop and enhance student teachers' experience of successful technology-based practice within core subjects, regardless of their specific school placement;
- demonstrate how schools' involvement in training can enhance pupils' progress in the core subjects;
- demonstrate how schools can organise effective training environments so that student teachers, pupils and school staff can benefit;
- further develop and strengthen partnerships between providers of Initial Teacher Education (ITE) and leading practitioners in the use of ICT in teaching; and

Task 4.1 Exploring online tools that promote creativity and collaboration

The web resources listed below provide real-time collaborative writing and planning spaces that can be accessed by fellow contributors through the sharing of the Uniform Resource Locator (URL) of the original page. Explore the following online tools and identify how you and your pupils could use the resource to promote creativity and collaboration in the core subjects. Possible ideas may include: using the tool for writing a collaborative poem; planning for a group or class project; posing a discussion question at the start of a lesson or an assessment question at the end.

- http://padlet.com/
- http://popplet.com/
- http://primarypad.com/
- http://abcict.wikispaces.com/

Consider using one or more of these online tools in one of your lessons. When planning the lesson, think about the following questions:

- How will the use of ICT enhance teaching and learning?
- How will it enhance the subject area you are teaching?
- Which ground rules will you need to set for your pupils?
- Are there any potential barriers or issues with using the tool?
- Can the work be developed into a sequence of lessons?

After the lesson, evaluate its success by responding to the questions above. The use of collaborative writing can feed into meaningful production of pupils' own texts. Here are some options to allow pupils to create a finished product:

- Get pupils to design and create a flip book. Using ReadWriteThink (www. readwritethink.org/files/resources/interactives/flipbook/) provides different page templates to allow easy organisation of content. Alternatively, get them to design and create an interactive book that can be shared with an online audience (http://storybird.com/).
- Employ Picture Book Maker (www.culturestreet.org.uk/activities/picture bookmaker) or a tablet app (such as Book Maker or Book Writer) to organise storyboards into a final format.
- Create a Portable Document Format (PDF) file using Word or Adobe software, and share it via a school website, Dropbox, or even Google Play Books.

Don't forget that electronically-generated images and illustrations play an important step in the creative process, whether these are created digitally or whether original artwork is scanned in.

Figure 4.1 Student teachers and pupils engaging with mobile technologies at Scargill Junior School.

- build coherence across training programmes in relation to student teachers' exposure to excellent teaching with ICT, including more coherent approaches to the way technology can be used across core subjects and improved integration of school and centre-based training.

UEL worked with Havering partnership schools (Engayne Primary School, The Mawney Foundation School, Scargill Junior School and Scotts Primary School), where wrap-around ICT provision and practice in the use of technologies to support learning and teaching in the core subjects were considered to be outstanding. This case study exemplifies examples of the creative use of ICT in supporting learning and teaching in the core subjects and is aimed to help guide you on how to employ a range of technologies in order to assist creativity in the classroom. The teaching activities outlined in this chapter represent some of the lessons that student teachers experienced using a range of technologies such as Quick Response (QR) Codes and video conferencing while working at Scargill Junior School and The Mawney Foundation School.

To find out more about the nature of this case study and the impact it has had on learning and teaching, please visit the following website: www.uel.ac.uk/ks2ictproject/

Quick Response (QR) codes

Scargill Junior School in the London borough of Havering has been recognised for its innovative use of ICT across the curriculum and specifically for its use of mobile technology (Ofsted, 2010; Naace, 2011). The school places significant value on the motivational impact of mobile technologies on supporting and enhancing teaching and learning and utilises an assortment of devices including, smartphones, Nintendo DS, Sony PSPs, iPod Touch and iPad tablets. The ICT coordinator is supported by a team of digital leaders – pupils whose responsibilities include testing and evaluating apps, as well as supporting peers and staff with their use of technology. Evidence of the school's integrated approach to the use of new technologies can be found in corridors as well as the classrooms, where QR codes bring displays to life and provide additional avenues of interaction for pupils. In your daily life you may well have come across, or even scanned and used, QR codes that frequently appear in the media and which look like the images in Figures 4.2 and 4.3.

Figure 4.2 A QR code linking to plain text.

Figure 4.3 A QR code linking to a QR code generator website.

QR codes are two-dimensional barcodes that can be read using the camera function on smartphones and tablets to provide links to websites, text and videos, as well as other forms of content. QR codes are commonly used in print marketing and their ease of use makes QR codes an ideal resource for teachers and pupils to use. Getting started with QR codes is simple, there are many websites that can be used to generate and print QR codes, such as www.qrstuff.com. Once a QR code has been created, anyone wishing to read and follow the code will require a QR code reader application on a smartphone, handheld device or tablet – alternatively a webcam can be used to read the code, in which case additional software will be required. Examples of QR code readers include Qrafter, Qmark, QRReader and QR Droid.

At Scargill Junior School, QR codes are used on displays to provide additional information and questions about what the pupils have been studying. The QR codes can be used by pupils in the form of a learning trail, while parents and visitors are able to discover more about the processes behind the work on display. The educational uses for QR codes across the curriculum are broad in their scope, and their use in the core subjects of English and mathematics could include:

- Teachers generating and placing question-based QR codes inside reading books, linking to comprehension questions about the text;
- Pupils placing QR codes inside books, linking to audio clips of book reviews they have created;
- Placing QR codes on homework sheets, providing a link to online support materials or video clips that explain strategies concerned with teaching and learning;
- Using QR codes for self-assessment and checking of calculations in mathematics;
- Pupils could create a mathematical treasure hunt for one another using QR codes linked to mathematical word problems;
- Using QR codes in the classroom shop role-play area, allowing pupils to scan grocery items for product information and pricing.

Video collaboration

There are many potential benefits of using video collaboratively, for learning and digital cameras are easily available on smartphones and tablets. Pupils can record each other presenting their work, recording learning within a classroom, or video-conferencing technology can be used to open up global learning opportunities for them.

Using video-conferencing equipment as part of a topic opens up the world to young learners. With relatively little preparation, discussions can be held with subject experts, in distant locations, saving time, money and resources. One school that has made the initial commitment to investing in the technology required for video conferencing is Mawney Foundation School.

The Mawney Foundation School is a two-form entry primary school situated in Greater London. The pupil cohort is well above national averages in terms of:

- pupils eligible for free school meals;
- pupils from minority ethnic backgrounds;
- pupils learning English as an additional language;
- pupils with special educational needs (Ofsted, 2011).

Despite the needs of its pupils, Mawney has been identified in the government's top improving schools based on performance in English and maths from 2008 to 2010 (Richards, 2011).

Task 4.2 Using QR codes to create a mathematics-based treasure hunt

QR codes can be used in innovative ways to support and motivate pupil learning. A QR code treasure hunt can provide an engaging approach to learning where pupils can work together to follow a trail of QR code questions or clues to accomplish a given task. Follow the steps outlined below to create your own QR code treasure hunt, or alternatively pupils can create treasure hunts for each other.

1   Start by creating a list of questions that relate to your class's current mathematics topic – between five to ten questions is sufficient. Although any topic can lend itself to this task, practical mathematics topics such as those of measures and geometry will provide an ideal opportunity to take learning outside the classroom.

2   Use a QR code generator website such as www.qrstuff.com to create a QR code for each question. It is advisable that QR codes are printed at a size that is easy to capture, especially by young pupils. You may also wish to add additional start and finish QR codes that contain instructions or prompts. For example, how would you like pupils to record their answers? Many handheld devices and tablets have a camera function that could be used to record answers.

3   Print the QR codes and display them around the classroom or the school. Colour coding or numbering the QR codes allows for the task to be differentiated through directing your pupils to specific codes.

4   In groups, pupils complete the treasure hunt by using a QR code reader application on a handheld device or tablet to access each question, before collaboratively solving the problem and recording or photographing the evidence.

5   At the end of the treasure hunt teams can peer assess their results or present evidence to the teacher before winners are announced.

The task above could be adapted by substituting the QR codes, which link to questions, with links to multiple choice answers, or to clues that provide further guidance where needed.

The school, its teachers and pupils benefit from an ongoing commitment to investment in technology to support teaching and learning. A systematic investment programme and staff training have resulted in an environment in which ICT is embedded and pupils use a range of technologies with confidence. For example, pupils run the daily school radio station, welcoming their peers at the start of the day and sharing school news and views.

The school uses the video-conferencing (VC) equipment to connect with other schools both within the local area and internationally. An annual opportunity to VC with Father Christmas is hosted by the school, giving pupils in partner schools the opportunity to talk through their expectations of Christmas, which fosters and develops their communication skills in a virtual setting where they have to deal with the challenges of online interaction as opposed to being one to one in a physical space.

Video motivates and engages pupils and can bring various benefits in learning outcomes. While some pupils will only have watched video or Digital Versatile Discs (DVDs) some will have had a broader experience, watching video clips online, or perhaps recording their own videos. Certainly, ICT hardware manufacturers – such as V-tech www.vtechuk.com – have produced a good range of child-friendly hardware, but do check the quality produced by these robust video cameras.

The opportunities for pupils to create videos in English and mathematics in cross-curricular ways could include:

- Small groups of pupils could record a synopsis of the beginning, middle and end of their story. Then other pupils could peer assess and the video can form a resource to support the drafting process.
- Taking hot-seating to a new level, by recording interviews with pupils acting as, for example, Mary Seacole, Michael Morpurgo and The Gruffalo (dressing-up optional, but encouraged!).
- Pupils could present a worded maths problem and demonstrate how they achieved the answer by illustrating or describing the steps.
- Booking a session with a JANET content provider, http://vccontentdirectory.ja.net, can provide pupils in all key stages with the opportunity to interact with experts from many organisations, for example in meteorology and history, or to ask questions of historical figures.

Marc Prensky (2007, p. 45) stresses the importance of cameras being in the hands of pupils and how the captured footage allows them to gain greater self-awareness. The task below outlines examples of how digital video can be used by pupils to record and evaluate their work.

Task 4.3 Using digital video

Using digital stills or video, either:

- Get pupils to take photos of their work in progress, before compiling them (Using YouTube Photo Slideshow, Animoto or Windows Movie Maker or the iMovie app on iPad) to document the process behind completed work, or
- Produce a video as the outcome of a piece of work, instead of writing in exercise books. For example, pupils could record a video explaining how to use and apply the 'chunking method' in numeracy.

Overcoming barriers to using ICT

Resource settings in schools vary widely. You may find yourself with state-of-the-art equipment, for example computer suites or portable laptop trolleys and mobile devices such as tablets and handheld devices, or you may find yourself with just one computer in your classroom. Even if you do not have Internet access you can still:

- record pupils' ideas as text, voice or video;
- display images as a stimulus for learning;
- create or get pupils to create presentations that assist with learning and teaching.

If do you have Internet access then you can use:

- Web 2.0 technologies (for example, social networking tools that allow the sharing and collaboration of ideas or information);
- video streaming;
- video conferencing. This is attainable through various free software downloads (such as Skype and Tango), so long as you have access to a webcam, speakers and a microphone. These features are provided as standard on most current laptops and other mobile devices, such as tablets and smartphones.

You may also like to consider using an additional range of resources:

- digital cameras;
- mobile phones;
- mobile devices;
- sound recording devices;
- programmable toys, for example bee bots or roamers.

Providing you have Internet access, there are many tools that allow you to be creative. For example, you can use an online post-it board where pupils can share their thoughts and ideas:

- http://primarywall.com

This can be used to generate initial ideas or assess pupils' existing knowledge before or at the end of a unit of work.

As teachers it is important to gain an insight into the recreational technologies that pupils are using, as some of these tools may have educational value too.

The use of digital video can also be used to document the process behind the completion of pieces of work, enabling an audience to gain an insight into the skills that pupils have used.

Case study 4.3 Extra-curricular example (2)

In Year 5 as part of a celebration assembly, pupils used a digital camera to record their class work. They were confident in both the use of the camera and their file management skills. The pupils decided that rather than hold up pieces of their work, they would show their parents the process behind their work. So, for each of three half-term topics the pupils created and then played a video comprising the photos in order to showcase their work to a specific audience.

Access to Web 2.0 and mobile technologies

It is worth noting that 'a lot of children and young people' learn a lot about computers and technology outside of the classroom (Schön, 2001, p. 11). When considering how your pupils have or might benefit from this kind of extra-curricular activity it is also worth considering the needs of low-income communities. Although schools can provide 'access points' and a gateway to technology, this still may mean that children from some families may not have access to technologies.

Task 4.4 Learning in literacy and numeracy using ICTs (M-level task)

Begin by compiling a list of between fifteen and twenty different technologies that your pupils may use in school or recreationally, for example: mobile phone, a camera device on a phone, apps on phones, tablets, MP3 players, games consoles, laptops, digital cameras, Kindles, etc.

Conduct a survey using Survey Monkey www.surveymonkey.com or by employing alternative data-gathering methods. The purpose of the survey will be to determine how many pupils use the technologies you have identified, in what ways and for what purpose. Analyse your findings and provide a rationale for the use of a particular technology or technologies that have emerged from your survey.

When completing this task, you will need to consider and comment upon the socio-economic factors that define the school and the community where you are working. In England, this may involve you reading your school's Ofsted report, accessing RAISEonline or Ofsted Dashboard data in order to establish the profile of your school. Ofsted Dashboard, released in February 2013, was designed to provide stakeholders with easier access to their school's data. Information is summarised in graph-form, and based on end of key stage results for reading, writing and mathematics, and attendance data. Although originally designed for use by school governors, it allows public comparison of the school nationally, or with 'similar schools' – those whose cohort attained similar results on entry to the key stage. Significantly, it allows class teachers to evaluate their school's performance and consider how their planning and teaching might help to impact upon pupils' learning.

Details of any English primary school's performance can be found at: www.education.gov.uk/schools/performance/index.html

1 Using the literature referenced in this chapter as well as your own wider reading, consider how technologies used by pupils may be integrated to support creative teaching and learning in literacy or numeracy. This should be approximately 1000 words.

2 Selecting up to two or three technologies from your survey, write a 500–750 word rationale and proposal explaining why you consider a particular technology (e.g., a downloadable app, or a social networking site) may be conducive to fostering creativity and supporting the teaching and learning of literacy or numeracy in your school. This rationale should be written with your mentor and/or school leadership team in mind and should be something that you

continued ...

may wish to share with them in terms of informing school policy. In doing so, you should identify both a year group and key stage.

3   In your proposal you should aim to outline the key objectives for the delivery of a unit of work, making reference to the revised government's schemes of work.

You should aim to make your appraisal critical by supporting your rationale and arguments with reference to relevant theory and literature.

You should also consider the following:

- learning objectives;
- levels of pupil engagement;
- pupil attainment;
- issues which may relate to pupil safety.

Summary and key points

Good practice depends on motivating and engaging pupils in meaningful, creative learning activities. ICT can help you to achieve this, as a lesson outcome or as part of a learning journey, by facilitating independent or collaborative practices, exploration, and problem solving requiring higher-order thinking. You should not have to depend on high levels of investment in ICT, as limited resourcing can be easily overcome. Once you have read this chapter, and carried out the tasks, you should be able to use ICT creatively to support teaching and learning, with an emphasis on the core subjects. You will also know how to use ICT to motivate and engage pupils in order to enhance their literacy and numeracy skills, as well as understand how technology can assist with assessing pupil progress.

Finally, you should consider this chapter as a starting point and it should enable you to realise the pedagogical value of using technology.

If you are a student teacher, check which requirements for your course you have addressed through this chapter.

Further reading and additional resources

Quick Response codes:

www.qrstuff.com
http://zxing.appspot.com/generator
www.quickmark.cn/En/basic
http://qrdroid.com
www.qrreaders.net
www.classtools.net/QR

Mathletics:

www.mathletics.co.uk

Collaborative writing and publishing tools:

http://popplet.com
http://primarypad.com
http://padlet.com
www.readwritethink.org/files/resources/interactives/flipbook
www.culturestreet.org.uk/activities/picturebookmaker
http://storybird.com

Blogs and wikis:

http://pbworks.com
http://edublogs.org
http://wordpress.com
www.blogger.com

Video, media and video conferencing:

www.youtube.com
http://windows.microsoft.com/en-gb/windows-live/movie-maker
http://vccontentdirectory.ja.net
http://animoto.com

Online school information sources:

http://dashboard.ofsted.gov.uk
www.raiseonline.org
www.education.gov.uk/schools/performance

Other online resources:

www.freetech4teachers.com
www.vtechuk.com

Please note – Internet Explorer 7 may no longer support some of the above sites and you will need to use an alternative web browser.

Further reading

Barber, D. and Cooper, L. (2011) *Using web tools in the primary classroom – A practical guide for enhancing teaching and learning.* London: Routledge.
> This text explains how Web 2.0 tools such as those for podcasting, blogging and social networking can enhance teaching and learning. As well as providing ideas for the classroom, this book provides discussion around learning, policy and curriculum, as well as tasks and reflective prompts for the reader.

Jesson, J. and Peacock, G. (2011) *The really useful ICT book: A practical guide to using technology across the primary curriculum.* London: Routledge.
> This is a highly accessible guide to using ICT inside and outside the primary classroom – providing ideas for discrete and cross-curricular use of ICT.

Richardson, W. (2010) Blogs, wikis, podcasts, and other powerful web tools for classrooms (3rd edn). California: Corwin.
> This book provides real case studies outlining how teachers have introduced new technologies into their classrooms and advice for teachers who wish to do so.

Rising Stars (2012–2013) *Switched on ICT schemes of work*. Rising Stars UK.
> Switched on ICT is a published scheme of work adopted by many schools in the London Borough of Havering. The scheme provides EYFS and primary teachers with planning for creative ICT projects with clear cross-curricular links.

References

Becta (2010) *21st century teacher*. Coventry: Becta. Available online at: http://webarchive.national archives.gov.uk/20101102103654/ http://publications.becta.org.uk/download.cfm?resID= 41521. Accessed on 31 January 2014.

Department for Education (DfE) (2013) *The National Curriculum in England: Key Stages 1 and 2 framework document*. Available online at: www.gov.uk/government/uploads/system/ uploads/attachment_data/file/260481/PRIMARY_national_curriculum_11-9-13_2.pdf. Accessed on 31 January 2014.

Department for Education and Employment (DfEE) (1997) *White paper: Excellence in schools.* HMSO.

Department for Education and Employment (DfEE) and Qualifications and Curriculum Authority (QCA) (1999) *The National Curriculum: Handbook for primary teachers in England*. London: HMSO. Available online at: www.educationengland.org.uk/documents/pdfs/ 1999-nc-primary-handbook.pdf. Accessed on 1 February 2014.

Edwards, A. (2012) *New technology and education*. London: Continuum.

Green, M. (2012) 'An introduction to Information Communication Technology'. In P. Driscoll, A. Lambirth and J. Roden (eds) *The primary curriculum: A creative approach*. London: Sage.

Hargreaves, L., Moyles, J., Merry, R., Paterson, F., Pell, A. and Esarte-Sarries, V. (2003) 'How do primary school teachers define and implement "interactive teaching" in the National Literacy Strategy in England?'. *Research Papers in Education*, 18(3): 217–36.

National Advisory Committee on Creative and Cultural Education (NACCCE) (1999) *All our futures: Creativity, culture and education*. Available online at: http://sirkenrobinson.com/pdf/ allourfutures.pdf. Accessed on 1 February 2014.

National Association of Advisors for Computers in Education (Naace) (2011) *Naace impact ICT awards 2011*. Nottingham: Naace. Available online at: www.naace.co.uk/conference2011/naace impactawards2011/shortlist. Accessed on 1 February 2014.

Office for Standards in Education (Ofsted) (2009) *The importance of ICT: Information and communication technology in primary and secondary schools, 2005/2008*. London: Ofsted. Available online at: www.ofsted.gov.uk/sites/default/files/documents/surveys-and-good-practice/t/ The%20importance%20of%20ICT.doc. Accessed on 1 February 2014.

Office for Standards in Education (Ofsted) (2010) *Scargill Junior School – inspection report*. London: Ofsted. Available online at: www.ofsted.gov.uk/provider/files/947113/urn/102281. pdf. Accessed on 1 February 2014.

Office for Standards in Education (Ofsted) (2011) *The Mawney School – inspection report*. London: Ofsted. Available online at: www.ofsted.gov.uk/schools/for-parents-and-carers/find-school-inspection-report. Accessed on 31 January 2014.

Prensky, M. (2007) 'How to teach with technology: Keeping both teachers and students comfortable in an era of exponential change'. *Emerging technologies for education*, Vol. 2. Coventry: Becta. Available online at: http://dera.ioe.ac.uk/1502/2/becta_2007_ emergingtechnologies_vol2_ report.pdf. Accessed on 1 February 2014.

Richards, L. (2011) 'Romford school named in top 100 of most improved in country'. *Romford Recorder*. Available online at: www.romfordrecorder.co.uk/news/romford_school_named_in_top_100_of_most_improved_in_country_1_771609. Accessed on 31 January 2014.

Royal Society (2012) 'Shut down or restart? The way forward for computing in UK schools'. Available online at: http://royalsociety.org/education/policy/computing-in-schools/report/. Accessed on 31 January 2014.

Schön, D. (2001) 'Introduction'. In D. Schön, B. Sanyal and W.J. Mitchell (eds) *High technology and low-income communities*. London: MIT Press.

Tanner, H. and Davies, S. (2011) 'How engagement with research changes the professional practice of teacher-educators: A case study from the Welsh Education Research Network'. In I. Menter and J. Murray (eds) *Developing research in teacher education*. Oxon: Routledge.

Wheeler, S., Waite, S.J. and Bromfield, C. (2002) 'Promoting creative thinking through the use of ICT'. *Journal of Computer Assisted Learning*, 18: 67–378.

Williamson, B. and Payton, S. (2009) *Curriculum and teaching innovation: Transforming classroom practice and personalisation*. Bristol: Futurelab.

5 Visual literacy for all teachers and learners

Essential knowledge and skills to create, use and assess concept maps and graphic organizers

Jeff Beaudry

Introduction

The chapter is developed around a series of provocations. First, what is visual literacy? What do we know about visual literacy, in particular concept maps and graphic organizers? Second, how do visual literacy strategies such as concept maps and graphic organizers play a role in teaching, learning and assessment in the primary classroom? What evidence is there that visual literacy strategies affect pupil engagement, cognitive growth and achievement? Are the potential effects consistent for learners at all ages and grades? Finally, what roles do technological tools play in the use of visual literacy for the benefit of teaching, learning and assessment in the primary classroom?

Objectives

At the end of the chapter you should:

- understand the definition of visual literacy;
- understand the need for a deeper understanding and mastery of visual literacy;
- understand and be able to use 7–8 teaching, learning and assessment strategies based on the construction and use of maps and graphic organizers;
- understand the value of maps and graphic organizers on assessment for learning (formative) and the potential for assessment of learning (summative).

What is visual literacy?

Visual literacy represents a variety of approaches to teaching, learning and assessment that stems from pictures, drawings, photographs, concept maps, graphics, videos and multimedia. As visual literacy emerged in the educational field in the 1960s through the 1990s, proponents of visual learning such as Tony Buzan (mind mapping), Joseph Novak (concept mapping), Richard Sinatra (semantic mapping and thinking networks), Gabrielle Rico (clustering), Nancy Margulies (mindscaping), and David Hyerle (thinking maps and cognitive map primitives) provided examples, evidence of the effects, and created software programmes to support visual literacy for creative problem solving, thinking, reading and writing. Graphicacy is a term very closely associated with visual literacy. Here is my operational definition of visual literacy: The ability to view, understand, analyze and evaluate, design and create, and use visuals and visual representations for acquisition, consolidation and communication and transfer of knowledge. Visual literacy involves both intra-personal and meta-cognitive, as well as inter-personal, collaboration. Visual literacy combines the use of a variety of visual products (lists, tables, graphics, graphic organizers, concept maps, mind maps, argument maps, timelines and systems maps) with teaching, learning and assessing processes, and creates interconnections of visual, oral, written, visual representation, numeracy and technological literacy (see Figure 5.1).

Visual literacy has a unique and positive role as a twenty-first century competency, especially the development of creative problem solving and innovative thinking, see for example https://sites.google.com/a/maine.edu/visualliteracy20/. For example, teachers and learners should be able to brainstorm and generate ideas, and then consolidate information into conceptual maps, create effective lists, timelines (e.g., lesson plans, historical sequences) and system maps (e.g., ecological systems, organizational systems, and process diagrams). Visual literacy strategies help teachers and learners explore a variety of cognitive, reasoning processes such as classification, comparative thinking, as well as analysis, evaluation and design thinking. Visual literacy develops 'the capacity of our pupils to use visual tools for seeking isolated definitions in context with while also consciously seeking the form in text structures across whole passages and books' to strengthen vocabulary, reading comprehension and writing (Hyerle, 2009: 26). The fundamental understanding and mastery of concept maps and graphic organizers are

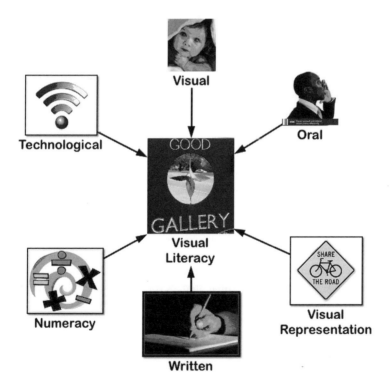

Figure 5.1 Elements of visual literacy system.

essential competencies for educators who seek to utilize and strengthen choices in their 'toolkit' of strategies (Sinatra, Beaudry, Pizzo, and Geisert, 1994).

Visual literacy is especially important in the elementary or primary school years as learners make the transition from viewing and speaking to formal language acquisition and incorporate the rules of speaking and writing, and from making marks and drawing to letters, language and text-based learning. Concept maps and graphic organizers are effective tools for meaningful learning (Novak and Cañas, 2006), critical thinking (Shedletsky and Beaudry, 2014), engaged, high-quality reasoning processes (e.g., comparison, analysis, design) and products that mark the progression of knowledge for teachers and learners (Gorman and Heinze-Fry, 2014).

From haphazard visual learning experiences to twenty-first-century competencies

Welcome to the twenty-first century, described by some as a visually-saturated world. I have heard many of my colleagues say, 'I am not a visual person.' What does it mean, that 'I can't draw' or 'I'm no good at art'? Learners are beset by the cognitive dissonance between the dominant model of 'highly constrained linear presentation of information in classrooms as text blocks', as opposed to 'multidimensional mapping of mental models that the brain naturally performs' (Hyerle, 2009: 12). In the twenty-first century we need to expand the visual thinking or mapping and mapping skills. The access to and use of media, software, games, and apps displayed on a wide variety of desktops, laptops, tablets, mobile phones and large flat-screen monitors are exerting tremendous influences on learning and education, not to mention social media, mobile apps and gaming. Pupils are being forced to view, interpret and create media, mixing text, photo images and video in a variety of formats and visual representations. Visual literacy plays an implicit role in our daily lives, what Carlin Flora says contributes to our 'everyday creativity' (2009: 1). It is not enough to read and write; it is likely that you are asking pupils to design and create new media forms.

Technological tools help us gain competence, but for most of us we are struggling at the beginning of a very important, but rather haphazard process (Metros and Woolsey, 2006). Metros (2009) suggested that our experience of living in a visually-saturated world may be described in three stages of visual literacy: 1) stimulated, 2) literate, and 3) fluent. Being stimulated means we are interacting with visuals constantly, but more as a passive consumer; strictly reading and interpreting visuals; more likely to imitate others and reproduce existing visuals. Next is the visually-literate phase, in which we understand the visual vocabulary and concepts and begin to learn how to construct visuals by imitation of others. Visual literacy is described by Sinatra (1986), Novak and Gowin (1986), Hyerle (1996; 2009), Trowbridge and Wandersee (1998), Kinchin (2001), and Beaudry and Wilson (2010), but the dissemination of visual literacy into practice is not very systematic. The final step beyond the visually-literate phase is the fluent phase, in which we contribute to the visual vocabulary, we are expert viewers, de-coders and consumers and we can create and produce visuals.

The use of templates is considered a literate use of visuals, and not yet fluent. Fluent users create unique visual representations and concept maps to solve new problems. The ability to judge the quality of pupils' work has come a long way due to the continuing emphasis on assessment in education (Stiggins *et al.*, 2004; Black *et al.*, 2004), but there needs to be more specific emphasis on the judgment of visuals (Beaudry and

Wilson, 2010). To this end there are examples of how maps fit with formative and summative assessment.

To sum up, the use of templates is considered a literate use of visuals, and not yet fluent. Fluent users create unique visual representations and concept maps to solve new problems. The ability to judge quality of academic work has come a long way due to the continuing emphasis on assessment in education (Stiggins *et al.*, 2004; Black *et al.* (2004), but there needs to be more specific emphasis on the judgement of visuals (Beaudry and Wilson, 2010). To this end there are examples of how maps fit with formative and summative assessment.

Standards and visual literacy: more room for improvement!

The evidence supporting concept mapping and visual literacy is strong but seems to run counter to the experience and practice of educators, many of whom don't acknowledge the value of visual literacy and do not incorporate it into their classrooms. Contrast this with educational systems in countries in Latin America, where the value of visual literacy has been directly incorporated into efforts to promote shared expertise in schools (Cañas *et al.*, 2001). Educational mandates – such as standards-based learning and common core standards in the traditional content areas such as reading, writing, mathematics, science and the arts – tend to focus on separate strands of learning and reinforce linear, text-based information. In the USA the push for the Common Core Standards, with the emphasis on reading and mathematics, minimizes the role visual literacy can have

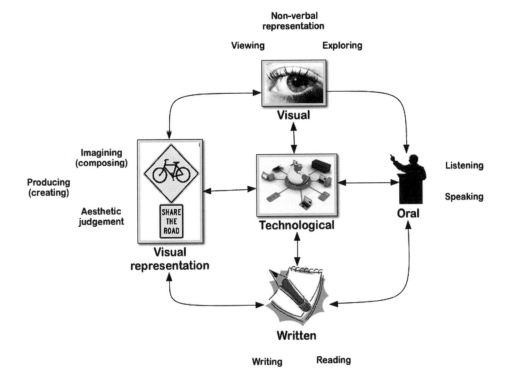

Figure 5.2 Sinatra's conception of visual literacy (1986).

in teaching, learning and assessment. Whether by lack of understanding or by design this may impede a broader conceptual understanding and practical use of visual literacy by teachers across the grade spans.

In the detailed and integrated definition of literacy presented by Sinatra (1986) (see Figure 5.2) technological literacy is the central component to integrate the traditional (written and oral spoken) and the emerging, non-traditional (visual and visual representation) forms of literacy. The model is important because it suggests that visual and visual representation are equals to the traditional modes of literacy, and that in any model literacy is best understood as an integrative and complex concept that must be maintained and developed to maximize learning for all.

In the two literacy models, Figure 5.1 and Figure 5.2, text and words are important but are not the dominant or more important literacy mode; visual representations in pictures, videos and graphics are just as necessary for learning. In addition, numbers can be represented graphically in sets, lists, formulas and tables. The concept of numeracy can be added to visual literacy to create a more holistic model for teaching, learning and assessment in early childhood and the primary grades. This synthesis of these models provides a systems view of literacy approaches. Ahead are more specific examples of teachers' planning and pupils' products to illustrate visual literacy throughout the grades.

Technological tool as visual representations

The literacy model by Sinatra (1986) placed technology at the centre of visual literacy (see Figure 5.2). As the power and affordances of technological tools such as computers and visual learning software like 'Inspiration', 'Mind Meister' and 'FreeMind' keep growing visual literacy is likely to be propelled into new prominence for learning. With over forty visual, concept mapping programmes available (www.dzinepress.com/2010/03/40-ultimate-useful-mind-mapping-tools/), new, low-cost programmes are accessible to teachers and learners. While visuals can be created with glue-paper-scissors (GPS) and markers (Beaudry and Wilson, 2010), computer software allows for digital storage and sharing of concept maps. There are Web 2.0 concept mapping systems such as 'Webspiration©' (www.mywebspiration.com/) and 'CMap Tools' (http://cmap.ihmc.us/) to instantly collaborate and share with international partners. Concept mapping programmes are available as mobile apps such as 'Kidspiration Maps' and 'Inspiration Maps' (www.inspiration.com/go/ipad). The essential components of a concept mapping programme are the text in shapes/symbols and links, arrows or lines, but programmes like 'Inspiration' products allow for users to annotate and write directly on the concept map with 'notes' and create hyperlinks to URLs. One product stands out as a leader in accessibility for learners with special needs; 'Inspiration' has audio capacity to read text, making spoken version concept maps, and can be quickly exported to a word document, portable graphic (.png) file or portable document (.pdf) file. In addition programmes such as 'Inspiration' offer a large selection of templates, ready to scaffold learners if they need assistance with overall forms.

At the heart of these technological tools is the new, blank page, what I call the 'problem-solving space'. Once learners are confident with the affordances and capacity of these technological tools they have a powerful new thinking strategy that, with time and practice, will become highly effective and a time-saver. In one case study (Gomez, Griffiths, & Pooshan, 2014), researchers compared the time it took to read and score complex essays, an average of 15 minutes, to the time it took to read and score concept maps, an average of 1.5–2 minutes. Teachers and students should have a flexible approach to concept mapping and visual literacy, so that they can adapt the essential visual, concept mapping skills to new learning environments.

Empirical research on concept mapping and graphic organizers

Visual literacy can be a very engaging and productive set of strategies that can have a positive impact on pupil engagement and achievement. According to research reviews by Nesbit and Adesope (2006), Hattie (2009) and Adesope and Nesbit (2010) there is consistent evidence of the positive effects of visual strategies like concept mapping on pupil outcomes such as achievement and engagement. Further analysis underscored the impact of concept maps when used as a tool for collaborative dialogue.

Evidence from the meta-analyses of over 100 empirical studies indicates the following:

- A large impact is found when a student constructs and re-constructs his/her own map;
- pupils exhibit high levels of learner engagement in the content with maps;
- pupils who use their maps for collaborative dialogue are more engaged with the content and achieve at a higher level;
- pupils must have sufficient opportunity to learn and practice concept mapping in order to use it effectively;
- learners with reading difficulties and lower organizational skills can increase reading comprehension;
- pupils benefit the most from the collection and reflection on the progression of mapping and re-mapping concepts on their own maps;
- students using mapping tend to have greater recall of concepts than students who use lists and outlines;
- both teacher-generated (expert) maps and student-generated (novice) maps are essential to maximize learning;
- pupils who lack prior knowledge may benefit from mapping more than students with greater prior knowledge;
- effects of concept maps may have the greatest impact in areas where there is a great deal of vocabulary and language to be learned;
- pupils with low verbal ability may benefit from mapping more than students with high verbal ability (Nesbit and Adesope, 2006; Hattie, 2009; Adesope and Nesbit, 2010).

As you would expect, concept mapping and visual literacy requires practice and preparation to be successful. Proponents of visual literacy may over-state the ease with which learners master their own visual literacy, an issue raised by the research study on practice retrieval by Karpicke and Blount (2011). The critical element for future research is to design more rigorous experimental studies to examine the time needed to develop visual literacy competencies. While that will take time the immediate concern for teachers is how much time and what variety of tasks contribute to the effective use of concept maps and graphic organizers. Based on a series of case studies about critical thinking and visual representation we recommend that students produce at least five to ten concept maps to master the skills and the technological tools in order to transfer the impact to academic outcomes (Beaudry, 2014; Shedletsky and Beaudry, 2014).

Visual literacy and concept mapping: phases of learning

How do concept maps and graphic organizers fit into the phases of teaching and learning? The model for self-directed learning by Meichenbaum and Biemiller (1998) includes three phases of learning: 1) acquisition, 2) consolidation, and 3) consultation, while Hyerle 's model includes learning engagement (acquisition, brainstorming), consolidation (sorting, organizing, analyzing and expressing ideas in speech and writing) and transfer to new media (design and production). The concept map of phases of development in Figure 5.3 is a synthesis of the two models and includes the effect size estimates from research syntheses (Nesbit and Adesope, 2006; Hattie, 2009; Adesope and Nesbit, 2010). In this new model the phases are:

1   the engagement phase with generative flow;
2   the consolidation phase with critical thinking flow; and
3   the transfer phase with design and creative flow (Csikszentmihalyi, 2009).

Brainstorming is the best example of the acquisition phase as these energetic activities generate what pupils know, a good start to understanding students' prior knowledge. Maps can be a detailed and easily revised visual representation of prior knowledge (Novak, 1998). Having a map as a visual representation of prior knowledge provides learners and teachers with a starting point for formative (self-assessment, meta-cognition) and summative assessment (pre- and post-assessments). The first map can be read and modified to incorporate new learning and dynamically revised to address unclear language, mistakes and deep misconceptions (see Visual literacy scenario #1 for a detailed example).

   With one engaging activity teachers can learn more about and accommodate learners' preferences and build confidence by presenting information in both formats, as the front and back of a single page, with the outline on one side and the concept map on the other. In this way, pupils can get used to the idea of multiple representations of information and make their own choice according to their own preference, facilitated by your instructional design. Challenge yourself to present information to align with the universal design for learning (see www.udlcenter.org).

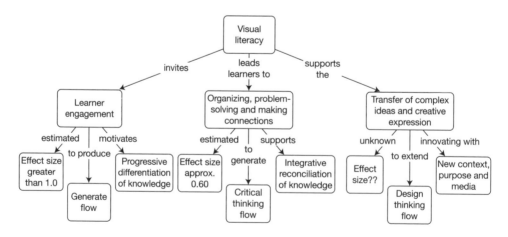

Figure 5.3 Phases of visual thinking and concept mapping.

Task 5.1 Am I a visual learner?

As you think about visual literacy, you can ask some very important questions and address one of the misconceptions. So far you may have treated this as an abstraction. This assessment sets the stage for you and your students by asking about your preference for text/outline versus visual representation. Take a look at the two graphic organizers (see the website https://sites.google.com/a/maine.edu/visual literacy20/) and compare a concept map with an outline for the same information. If you were given the choice of visual, outline, or no preference, what would you choose? Do you have a strong preference for either one? Do you know what your learners' dispositions are for the outline versus the concept map? Are there learners with strong preferences?

The visual assessment of preferences gives you a place to start thinking about how you view visuals, and reflects on your background, prior knowledge and your engagement with visual literacy. As a teacher your visual literacy challenge is to learn how to design maps that transfer directly to outlines, or vice versa. Software programmes are designed with these two visual choices in mind and have a toggle button for immediate conversion from map to outline.

Visual literacy scenario #1
Radiating thoughts: starting in the middle

Young learners are in the transition stages of language development and already oriented to viewing pictures. Buzan suggests that we think from a central picture or word/idea and radiate outwards into spokes (1996). According to Buzan you should use one word per line, make the lines curved, use colours for different concepts, and connect the main branches to the central concept and link secondary terms to the secondary terms. In the example below first grade pupils have begun to work on the unit on bats. The map in Figure 5.4 began with the image of the black bat with wings spread as the central concept. In this visual the ideas have been represented as direct links to the central image and ready for the next stage, sorting and categorizing. The power of the first map is that it is inclusive of pupils' writing skills and captures the breadth of their diverse thinking. The teacher is allowing the pupils to create their own map with an image at the centre.

The next step is for pupils to talk about the concepts. Hand-drawn maps are necessary for very young learners who are in the early stage of technology use and are a straightforward way to represent knowledge. Hand-drawn maps require the teacher to pay attention to letter formation, spelling and to interpret phrases. Take a look at the hand-drawn map and ask yourself some questions about this map. Overall, what does the map tell you about the prior knowledge of your pupils? What else does it tell you about the language skills of the first graders?

As mentioned, whole-group and small-group discussions with guiding questions can assist students to dig deeper into their understanding. One possible choice is to use the Visual Thinking Strategies approach (www.vtshome.org/what-is-vts/method-curriculum–2).

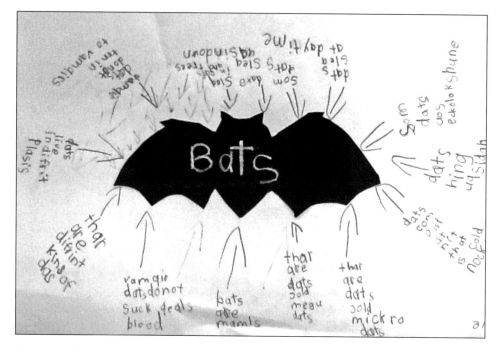

Figure 5.4 Hand-drawn, radiating concept map of bats.

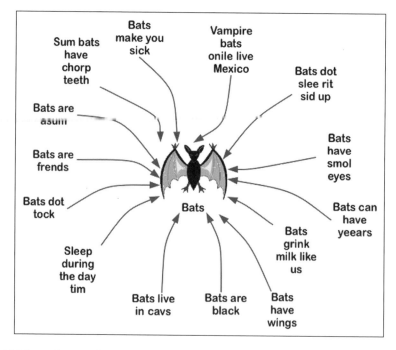

Figure 5.5 Map of bats re-drawn with visual mapping software, with the original spelling preserved.

In this approach the teacher asks three questions and facilitates a discussion with the whole class:

- What is going on in this picture (map)?
- What do you see that makes you say that?
- What more can we find?

The power of mapping and visual strategies is that there is less to read, with plenty of space to make additional notes, comments and corrections.

I took the step to re-draw the hand-drawn map of the bat using concept mapping software, in order to show the details (see Figure 5.5). Overall the effect on conceptual development is that there is no advantage to the use of a computer-drawn map when compared directly with the hand-drawn map, but the advantages are apparent when you make the crucial next step – revision and re-drawing. The question to pupils would be, 'How can you reorganize this information for better understanding?' The next challenge to the class would be for each pupil to re-draw this map, thus asking each pupil to integrate the new understanding of bats with prior knowledge. The technological tools help you revise and save new versions of your work. Ultimately the map can be saved and included as an image or figure in written work.

Visual literacy scenario #2
Moving from brainstorm lists to a concept map

Pupils get very excited when you ask them to brainstorm ideas. The level of engagement is predictably very high because they are participating directly in the construction of ideas, but what happens after the brainstorming is vital to the progression of learning. The essential difference from a visual literacy perspective is to create the brainstorm list as individual, movable words and concepts, and not as a list. Teachers can hand out index cards or cut-out pieces of paper that allow you to sort, categorize and re-categorize concepts into a meaningful hierarchy. Beaudry and Wilson (2010) recommend that the initial maps be done in small groups to promote collaborative learning. The low-tech strategy was nicknamed GPS, which means 'group-paper-scissors'. Technological tools have their advantage but you can begin with an active learning strategy such as cut-outs or expanding the open space to include a classroom floor. You could stop there or proceed to add words, usually verbs or prepositions, to the linking lines – a step unique to concept maps as originated by Novak and Gowin (1984). In this step the mappers are constructing propositions, basic sentences and further extending the mapping activity for development of language. This step is challenging for the map creator because a concept–link–concept structure requires a deeper understanding of key concepts and an explanation of the nature and direction of the linkage.

The following scenario is based on the strategy known as the 'parking lot' (Novak and Cañas, 2006) and it is used to model the map-building process with an analogy with pupils. The list of words is called the 'parking lot' because the words look as if they are parked on a line. The list begins the focus question 'What are things we eat?' and included:

1 Jam
2 Bread
3 Candy
4 Carrots
5 Cookies
6 Meat
7 Chicken
8 Cheese
9 Gravy
10 Potatoes.

The idea of creating a structure of knowledge is challenging and students may be unable to sort and categorize information into coherent 'chunks' or maps. After working in small and large groups the results looked like the map in Figure 5.6, still a list. Kinchin (2001) identifies three types of maps: the list or chain of concepts; the wheel in which concepts radiate from a central concept; and the network or system of ideas, as in a fully developed concept map with multiple levels of concepts and cross-links (see Figure 5.7).

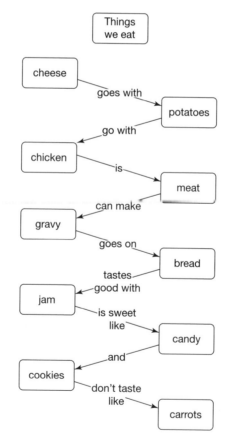

Figure 5.6 Concepts of 'things we eat' arranged in a chain of ideas.

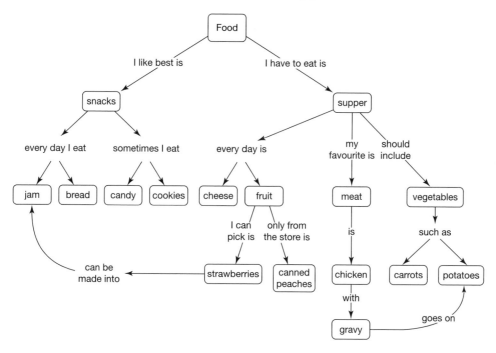

Figure 5.7 Concept map with new concepts, linking words, and cross-links of concepts arranged as a network.

Visual literacy scenario #3
Using a concept map to make comparisons and to understand similarities and differences of concepts

Making comparisons is one of the most powerful reasoning strategies according to Marzano (2001), and it provides an opportunity to apply visual literacy to improve on a familiar approach, the Venn diagram. A popular visual template for a Venn diagram is two, intersecting circles (see Figure 5.8). A more precise visual, named the 'double bubble', allows you to provide more specific language development (see Figure 5.9 and Figure 5.10). A suggestion would be to use the Venn diagram initially to make the comparisons between concepts, and to progress to the double bubble once you have established definitions of key concepts. The double bubble now offers the next step in vocabulary development with the linking words. The development of propositions with nodes–link–node connections challenges learners to integrate cognitive structures.

Case study 5.1 Creating concept maps as multimedia

As teachers we want to capture pupils' interests, to connect with a positive disposition to sustain pupils' attention. In this example of a sixth-grade classroom the teacher asked this essential question: 'How can I improve my practice through the use of concept mapping, technology, rubrics and pupil involvement in assessment?' (B. Connolly, personal communication, May, 2012). In this case the topic, ancient Egypt, was interesting (at least as far as the teacher was concerned), as the teacher asked pupils to write a paper

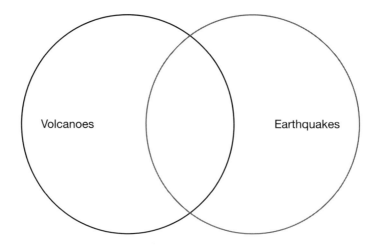

Figure 5.8 Venn diagram as a template for comparison of volcanoes and earthquakes.

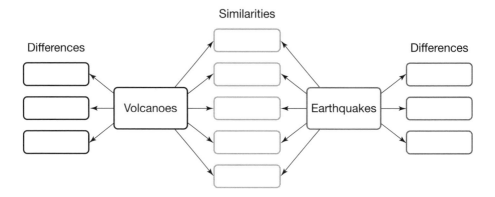

Figure 5.9 Double bubble map as a template for comparison of volcanoes and earthquakes.

about some aspect of life in ancient Egypt. In order to help pupils focus on the project the teacher assembled texts and videos about Egypt on a website, but was seeing a large proportion of pupils' work that lacked focus, rigour and organization. To begin she reduced the range of topics on the unit from ten to six (i.e., pyramids, daily life, modern Egypt, inventions, ancient Egyptian religion/gods and goddesses, and pharaohs). The two strategies she employed were the formative use of concept mapping to help provide focus and organization and student involvement in the use of the rubric to help pupils understand how to use a rubric to judge quality of the Egypt projects. Attributes to be assessed included the following: main idea, essential questions, use of class time, use of arrows (links), images, and 'sticky' notes.

The software tool, 'Webspiration©', contains the basic features of the standard 'Inspiration' programme – symbols (nodes), links, notes, hyperlinks, colours, shapes, templates and clip art. In addition, it is the web-based version of a concept map software

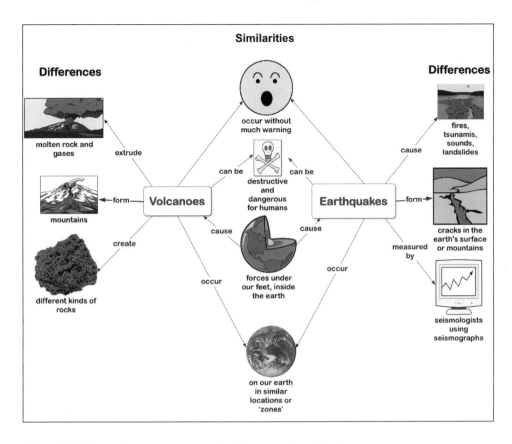

Figure 5.10 Comparison concept map of volcanoes and earthquakes.

programme, which allows users to create and share access to concept maps with a community of learners who use the same concept map. First of all she practised with her pupils, asking each one to create a concept map with the following directions:

1 You are the 'main idea'.
2 Create at least three categories (sub-topics) branching off to describe yourself.
3 Break down each category into even more detail – add a 'sticky' note!
4 Use colour to make your map clearer.
5 Experiment with finding pictures that go along with your topic.
6 Organize your map and 'stickies' in a neat, easy-to-understand design.

She gave the pupils fifteen minutes to build their person map, an event that both energized pupils and built pupils' capacity. Concept mapping with the technology tool was a specific strategy to organize and focus writing, and collect the digital media in a single, easily accessible location.

Summary and key points

Visual literacy is an integrative approach that seeks a better balance of text and images to develop multiple literacies. Current standards-based thinking may foster a reinforcement of traditional modes of literacy, reading, writing and speaking, unless we support the evolution of twenty-first century skills such as collaboration, social identities, creativity and systems thinking (Shute, 2008). Research on visual literacy, especially concept maps, provides strong evidence for improvements in memory, identification of main ideas, scaffolding organization of written products, systems thinking and collaboration. Visual literacy, especially concept mapping, provides strategies to improve short-term memory by allowing individuals to develop his/her own customized framework or scaffold of concepts representing a memory path to follow to communicate ideas to others. Teachers gain an efficient strategy to review and provide feedback on students' summaries. At the same time these visual representations reveal the boundaries of knowledge to both the expert and the accomplished novice, and the points of further learner engagement for future understanding and meaningful learning. With the affordances of multimedia and the Internet, coupled with the increasing demands on learners to make sense of the rapidly developing knowledge base, the promise for visual literacy is clear – can we see it and deliver?

Further reading

Buzan, T. (1996) *The mind map book: How to use radiant thinking to maximize your brain's untapped potential.* New York: Penguin Books.
>   This is a must-read book about visual literacy. Written for a popular audience with visual examples of the benefits for memory, writing, and planning.

Novak, J. and Gowin, D. (1984) *Learning how to learn.* New York: Cambridge University Press.
>   This describes concept mapping devised to help primary-grade pupils to remember complex scientific concepts and provide a scaffold for teacher–pupil interviews. The basic use of the node-link visual has been validated by almost thirty years of research.

Shedletsky, L. and Beaudry, J. (2014) *Cases on teaching critical thinking through visual representation strategies.* Hershey, PA: IGI Publications.
>   These are case studies by teacher-researchers who are using visual representations such as mind maps, concept maps and argument maps to improve pupils' critical thinking. The impact on writing, oral communications, collaboration and construction of knowledge is emphasised.

Additional resources and websites

www.inpsiration.com
Inspiration©, Webspiration©, InspirationMaps©
http://cmap.ihmc.us/
CMap Tools construction and modeling
Forty Ultimate Useful Mind-mapping Tools
www.dzinepress.com/2010/03/40-ultimate-useful-mind-mapping-tools/
https://sites.google.com/a/maine.edu/visualliteracy20/

References

Adesope, O. and Nesbit J. (2010) 'A systematic review of research on collaborative learning with concept maps'. In R. Marriott and P. Torres (eds) *Handbook of research on collaborative learning using concept mapping*. Hershey, PA: IGI Publications.

Beaudry, J. and Wilson, P. (2010) 'Concept mapping and formative assessment: Elements supporting literacy and learning'. In P. Torres and R. Marriott (eds) *Handbook of research on collaborative learning using concept mapping*. Hershey, PA: IGI Publications.

Beaudry, J. (2014) 'Thinking critically about visual representations: A visual journey to understand critical thinking'. In L. Shedletsky and J. Beaudry (eds) *Cases on teaching critical thinking through visual representation strategies*. Hershey, PA: IGI Publications.

Black, P., McCormick, R., James, M. and Pedder, D. (2004) 'Learning how to learn and assessment for learning'. *Research Papers in Education*, 21(2): 119–32.

Buzan, T. (1996) *The mind map book: How to use radiant thinking to maximize your brain's untapped potential*. New York, NY: Penguin Books.

Cañas, A.J., Ford, K.M., Novak, J.D., Hayes, P., Reichherzer, T. and Suri, N. (2001) 'Online concept maps: Enhancing collaborative learning by using technology with concept maps'. *The Science Teacher*, 68(4): 49–51.

Csikszentmihalyi, M. (2009) *Flow*. New York, NY: HarperCollins.

Flora, C. (2009) 'Everyday creativity'. *Psychology Today*: November. www.psychologytoday.com/articles/200910/everyday-creativity. Accessed in October 2013.

Gomez, G., Griffiths, R. and Pooshan, N. (2014) 'Concept maps as replacements of written essays in efficient assessment of medical knowledge'. In L. Shedletsky and J. Beaudry (eds) *Cases on teaching critical thinking through visual representation strategies*. Hershey, PA: IGI Publications.

Gorman and Henize-Fry, J. (2014) 'Conceptual mapping facilitates coherence and critical thinking in the science education system'. In L. Shedletsky and J. Beaudry (eds) *Cases on teaching critical thinking through visual representation strategies*. Hershey, PA: IGI Publications.

Hattie, J. (2009) *Visible learning: A synthesis of over 800 meta-analyses relating to achievement*. London, UK: Routledge.

Hyerle, D. (1996) *Visual tools for constructing knowledge*. Alexandria, VA: Association for Supervision and Curriculum Development.

Hyerle, D. (2009) *Visible tools for transforming information into knowledge*. Newbury Park, CA: Corwin Press

Karpicke, J. and Blount, J. (2011) 'Retrieval practice produces more learning than elaborative studying with concept mapping'. *Science*, 331(6018): 772–5.

Kinchin, I. (2001) 'If concept mapping is so helpful to learning biology, why aren't we all doing it?'. *International Journal of Science Education*, 23(12): 1257–69.

Marzano, R. (2001) *What works in schools: Translating research into action*. Reston, VA: Association for Supervision and Curriculum Development.

Meichenbaum, D. and Biemiller, A. (1998) *Nurturing independent learners: Helping students take charge of their learning*. Newton, MA: Brookline Books.

Metros, S. (October, 2009) 'Stages of visual literacy'. Keynote address at the International Visual Literacy Association, Chicago, IL.

Metros, S. and Woolsey, K. (2006, May/June) 'Visual literacy: An institutional imperative'. *EDUCAUSE Review*, 41(3): 80–2.

Nesbit, J. and Adesope, O. (2006) 'Learning with concept and knowledge maps: A meta-analysis'. *Review of Educational Research*, 76(3): 413–48.

Novak, J. and Gowin, D. (1984) *Learning how to learn*. New York: Cambridge University Press.

Novak, J. (1998) *Learning, creating, and using knowledge: Concept maps as facilitative tools in schools and corporations*. Mahwah, NJ: Lawrence Erlbaum Associates.

Novak, J. and Cañas, A. (2006) *The theory underlying concept maps and how to construct them*. Technical Report IHMC CmapTools 2006–01, Florida Institute for Human and Machine Cognition.

Shedletsky, L. and Beaudry, J. (2014) *Cases on teaching critical thinking through visual representation strategies*. Hershey, PA: IGI Publications.

Shute, V. (2008 'Focus on formative feedback'. *Review of Educational Research*, 78(1): 153–87.

Sinatra, R. (1986) *Visual literacy connections to thinking, reading, and writing*. Springfield, IL: Charles Thomas Press.

Sinatra, R. (2000) 'Teaching learners to think, read, and write more effectively in content subjects'. *The Clearing House*, 73(5): 266–73.

Sinatra, R., Beaudry, J., Pizzo, J. and Geisert, G. (1994) 'Using computer-based semantic mapping, reading, and writing approach with at-risk fourth graders'. *Journal of Computing in Childhood Education*, 5(11): 93–112.

Stiggins, R., Arter, J., Chappuis, J. and Chappuis, S. (2004) *Classroom assessment for student learning*. Portland, OR: Assessment Training Institute.

Trowbridge, J. and Wandersee, J. (1998) 'Theory-driven graphic organizers'. In Mintzes, J., Wandersee, J. and Novak, J. (eds) *Teaching science for understanding*. London, UK: Elsevier Academic Press.

6 Delivering the mathematics curriculum through technology-enhanced learning

Andrea Holloway

Introduction

There is a well-used mantra for student teachers and Newly Qualified Teachers (NQTs): 'only use ICT if it enhances the learning outcomes.' In England, with the changes in the new curriculum and ever-advancing technology, there is a shift towards delivering the mathematical curriculum with a focus on the mathematical content, but one that encourages the use of technology-enhanced learning, unless it *detracts* from the learning outcomes. At a National College for Excellence in Teaching Mathematics (NCETM) Digital Technologies conference in 2013, David Murrells of The Ravensbourne School, Bromley, put forward the suggestion that 'in the past, ICT was considered a privilege; now it is a right.'

Dr Vanessa Pittard, responsible for science, technology, engineering and mathematics (STEM) education and technology in schools at the Department for Education, at the same NCETM 2013 conference, shared her belief that the national curriculum provides a clear rationale for the use of cross-curricular ICT. Pittard argues for the need to integrate devices, consider mobility and connectivity and make use of a range of interfaces to enhance and develop user skills. Pupils need to become confident and competent in a range of life skills, many of which relate to technology (Jisc, 2009). We need to seize the opportunity to embed technology across the curriculum and the new mathematics and computing curricula provide clear opportunities for this. As the Department for Education (DfE), 2012 p. 2 states,

> Consider how ICT can best be used to support the teaching of mathematics . . . a wider range of new technology should be considered . . . Many ICT tools allow pupils to use different mathematical representations (e.g. number, algebra, graphs) to aid conceptual development. As technology changes, teachers need to assess what the latest innovations offer in teaching mathematics.

Opportunities are there to exploit and develop in any curriculum; this chapter aims to empower you as a professional to develop strategies to meet these challenges.

Objectives

At the end of this chapter you should be able to:

- develop a clear rationale for the use of technology to enhance mathematical learning activities;
- develop a range of technology-enhanced mathematical learning activities;

- build on your current knowledge of research, to support your development in this area;
- refer to a range of reference points to support your own continuous professional development (CPD).

Overview

The requirement for delivering technology-enhanced learning activities is not only a UK governmental policy; the United Nations Educational, Scientific and Cultural Organisation (UNESCO) has recently published an 'ICT competency standards for teachers'; a framework that emphasises that:

> it is not enough for teachers to have ICT competencies and be able to teach them to their students. Teachers need to be able to help the students become collaborative, problem solving, creative learners through using ICT so they will be effective citizens and members of the workforce.
>
> (UNESCO, 2011)

This means technology needs to be used seamlessly in both teaching and learning, to ensure a country provides this future workforce with the requisite skills, knowledge and understanding needed for the twenty-first century.

Task 6.1 Self-evaluation against competencies

Access Appendix 1 (pages 23–8) of the UNESCO framework (see URL below), which lists modules for technology literacy. Reflect on your current practice in using technology-based learning in the delivery of mathematics and identify your level of confidence and capability in terms of the teacher competences listed. How can you evidence these specifically, e.g., lesson plans, observations? Which competences do you need to develop further? How can you do this while keeping a focus on the mathematical objectives? Map the outcomes to update your PDP and set targets for School Experience (SE) (www.unesco.org/new/en/unesco/themes/icts/teacher-education/unesco-ict-competency-framework-for-teachers/).

In terms of technology, it is crucial to consider how we can use resources to enhance children's understanding of the mathematical learning objectives for a lesson. One example is the use of the interactive whiteboard (IWB) to support the delivery of capacity, required in England in both KS1 and KS2 of the National Curriculum 2014. Capacity brings with it classroom management issues, as pupils need to develop their understanding of scale using practical resources, which can be problematic. Even in KS1, pupils need to have a range of opportunities provided: 'In order to become familiar with standard measures, pupils begin to use measuring tools such as a ruler, weighing scales and containers' (DfE, 2013a: 9).

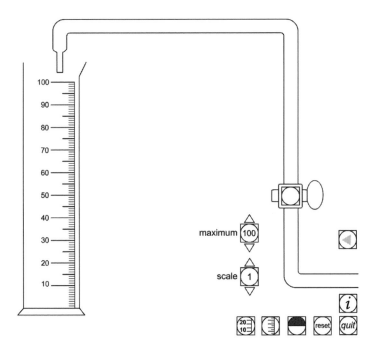

Figure 6.1 Mathematics ITP: measuring cylinder.

When making choices about teacher-led demonstrations or pupil-led investigations, it is clear that a combination of both strategies is best practice, to promote the highest possible outcomes for the development of pupils' understanding. However, when teaching capacity, teacher-led demonstration can prove ineffective due to the need for pupils to see clearly the range of scales, particularly the conversion of units. A useful strategy would be to use a IWB programme, such as the Interactive Teaching Program (ITP) 'Measuring Cylinder' (Primary National Strategy, 2004). While many of the ITPs have been superseded by arguably more engaging programmes, written with the digitally native generation in mind, this programme provides an extremely effective raft of features to enable pupils to see clearly the application and use of scale. See Figure 6.1 (Mathematics ITP: Measuring cylinder) for an example of this.

However, it must be remembered that the specific use of ITPs can vary: you can use them to simply engage and motivate and, while not the most effective use, this can still indirectly enhance outcomes; you can use them to ensure clarity of understanding in terms of visual impact and/or you can use them to develop Assessment for Learning (AfL) by building in questioning. However, a report published by CISCO (2008) (see Figure 6.2) into recent research on the impact of multimodal learning on learning demonstrates the effectiveness of using the multimodality functions of the IWB in conjunction with pupil interaction (this is in contrast to the teacher using it simply as a non-interactive teaching resource). The impact of implementing multimodal and interactive opportunities, on developing pupils' higher-order skills, are clear and impressive.

What this research suggests is that the pupils need to be engaging with the resource to gain the highest possible outcomes in terms of development of higher order and

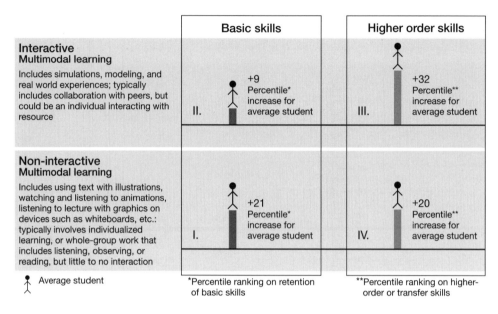

	Basic skills	Higher order skills
Interactive **Multimodal learning** Includes simulations, modeling, and real world experiences; typically includes collaboration with peers, but could be an individual interacting with resource	II. +9 Percentile* increase for average student	III. +32 Percentile** increase for average student
Non-interactive **Multimodal learning** Includes using text with illustrations, watching and listening to animations, listening to lecture with graphics on devices such as whiteboards, etc.: typically involves individualized learning, or whole-group work that includes listening, observing, or reading, but little to no interaction	I. +21 Percentile* increase for average student	IV. +20 Percentile** increase for average student

Average student   *Percentile ranking on retention of basic skills   **Percentile ranking on higher-order or transfer skills

Figure 6.2 The impact of multimodal learning in comparison to traditional, unimodal learning.
Source: Cisco, 2008.

transferable skills. In terms of the capacity ITP, this can clearly be gained by inviting pupils to come to the board and use the integrated tools to predict levels, identify intervals, convert scale, etc. This can be supported by traditional methods, such as the use of mini whiteboards and 'show me', with the rest of the class engaging in the same activity, comparing their answers to those of the pupil(s) at the IWB. This will also enable a social constructivist approach to learning (Vygotsky, 1978), through paired talk and group talk. Our awareness of the different ways that new knowledge can be constructed includes pupils engaging and interacting with others, not just IWBs. This mixed-method approach is crucial to maintain interest and engagement of all the pupils within the class and to retain opportunities for AfL.

Case study 6.1 The use of technology in delivering the EYFS curriculum

In my role as school experience tutor, I carried out an observation of a student (Louise Smith), based at a primary and nursery school, located near Birmingham. This is a one-form entry, urban primary school, with relatively low pupil premium numbers. The lesson was delivered in the spring term 2013 in the nursery. The student had planned a mathematics lesson using the Early Years Foundation Stage (EYFS) Development Matters (DM) materials and met the following recommendations for creating an enabling environment in early years:

- Plan opportunities for children to describe and compare shapes, measures and distance.

It also addressed the need for adults to:

• Introduce children to the use of mathematical names for 'solid' 3D shapes and 'flat' 2D shapes, and the mathematical terms to describe shapes.

The pupils carried out a treasure hunt around the classroom. An excellent pedagogical point was the student encouraging children to find both specific 2D shapes but also the shapes within objects, for example, a cuboid building block having some square faces. Before they began, the student modelled the use of the IWB, displaying a tally chart of the three shapes they were looking for: circle, triangle and square.

The pupils were asked, when returning with a shape, to put the shape in the box and make a mark on the tally chart. This activity clearly delivered the Early Learning Goal:

• Children recognise that a range of technology is used in places such as homes and schools. They select and use technology for particular purposes.

It also addressed further elements of the EYFS DM requirements relating to 'number'.

Classroom management had been carefully thought through as the student had anticipated the level of engagement and interest would be high. However, the student still needed to adjust her delivery, as a bottleneck of pupils wanting to record their findings on the board had developed; fortunately, the student was sufficiently confident to address this and designated additional treasure hunt roles.

The focus stayed on the mathematical content and the integration of the technology was seamless and effective.

Task 6.2 Contingency planning

Technology can and will fail; it is important to have a back-up plan in place for all lessons that have a significant element of technology incorporated into their planning. What plan would you put in place if the IWB failed in this lesson, to ensure the mathematical objectives were still being met?

Task 6.3 Implementing learning theories

Applying Vygotsky's social constructivist approach to learning (Vygotsky, 1978) can enhance outcomes. How could a set of six mobile tablet devices be used within this lesson to promote a social constructivist approach to learning?

Case study 6.2 Colley Lane Primary School: the use of voting technology in Year 1 and Year 6

This three-form entry primary school has taken bold steps in integrating technology in numeracy lessons to engage and focus their pupils when carrying out mathematical activities.

The school is set in an area of socio-economic deprivation. Assessment for Learning (AfL) (see AfL MESH Guide www.MESHguides.org) is seen as a crucial part of the pedagogical process and is embedded throughout the school. However, we were keen to make use of a range of strategies to keep pupils engaged. Previously we have used IWB to address AfL across the curriculum, by using PowerPoint presentations to scaffold questioning sessions. When we were given the opportunity to implement voting technology hardware and software linked with the IWB, we decided to make the focus on mental maths skills.

The voting resource was integrated into the Year 6 booster group, where it was hoped the resource would maintain pupils' focus and engagement in numeracy lessons and to identify specific areas pupils needed to consolidate to secure Level 4. The nature of mental maths skills and the pace required in numeracy lessons ideally suit this type of resource. The traditional methods of AfL were maintained but the use of the voting software again provided an additional level of interest to the tasks. The resource undoubtedly aided classroom management and resulted in these pupils, rapidly coming towards the end of their primary career, still being enthusiastic to take part in numeracy lessons. It crucially informed planning, supporting these pupils in consolidating a range of vital mental maths skills and enabling them to secure Level 4.

To engage very young pupils in focused assessment activities, we trialled the same technology in Year 1, with thirty children aged between five and six, who were developing mental maths skills, specifically addition. While the use of mini whiteboards and 'show me' activities was maintained, the addition of the voting activity definitely promoted engagement and gave value to the activities. The speed and accuracy of the response raised the effectiveness and, with a focus on a positive and supportive ethos, pupils were happy to share if they had answered incorrectly. When using mini whiteboards and 'show me' activities, pupils can be reticent to display their answers in case of error, which often has an impact on self-esteem. This did not appear to be the case with the voting software. We had drawn links to the different games children were familiar with on television and there appeared to be a raised level of enjoyment.

In both year groups and throughout the activities, we realised it was vital that questioning remained a focus, both from teachers and teaching assistants and peer-to-peer. The process was evaluated and changes made, as lower-attaining pupils needed additional support to enable them to answer the questions. Consequently, a range of resources such as blank number lines and 100 squares were provided, and integrating traditional resources with this technology proved highly successful, with all the pupils able to answer confidently.

On reflection, the cost of the voting software used was significant and could not be justified against other items in the school budget. However, as a school we have made the decision to purchase iPads; one of the justifications was the availability of a 'voting app' called Powervote, which will allow us to use this technology-enhanced learning strategy to deliver AfL not only in numeracy but in all curriculum areas.

This case study demonstrates how effectively the same technology can be used in very different year groups with very different rationales. In Year 6, it was to inform short-term planning and motivate and engage. In Year 1, it was used to provide an alternative to traditional methods, to promote engagement and interaction and to provide an

> **Task 6.4 To what degree can voting technology impact on learning?**
>
> Consider how the use of this technology could be evaluated in terms of impact on pupils' learning. Further information about this type of software is widely available, for example at www.powervote.com and www.rm.com.

opportunity to integrate technology in Year 1. The school is in England and is very aware of the focus on the use of technology in Key Stage 1 (KS1) in the National Curriculum 2014; this activity addresses several elements of the KS1 programme of study, such as developing the knowledge that 'programs execute by following a sequence of instructions' (DfE, 2013b).

Voting technology can clearly assist in the assessment process and, due to its immediacy and accuracy, can improve outcomes. However, the school clearly identified how important it is to maintain the traditional elements of AfL, particularly questioning.

Case study 6.3 Lord Scudamore Academy: the use of Scratch to deliver the geometry element of the mathematics curriculum, 2014

There is a raft of software to support teachers in delivery of the computing curriculum, for example 'Scratch', a piece of free computer programming software that enables pupils to create their own interactive games and animated presentations. Scratch 'helps young people learn to think creatively, reason systematically, and work collaboratively – essential skills for life in the 21st century' (MIT Media Lab, no date).

The Scratch programme uses sprites (personalised 'avatars') and blocks of instructions, which children of all ages in the primary setting can programme simply and creatively. The programme is based on the x and y axes and consequently can provide an innovative and exciting strategy to deliver the upper Key Stage 2 geometry element of the new English National Curriculum for Mathematics – that pupils should be taught to 'describe positions on the full coordinate grid (all four quadrants)' (DfE, 2013b, no page).

In addition, the programme can be used to deliver other aspects of the geometry curriculum and Assistant Headteacher, Johanna Brace, has made effective use of these links in KS2, in terms of angles and turns, in two schools in Herefordshire. The children used the programme to draw a square and then completed other shapes using a formula. Some of the younger children used calculators while higher-attaining pupils used their knowledge of angles and 'trial and error'. The children were able to work at a much higher level of shape and direction than they would normally be exposed to and there was a significant element of excitement when groups found the correct answers, raising engagement and consequently improving outcomes. The benefits of cross-curricular delivery are many and this is a clear example of the positive use in terms of technology and mathematics.

Summary and key points

The reform of the English National Curriculum has given a clear remit to integrate technology throughout the curriculum with a focus on practice that will 'allow teachers greater freedom to use their professionalism and expertise to help all children realise their potential' (DfE, 2013c: 3). The natural relationship between mathematics and technology, as seen in STEM projects, the similar language used in the objectives for the Mathematics and Computing National Curriculum 2014 and the importance of both subjects in ensuring we make progress towards improving our standing in world economies, must drive us forward in taking every opportunity to combine them in effective learning opportunities.

It must be remembered that it is crucial that traditional methods are used in combination with technology-based methods; to ignore these methods would reduce AfL opportunities, diminish opportunities for social constructivist approaches to learning and have a negative impact on speaking and listening skills. Research in this area is ongoing and it is important to stay aware of advances and developments, for example through joining a subject association. In particular, it is crucial to keep the requirement of the mathematics curriculum at the forefront of delivery, using technology to enhance through whatever means available.

If you are a student teacher check which requirements for your course you have addressed through this chapter.

Further reading

Jesson, J. and Peacock, G. (2012) *The really useful ICT book: A practical guide to using technology across the primary curriculum.* Oxon, UK: Routledge.
>   This text provides an insight into the delivery of technology and also provides powerful cross-curricular links.

References

CISCO (2008) 'Multimodal learning through media: What the research says'. Available online at: www.cisco.com/web/strategy/docs/education/Multimodal-Learning-Through-Media.pdf. Accessed on 11 February 2014.

Department for Education (2012) *National Curriculum for mathematics Key Stages 1 and 2 – Draft.* Available online at: http://dera.ioe.ac.uk/14671/1/draft%20national%20curriculum %20for%20mathematics%20key%20stages%201%202%20primary%20%20%20%2011%20june%2020 12.pdf. Accessed on 10 May 2014.

Department for Education (2013a) *National Curriculum in England: Computing programmes of study.* Available online at: www.gov.uk/government/uploads/system/uploads/attachment_ data/file/239129/PRIMARY_national_curriculum_-_Mathematics.pdf. Accessed on 10 January 2014.

Department for Education (2013b) *National Curriculum in England: Mathematics programmes of study.* Available online at: www.gov.uk/government/publications/national-curriculum-in-england-mathematics-programmes-of-study/national-curriculum-in-england-mathematics-programmes-of-study. Accessed on 9 February 2014.

Department for Education (2013c) *Reform of the National Curriculum in England.* Available online at: www.education.gov.uk/consultations/downloadableDocs/040713%20NC%20in% 20England%20consultation%20-%20govt%20response%20FINAL.pdf. Accessed on 13 February 2014.

JISC (2009) 'Spotlight on "Generation Y"'. Available online at: www.jisc.ac.uk/news/spotlight-on-generation-y-new-study-launched-21-jan-2009. Accessed on 11 February 2014.

MIT Media Lab (no date) 'About Scratch'. Available online at: http://scratch.mit.edu/about/. Accessed on 16 February, 2014.

Primary National Strategy (2004) 'Mathematics ITP: Measuring Cylinder'. Available online at: http://webarchive.nationalarchives.gov.uk/20110809101133 or www.nsonline.org.uk/node/47798. Accessed on 4 February 2014.

United Nations Educational Scientific and Cultural Organization (2011) *UNESCO ICT Competency framework for teachers*. Available online at: www.unesco.org/new/en/unesco/themes/icts/teacher-education/unesco-ict-competency-framework-for-teachers/. Accessed on 11 February 2014.

Vygotsky, L. (1978) *Interaction between learning and development*. Available online at: www.psy.cmu.edu/~siegler/vygotsky78.pdf. Accessed on 11 February 2014.

7 e-Learning and mathematics

A blended learning approach

Michael James Malone and
John O'Shea

Introduction

This chapter presents a case study (Malone, 2012) of an e-learning programme used to support the teaching of mathematics in a primary classroom. Specifically, the chapter addresses how an e-learning programme can effect pupils' motivation for doing mathematics, how mathematics learning can extend beyond the walls of the classroom and how using an e-learning programme can have a positive impact on pupil achievement in mathematics. The study emphasises that, under optimum conditions, e-learning blended with traditional instruction methods can enhance student motivation, achievement and engagement with mathematics. Technology has greatest effect when effectively integrated with the general work of the school, consequently, at its most effective; it is least possible to quantify (O'Leary, 2011). This case study aims to illuminate the benefits of using an e-learning programme in a primary classroom setting. It shows how teachers can support their teaching of mathematics both within and outside the boundaries of the classroom by integrating e-learning into their daily teaching.

At the end of the chapter you should be able to:

* understand what e-learning, an e-learning programme and blended learning are in the context of teaching and learning;
* identify the key role of the teacher in the successful implementation of e-learning in a classroom;
* evaluate an appropriate e-learning programme for your classroom and your pupils;
* have a clear understanding of how, under optimal conditions, e-learning can enhance pupil motivation, achievement and engagement with the learning process in mathematics.

Research on e-learning

Carliner and Shank (2008) describe e-learning as any element of teaching and learning that involves digital material and information communication technologies (ICT). Educational e-learning programmes contain learning activities, content related to a subject matter, and navigational features to guide learners through the content (Carvalho and Dong, 2010). It is a computer-based system that manages the delivery of curriculum materials to individual learners and is capable of providing comprehensive feedback to the learner and the teacher/parent (Fitzgerald and Fitzgerald, 2002). Therefore, an e-learning programme is the system through which e-learning is delivered. It is the content, activities and navigational features that manage the delivery of the curriculum, as well as the online space that the content occupies. Many researchers argue that since e-learning is about individuals and about using technology systems to support individual learners, it may work best when it is combined with some face-to-face classroom experience (Appana, 2008; Brown, 2001; Cavanaugh, 2001; Vaughan, 2007).

Think of traditional learning taking place in a classroom and a pupil learning on their computer at home – blended learning is somewhere in between these two. Blended learning is simply a blend of face-to-face teaching and twenty-first century tools. Martyn (2003) states that blended learning is the combination of two or more methods, which may include the blend of classroom instruction with online instruction, online instruction with access to teacher, or simulations with structured courses. Most definitions of blended learning follow the concept that it is a blended solution between e-learning (online or click) and classroom learning (face-to-face or brick) (Bonk and Graham, 2006; Martyn, 2003). The goal of a blended approach is to combine the best aspects of both face-to-face and online instruction (Rastegarpour, 2010). One clear advantage of blended learning in education is its connection with differentiated instruction, which involves custom-designing instruction based on student needs (Buckley, 2002). The need for blended learning is simple. Pupils learn differently, learning outcomes are achieved differently, and a single approach cannot possibly fit all needs (Hofmann and Miner, 2009). Rastegarpour (2010) warns that there is no perfect recipe for blended learning, there is only the selection of learning delivery channels that best meet the learning needs of the pupils. The challenge for educators is to create the right learning blend that focuses on the best learning style for each pupil.

Choosing an e-learning platform for the classroom – opportunities through games

Teachers constantly strive for balance between entertainment and learning in choosing online content to use in an educational setting. Many e-learning programmes, such as Mathletics, deliver their learning experiences to pupils through the format of games and activities for pupils to complete. Habgood and Ainsworth (2011) suggest that successful educational games are those that establish an intrinsic link between a core game mechanic and the target learning content. Kiili and Ketamo (2007) describe how the greatest challenge of learning-game design is implementing the sorts of game elements that trigger reflection. In practice, the process of reflection can be facilitated by providing 'cognitive feedback' to the player (Butler and Winne, 1995). Cognitive feedback aims to stimulate players to reflect on their experiences, problem-solving strategies and created solutions in order to further develop their mental models (Merrienboer and Kirschner, 2007).

Cognitive feedback can also be understood as being a trigger of cognitive conflict. According to Foko and Amory (2008), gaming plays only a limited role in the development of the individual mind. Therefore, social dialogue needs to be part of their design. Social dialogue can be game-world mediated or real-world mediated. The role of the teacher, other pupils and parents is fundamental to providing positive social dialogue regarding the value of the programme. Will pupils see a value with experiencing success using the e-learning programme? Will it facilitate healthy competitiveness within the class or will using the programme be perceived as a negative experience for pupils?

Furthermore, as Schön (1983) describes, reflection can be linked to time. Reflection-in-action refers to reflective actions performed during playing and reflecting-on-action refers to reflective actions performed after the playing session. By providing instantaneous feedback and results after and during interaction the e-learning programme aims to trigger reflection-in-action and reflection-on-action to develop pupils' mathematical understanding.

Currently there is a wide variety of e-learning programmes, both free and subscription-based, available. So how can a teacher decide which one is best suited to their classroom? One way to decide is to look at the list below as a checklist, as there is an increasing body of research that indicates that successful e-learning programmes have similar components (Alessi and Trollip, 2001; Handley, 2008; O'Leary and O'Mahony, 2010). These components are the critical factors responsible for the success and failure of many different e-learning platforms. The following list details the components of a successful e-learning programme:

- Is appropriate to the curriculum.
- Is appealing to the learner.
- Provides immediate unambiguous feedback to the user.
- Is adaptive and responsive to student response.
- Contains reward and feedback mechanisms.
- Media is presented in a variety of ways including audio and text.
- Facilitates support and guidance in the completion of a task.
- Has customisable levels.
- Has an assessment function.

Task 7.1 Evaluating e-learning environments

Choose an e-learning platform that you have access to and establish whether or not it contains the components of a successful e-learning programme, using the above as a guide.

Using an e-learning programme in the classroom

Rastegarpour (2010) states that there is no perfect recipe for blended learning; there is only the selection of learning delivery channels that best meet the learning needs of the pupils. The challenge for teachers is to create the right learning blend that focuses on the best learning style for each pupil.

In the case study underpinning this chapter, Malone (2012) adopted and tested a variety of pedagogical models in integrating the use of the Mathletics e-learning programme into everyday classroom teaching. Each model has advantages and disadvantages associated with it, which are described below.

Exploratory model of e-learning: Pupils are not given any prior in-class tuition surrounding the topic. Pupils are encouraged and given the opportunity to explore the new curricular content and mathematic activities associated with the topic in the e-learning programme. This approach highlights pupils' self-directed and self-paced learning. Pupils engage in questioning with the teacher in relation to an area of the new topic that they are having difficulty with. Malone (2012) found the benefit of the exploratory approach was that pupils' prior knowledge of a curricular area is established quite quickly and as a result you could identify the specific curricular areas that pupils are having difficulty with, which then need to be targeted during in-class tuition.

Traditional model of e-learning: The topic is introduced to the class in a traditional way through in-class tuition. The e-learning programme is then used to let the pupils build their core skills by attempting the curricular activities and practice to implement what they learn from class. The benefit of this approach is that pupils experience greater initial success than with the exploratory approach. This approach is teacher-led. However, as it develops it becomes more pupil-led as pupils try to improve their score in the related curricular activities to achieve mastery level. The 'help' function can be used as a stimulus by pupils to recall prior knowledge. The e-learning programme works to consolidate prior knowledge and learning that may have taken place in another setting, such as the classroom. Therefore, using an e-learning programme can help reinforce previous classroom learning.

Homework and revision/test model of e-learning: Homework activities can be assigned to pupils through the e-learning programme to reinforce concepts. This results in homework being completed in a self-paced personal environment. The benefit of this approach is that if pupils experience difficulty in a topic they can access the support offered through the programme using the 'help' button and the online tutorials. Teachers have noted that assigning homework in this way enabled access to the results of the activities the next morning and teachers could therefore plan what to cover in class, based on the results and identified areas of difficulty. This was noted as a great benefit in comparison to copybook homework, where lesson time has to be assigned to correcting homework and problems arising. The e-learning programme can also be used as a testing platform. Pupils were assigned specific curriculum activities on topics previously covered in class as revision work or a test to establish attainment and retention levels.

Task 7.2 Models of e-learning

Consider one particular unit of work explored in your classroom in the recent past. Evaluate the most useful model described above that you could employ in the future to explore such content.

Mathletics – a case study

For the purposes of the case study (Malone, 2012), pupils were subscribed to the Mathletics e-learning programme by the teacher. The Mathletics e-learning programme was chosen as it contained all the components for successful e-learning platforms, as previously outlined. This subscription-based e-learning programme allows pupils to take part in competitive mathematics games against other pupils and engage in activities aligned to the standards of the curriculum. The main features of the Mathletics e-learning programme are:

Activities that are closely aligned with the curriculum

The topics are selected by the teacher, and pupils are highly motivated to measure their progress against their peers and to gain virtual rewards by succeeding and improving their scores. Many pupils log in from their home computer so that learning and enjoyment is extended way beyond the boundaries and timetables of school. Pupils click on the module to see the activities it contains. The activities are aligned with the curriculum and the teacher controls which modules the pupil can see. If necessary the teacher can force a pupil to complete an activity before being allowed to use the other features of the programme. Pupils earn points for every correct answer, earning them rewards that unlock further mathematical games in their personalised area of the virtual learning environment.

Live virtual learning environment

The live element of the Mathletics programme allows pupils to take part in competitive mathematics games against other pupils in other schools and other countries in real time. The goal is to answer as many questions as possible in a time frame. Questions are based on number operations. Pupils can choose which level they compete at – if they play a level higher than they have attempted before they earn multiple rewards in an effort to encourage them to progress. Also, the teacher can block pupils from attempting lower levels.

Pupils' online identity in social media

When learners engage in cycles of creation and consumption as part of the participatory web culture, they are simultaneously developing online identities, or 'dynamic and shifting constructions and presentations of self' (Coiro et al. 2008, p. 526), which have implications for education. Developing one's identity online is a relatively recent cultural process, aided by the features of the participatory web (Greenhow, Robelia and Hughes 2009). Boyd (2007), an ethnographer and social media researcher, describes this process of initiation and acculturation in a social network. Boyd (2007) explains how users new to social networks learn to assimilate, customising the look of their online profiles to represent themselves and identify with their peers. Often, the results are animated with brightly coloured webpages covered with original artwork, photographs and writing.

The Matletics e-learning programme used for the purposes of the case study by Malone (2012) has recognised this trend and applied it to their platform. Each pupil has a personalised home page that they can change, as well as a personal avatar or character. Personalisation acts as a motivator for students to engage with the content. As the pupil uses the virtual learning environment, by completing teacher-assigned tests, live activities or playing mathematics games, they earn points. These points can then be used to develop their avatar/character or backgrounds for their home page and develop their online identity (Greenhow, Robelia and Hughes, 2009; Boyd, 2007; Coiro et al.,

2008). Their personalised avatar represents their online self when interacting with other users worldwide.

Pupil profile learning logs

Learning logs are capable of providing comprehensive feedback to the learner and the teacher/parent. Feedback to the teacher includes detailed information on the performance of individual pupils and defined groups of pupils, and diagnostic assessment of learning problems.

The case study methods

The case study by Malone (2012) was action-research based. The design was a mixed methods approach consisting of a pre-test–post-test control group design (Creswell 2009, Suter and Frechtling 1998). One group was given access to an e-learning programme and the other group was not (Suter and Frechtling, 1998). Various data collection methods and data sources, including pupils, teachers and parents, were utilised in this inquiry. The thirty pupils who participated in the study were all in the same class in a large urban primary school located in the mid-west of Ireland. Another group of participants comprised of six adults, all parents of the intervention group of pupils within the class and two teachers – one was the mainstream class teacher and the other was the learning-support teacher of the class.

The case study findings

The case study found the following in relation to attainment, developing mathematical understanding, self-directed learning, pupil attitude, motivation and assessment.

Attainment

Those pupils who had access to the Mathletics e-learning programme in conjunction with classroom tuition experienced a greater achievement in mathematics than their classmates who did not have access to the e-learning programme. The pupils who had access to the e-learning programme on average achieved an improvement of 5.07 per cent more than their control group counterparts in a mathematics measures test. Significantly, lower-ability pupils within this group made the greatest gains in achievement over the course of the study period.

Developing mathematical understanding

This case study identified that the Mathletics e-learning programme successfully developed pupils' mathematical understanding by providing cognitive feedback to the pupil during activities, prompting reflection-in-action and after activities prompting reflection-on-action, as described by Schön (1983). By triggering self-reflection during the activity, pupils can learn from their mistakes and the instant cognitive feedback provided by the programme can prompt pupils to adapt their strategies towards answering particular sets of problems. After each set of curriculum activities the pupil receives a graphic visual representation of how they performed during the task.

Self-directed learning

Pupils need to develop a range of new skills, such as managing their own pace of learning, becoming autonomous learners and taking greater responsibility for their own learning when engaging with e-learning (Boulton, 2008).

The Mathletics e-learning programme provided the opportunity for pupils to pursue learning in an individualised and self-paced way. 'You can do mathematics without a teacher telling you what to do' (Pupil Focus Group). The learner can instantly raise queries, doubts and receive feedback without delay, which might not be the case in the physical classroom. 'She really liked being able to figure out the answers on her own, and was really proud when she would use the help button to figure something out and then get 100% in the test, she would show me and say that she taught herself' (Parents Focus Group).

Pupil attitude

SELF CONCEPT

The construct of self-efficacy is distinctly different than one's attitude towards mathematics in that it signifies an individual's beliefs concerning their ability to perform mathematical tasks (McLeod, 1992). A pupil may have positive attitudes towards the field of mathematics, but low confidence in their ability to do mathematics, which can negatively impact their mathematical performance. The fact that pupils' self-efficacy in mathematics positively changed after the intervention provides further evidence that educational e-learning may positively influence the construct (Lu, Lee and Lien, 2008; Thomas, Cahill and Santilli, 1997).

PUPIL ENGAGEMENT

Chapman (2003) suggests that the term pupil engagement has been used to depict pupil willingness to take part in school activities while Skinner and Belmount (1991, p. 4) define engagement as the willingness of the pupils to 'exert intense effort and concentration in the implementation of learning tasks'. In response to the post-questionnaire question 'Do you like using the Mathletics e-learning programme?' 73.33 per cent of respondents said 'yes, a lot'. These responses indicate a willingness on the part of the pupils to engage and interact with the programme.

Motivation

Intrinsic motivation is characterised by learning that is driven from within by internal desires and interests. According to Bomia *et al.* (1997), intrinsically motivated pupils usually become engaged in learning as a result of curiosity, interest or enjoyment. Dev (1997: p. 13) suggests that this type of pupil is 'more likely to complete a chosen task and be excited by the challenging nature of an activity'. Evidence of intrinsically motivated pupils emerged from the pupil focus groups: 'I just liked learning mathematics, say if you had a test and you were not sure of it, you can just go on the help thing and learn off that and then I would be able to do them' (Pupil Focus Group).

Extrinsically motivated pupils are more interested in external influences such as incentives, loss of privileges and academic achievement (Dev, 1997). The Mathletics e-learning programme attempts to appeal to pupils by combining intrinsic as well as extrinsic motivators. Initially, the pupils must complete the tests and tasks assigned to them by the teacher. Intrinsically motivated children, according to Bomia *et al.* (1997) and Dev (1997), will be motivated by the challenge in the task and be engaged in learning as a result. The programme also utilises extrinsic motivators to engage the pupil in the learning process. The pupils can earn certificates if they achieve a prescribed number of points or successfully complete a certain number of tasks. The research by Malone (2012) indicated that the 'earning a certificate' aspect of the programme appealed to the respondents: 'The things I like about it is that you can earn points and when you get enough you get a certificate' (Pupil Focus Group).

Assessment and e-learning

The case study by Malone (2012) identified that one of the great advantages of the use of the Mathletics e-learning programme in the classroom was the availability of on-demand individual pupil records. These records give detailed information to the teacher regarding the pupils' use of the programme, how they are achieving in each task, when they are accessing the programme and an in-depth analysis of the pupils' relative strengths and weaknesses, determined from the results of the tests and challenges that they have undertaken. This information is constantly updated and over time individual pupil records and profiles are developed and expanded. One of the key findings of the study was the benefit of the record-keeping functions of the programme that facilitated teachers in the assessment 'for' and 'of' learning. The class teacher and the learning-support teacher commented on the advantages that this type of programme provided in the area of assessment. It meant that the class teacher was able to keep an interactive record of pupil progress.

The information made available by the e-learning programme changed the way the teacher approached planning and preparing for lessons. The Mathletics programme provided detailed analysis of areas that particular pupils may be underachieving in. These assessments, as noted by Stiggins (2005) are assessments for learning rather than of learning. Assessment for learning, as described by Hargreaves (2005), is categorized as meaning monitoring pupils' performance against targets or objectives, using assessment to inform next steps in teaching and learning, teachers giving feedback for improvement, children taking some control of their own learning and assessment, and turning assessment into a learning event. This information supplied in real time to the teacher can be used to re-direct the teaching focus over a period of time on particular areas in an effort to increase understanding among the pupils. The difference between this type of environment and a traditional teacher-designed test is the data analysis capabilities and the instantaneous feedback that it provides. The programme can detect and highlight 'trends' of questions that some pupils may be getting incorrect.

Pupils reported that they liked instantaneous feedback of their test results. 'It's good because it's not like in school where you have to wait for the teacher to tell you it's right or correct, you know straight away and can then do other stuff on it like live work and games' (Focus Group Interview). In a traditional classroom environment the pupil often has to wait for the teacher to correct the test and then see how they got on. In addition to this, it can be a very time-consuming and a difficult task for teachers to analyse test results at a whole-class level to ascertain overall analysis of areas where pupils are underachieving.

Summary and key points

This chapter has outlined general principles for successful e-learning environments and explored the use of the Mathletics e-learning programme. An important characteristic of e-learning in comparison to other methods of instruction is that instruction and assessment can be seamlessly integrated into the same environment. The use of e-learning in the classroom offers many advantages not directly related to pupil grades. Teachers are relieved of some of the time associated with correcting and pupils are able to receive instant feedback and immediate help at any time on any mathematical task. The results of this case study (Malone, 2012) indicate that pupils who had access to the Mathletics e-learning programme experienced greater gains in achievement in comparison to the control group. Also, the e-learning programme has a positive effect on many pupils' attitude and self-concept towards mathematics. This supports the research that suggests that when the optimum conditions are in place ICT, such as e-learning programmes, do enhance pupils' motivation, achievement and engagement in the learning process. While not advocating a move away from traditional face-to-face teaching, we recommend supplementing 'traditional' teaching methods with a blended-learning model utilising technological tools in an effort to improve pupils' experience with mathematics and in turn their achievement.

Websites

Mathletics is a subscription-based e-learning programme. Live Mathletics area matches students against others from around the world in real-time arithmetic races, powering towards mathematical fluency. www.mathletics.eu/

Mangahigh is a comprehensive and powerful online maths teaching resource offering full coverage of the UK National Curriculum with more than 400 different challenges ranging from addition to quadratic factorisation. www.mangahigh.com/en-gb/

Kahn Academy allows pupils to make use of an extensive library of content, including interactive challenges, assessments and videos across a range of subjects including maths and science. www.khanacademy.org

The PDST Technology in Education (Professional Development Service for Teachers, Ireland) website has extensive information and resources for teachers. www.pdst technologyineducation.ie/

Further reading

Boulton, H. (2008) 'Managing e-Learning: What are the real implications for schools?'. *The Electronic Journal of e-Learning*, 6(1): 11–18.
> The paper considers the current research in e-learning and identifies the challenges faced by teachers, the changing role of the learner, and the impact e-learning can have on pupils.

Greenhow, C., Robelia, B. and Hughes, J.E. (2009) 'Learning, teaching and scholarship in a Digital Age: Web 2.0 and classroom research: What path should we take now?'. *Educational Researcher*, 38(4): 246–59.
> Several important themes that are key areas in the future of e-learning are addressed in this paper, including learner participation and creativity and online identity formation.

References

Alessi, M. and Trollip, S.R. (2001) *Multimedia for learning: Methods and development* (3rd edn). Boston, MA: Allyn and Bacon.

Appana, S. (2008) 'A review of benefits and limitations of online learning in the context of the student, the instructor, and the tenured faculty'. *International Journal on e-Learning*, 7(1): 5–22.

Bomia, L., Beluzo, L., Demeester, D., Elander, K., Johnson, M. and Sheldon, B. (1997) *The impact of teaching strategies on intrinsic motivation*. Champaign, IL: ERIC Clearinghouse on Elementary and Early Childhood Education.

Bonk, C. and Graham, C.R. (2006) *The handbook of blended learning*. San Francisco, CA: Pfeiffer.

Boulton, H. (2008) 'Managing e-learning: What are the real implications for schools?'. *The Electronic Journal of e-Learning*, 6(1): 11–18. Available online at: www.ejel.org/volume6/issue1/p11. Accessed on 18 March 2013.

Boyd, D. (2007) 'Why youth love social network sites: The role of networked publics in teenage social life'. In D. Buckingham (ed.) *The John D. and Catherine T. MacArthur foundation series on digital media and learning: Youth, identity and digital media* (119–42). Cambridge, MA: MIT Press. Available online at: www.mitpressjournals.org/toc/dmal/-/6?cookieSet=. Accessed on 30 March 2013.

Brown, R.E. (2001) 'The process of community-building in distance learning classes'. *Journal of Asynchronous Learning Networks*, 5(2): 18–35.

Buckley, D.P. (2002) 'In pursuit of the learning paradigm: Coupling faculty transformation and instructional change'. *EDUCAUSE Review*, Vol. 37, No. 1, 2002: 29–38.

Butler, D.L. and Winne, P.H. (1995) 'Feedback as self-regulated learning: A theoretical synthesis'. *Review of Educational Research*, 65: 245–81.

Carliner, S. and Shank, P. (2008) *e-Learning handbook: Past promises, present challenges*. San Francisco, CA: John Wiley & Sons.

Carvalho, L. and Dong, A. (2010) 'Bringing a social realist approach into computer supported learning environments: The Design Studio case study'. Presented at The 6th Basil Bernstein International Symposium, Brisbane.

Cavanaugh, C.S. (2001) 'The effectiveness of interactive distance education technologies in K-12 learning: A meta-analysis'. *International Journal of Educational Telecommunications*, 7(1): 73–88.

Chapman, E. (2003). 'Alternative approaches to assessing students' engagement rates'. *Practical Assessment, Research and Evaluation*, 8: 13. Available online at: http://PAREonline.net/getvn.asp?v=8&n=13. Accessed on 23 October 2012.

Coiro, J., Knobel, M., Lankshear, C. and Leu, D. (2008) 'Central issues in new literacies and new literacies research'. In J. Coiro, M. Knobel, C. Lankshear and D. Leu (eds.) *Handbook of research on new literacies* (1–21). New York: Lawrence Erlbaum Associates.

Creswell, J.W. (2009) *Research design: Qualitative, quantitative and mixed methods approaches* (3rd edn). Thousand Oaks, CA: Sage Publications.

Dev, P.C. (1997) 'Intrinsic motivation and academic achievement: What does their relationship imply for the classroom teacher?'. *Remedial and Special Education*, 18(1): 12–19.

Fitzgerald, D. and Fitzgerald, R.N. (2002) *The use of integrated learning systems in developing number and language concepts in primary school children: A longitudinal study of individual differences*. Griffith University, Australia: DEST Clearinghouse.

Foko, T. and Amory, A. (2008) 'Social constructivism in games based learning in the South African context'. In *World Conference on Educational Multimedia, Hypermedia and Telecommunications*, pp. 5757–64. Available at: www.editlib.org/toc/index.cfm/. Accessed on 12 April, 2013.

Greenhow, C., Robelia, B. and Hughes, J.E. (2009) 'Learning, teaching and scholarship in a Digital Age: Web 2.0 and classroom research: What path should we take now?'. *Educational Researcher*, 38(4): 246–59. Available online at: http://edr.sagepub.com/content/38/4/246.full.pdf+html. Accessed on 30 March 2013.

Habgood, M.P.J. and Ainsworth, S.E. (2011) 'Motivating children to learn effectively: Exploring the value of intrinsic integration in educational games'. *Journal of the Learning Sciences*, 20(2): 169–20.

Handley, R. (2008) 'Using technology to motivate student learning'. In I. Olney, G. Lefoe, J. Mantei and J. Herrington (eds.) *Proceedings of the second emerging technologies conference*, 2008 (82–91). Wollongong: University of Wollongon. Available online at: http://ro.uow. edu.au/etc08/10/. Accessed on 31 October 2012.

Hargreaves, E. (2005) 'Assessment for learning? Thinking outside the (black) box'. *Cambridge Journal of Education*, 35(2): 213–24. Available online at: www.tandfonline.com/doi/pdf/10. 1080/03057640500146880. Accessed on 30 March 2013.

Hofmann, J. and Miner, N. (2009) *Tailored learning: Designing the blend that fits*. Alexandria, VA: American Society for Training and Development Press.

Kiili, K. and Ketamo, H. (2007) 'Exploring the learning mechanism in educational cames'. *Journal of Computing and Information Technology*, 15: 319–24.

Lu, Y., Lee, I. and Lien, C. (2008) 'A preliminary study of student's self-efficacy on problem solving in educational game context, digital', 23–7. Second IEEE International Conference on Digital Game and Intelligent Toy Enhanced Learning.

Malone, M.J. (2012) 'Exploring the use of a virtual e-learning environment for the teaching and learning of mathematics in a primary classroom'. Unpublished thesis. Limerick: Mary Immaculate College, University of Limerick.

Martyn, M. (2003) 'The hybrid online model: Good practice'. *EDUCAUSE Quarterly*, (26): 1.

McLeod, D.B. (1992) 'Research on affect in mathematics education: A reconceptualisation'. In D.A. Grouws (ed.) *Handbook of research on mathematics teaching and learning: A project of the National Council of Teachers of Mathematics*. New York: MacMillan.

Merrienboer, J.J.G. and Kirschner, P.A. (2007) *Ten steps to complex learning: A systematic approach to four-component instructional design*. London: Lawrence Erlbaum Associates.

O'Leary, R. and O'Mahony, J. (2010) *ICTs in the primary school teaching and learning for the 21st century*. Dublin: Dublin West Education Centre.

O'Leary, R. (2011) *Enhancing literacy and numeracy with ICTs*. Dublin: Dublin West Education Centre and Navan Education Centre.

Rastegarpour, H. (2010) 'What is the hoopla about blended learning: Something old is new again'. The Second International Conference on e-Learning and e-Teaching (ICELET 2010). Available online at: http://ieeexplore.ieee.org/stamp/stamp.jsp?tp=&arnumber=5708381. Accessed on 28 March 2013.

Schön, D.A. (1983) *The reflective practitioner: How professionals think in action*. New York: Basic Books.

Skinner, E. and Belmont, M. (1991) *A longitudinal study of motivation in school: Reciprocal effects of teacher behaviour and student engagement*. Unpublished manuscript. Rochester, NY: University of Rochester.

Stiggins, R.J. (2005) *Classroom assessment for student learning: Doing it right – Using it well*. Portland, OR: Assessment Training Institute.

Suter, L.E. and Frechtling, J. (1998) *Guiding principles for mathematics and science education research methods: Report of a workshop*. National Science Foundation, November 19–20, Arlington, Virginia. Available online at: www.nsf.gov/pubs/2000/nsf00113/nsf00113.html. Accessed on 26 February 2013.

Thomas, R., Cahill, J. and Santilli, L. (1997) 'Using an interactive computer game to increase skill and self efficacy regarding safer sex negotiation: Field test results'. *Health Education and Behavior*, 24: 71–86.

Vaughan, N. (2007) 'Perspectives on blended learning in higher education'. *International Journal on e-Learning*, 6(1): 81–94.

8 Using technology in primary science

Paul Hopkins

Introduction

> In order for technology to be useful in the classroom it must be appropriate for what you are wanting to accomplish and implemented efficiently.
>
> (Harry G. Tuttle, Twitter, @HarryGTuttle)

Science and technology are natural bedfellows and we start by defining what we mean by technology. The young pupils in today's primary classrooms will have grown up in a world where technology will have meant the laptop, the notebook and the interactive whiteboard more than the desktop and they are truly 'digital natives' (Prensky, 2001) or 'HomoZappiens' (Veen, 2004), happy and familiar with technology as an integral part of their and their parents' lives. Much of this technology will be mobile and portable and as more and more primary schools around the world are introducing tablet computers (see studies such as Burden *et al.*, 2012; Webb, 2012), this chapter considers how the mobile computer will lie at the heart of technology use to support science in the primary classroom of the near and continuing future, and the affordances that such mobile devices give over the fixed computer (Traxler, 2007). While we recognise that not all schools will have invested yet in these mobile technologies, others have written about the use of existing technology and in the space available this chapter we will focus on the use of mobile technologies. Think back to your own time in the primary classroom. What technology did you use in your primary classroom? Digital cameras? Dataloggers? Video? Computers? The rate of change has been incredible and it is for this reason that this chapter focuses on the most recent technology – that of the mobile learning devices and the affordances that such devices offers. In this chapter we explore some core pedagogic ideas for using the technology of the near future in the primary classroom.

Objectives

At the end of this chapter you should:

- understand how mobile technology can enhance and/or transform the learning and teaching of science in the primary classroom;
- explore some key activities and ideas for using mobile technology in the classroom to teach science;
- feel confident to introduce the available technology into your teaching of science and consider the introduction of mobile technologies.

Good practice in teaching science in the primary classroom

Before looking at the technology we need to consider what is good science in the primary classroom. I argue three core principles for the science that takes place in the primary classroom; these are similar to those argued by Harlen (2010).

1   *It is real science*: The science that takes place in the primary classroom has at its heart the same scientific method used by all scientists. It may not be new to the world but it is likely to be new, creative and original to the pupils and thus has real value (NACCCE, 1999) and is 'science that builds on the children's natural curiosity, inventiveness and wonder' (Rose, 2008: 8).
2   *It is rooted in investigative work*: While there is an important place for learning information and facts about science the best science in the primary classroom is the hands-on, investigative work, 'primary schools should ensure that pupils are engaged in scientific enquiry, including practical work' (Ofsted, 2011: 8), where children are exploring questions that have relevance and meaning to them: 'children need time to pursue their own ideas in science' (Harlen and Qualter, 2009: 48).
3   *It develops models and criticality*: Concepts that can be built upon and developed rather than teaching immutable facts about science that might have to be 'unlearned' later in their science learning life, 'children must be given the opportunity to challenge their existing ideas' (SCORE, 2013: 7).

So we need to consider how technology use by the teacher and by the pupils can enhance and support these core ideas. Becta (2009: 2) suggested nine main applications for ICT in science:

1   providing information;
2   supporting fieldwork;
3   assisting observation;
4   recording and measuring;
5   sharing data with others;
6   facilitating interpretation;
7   simulating experiments;
8   providing models or demonstrations;
9   enhancing publishing and presentation.

Considering these three core principles and the nine areas we can consider the use of technology in three areas:

1   by pupils as a tool for data capture, analysis and evaluation including video, audio, data logging and presentation and for the development and expansion of their own subject knowledge;
2   by teachers as a tool for information presentation and demonstration, simulations and virtual experiments and developing resource;
3   as a tool for knowledge enhancement, planning and assessment.

There are a number of frameworks that consider the interface between technology and pedagogy, including the Technological, Pedagogical and Content Knowledge (TPACK) model (Mishra and Koehler, 2009), the Enhancement, Efficiency and Transformation (EET) model (McCormick and Scrimshaw, 2001) and the Substitution, Augmentation, Modification and Redefinition (SAMR) model (Puentedura, 2011). The use of technology should never be just for the sake of using the technology – there should always be a pedagogic driver, a reason why the use of the technology improves the teaching or the learning or both. We can think of these drivers in two ways:

1 technology that *enhances* the experiences in the classroom;
2 technology that *transforms* the learning in the classroom.

In the Table 8.1 below I have combined the EET and the SAMR models, while taking note of TPACK, to give us the key drivers of enhancement and transformation of learning.

Table 8.1 Frameworks for change (based on Burden *et al.*, 2012: 102)

	McCormick and Scrimshaw, (2001)	*Puentedura model (2011) SAMR*
Enhancement		Substitution (technology acts as a direct tool substitute with no functional change or improvement)
	Technology used to do things more efficiently (productivity)	Augmentation (technology acts as a direct tool substitute with functional improvement)
Transformation	Technology used to extend the reach of teaching and learning the task (e.g., using the Internet to work with experts or other students abroad)	Modification (technology allows for significant task redesign)
	Technology used as transformational device (e.g., allowing you to do things that were (to all intents) impossible or impractical before the technology)	Replacement (technology allows for creation of new tasks previously inconceivable)

Pupils' use of technology

In this section we explore a number of ways in which pupils can use mobile technologies to support their understanding and learning in science. However, before you start you should explore, through Task 8.1, how technology is being used in your classroom or the classroom you are in while on your teaching practice.

Using technology to record pupils' investigations

Pupils are naturally curious and enjoy conducting investigations. An essential part of this is for them to carefully and accurately record what is happening as they carry out their explorations. For the youngest pupils, having to record things in writing can be physically quite difficult. While is possible for one pupil to take on the role of the

---

Task 8.1 Where are we at?

Talk to the teacher and the pupils in a class you have access to about the technologies that they use in their science lessons. Especially ask them if they:

- use technology to record their investigation,
- use technology as a data capture during investigations,
- use technology to develop their subject knowledge,
- use technology to analyse, evaluate and model data,
- use technology to show their findings when reporting back.

Consider how the technology is used in other parts of the curriculum. When you have had these conversations go back to your medium-term plans to consider what needs to be changed.

---

recorder while the other is the experimenter, most pupils want to be involved in the hands-on activity. This is where video is an excellent tool. Many primary schools will already have small hand-held video recorders such as Digital Blue (www.digitalblue.org.uk) or FlipCams©, but all modern mobile devices come with a good-quality still and video camera and video editing software is available for very low cost. The only limitation of these devices is the quality of the audio recording.

The use of video to record has a number of advantages that can be seen in the case study below.

Case study 8.1 A fruit olympics

A reception teacher is exploring with a small group of pupils ideas around floating and sinking and wants to challenge the pupils' ideas about what might float and what might sink. They begin with a class discussion about objects in their house that they think will float or sink. The teacher has developed a carousel of activities, one of which is to explore the floating and sinking properties of common fruits and vegetables. She shows the pupils a selection of fruits and vegetables and asks them to discuss which of these they think will float and which of these they think will sink.

Each group is asked to discuss and then to record a short piece of video where they explain (a) what they think will happen and (b) why they think this will happen. Once they have recorded this video they are given their fruits and vegetables and they then carry out the investigation by carefully putting the fruit or vegetable into the tank of water and seeing if it floats or sinks. Each time they put one of the objects into the tank they video the process and their discussion.

When they have explored all their objects they can compare their initial predictions with their observed results and they are then asked to draw some conclusions from their results and again video this, so that they can present this to the teacher and to the rest of the class when they feedback later in the sequence of lessons. This activity (based around the POE (predict, observe, evaluate) principle (Kearney and Treagust, 2001) is part of a carousel exploring floating and sinking and the teacher uses the video later in the sequence of lessons.

---

a

b

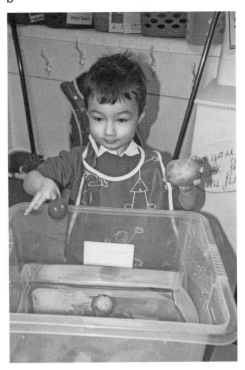

Figures 8.1a and b A fruit olympics: reception children undertaking investigations into floating and sinking.

Task 8.2 Using video to capture pupils' thinking

Consider this use of technology using the enhancement and transformation framework above. What are the advantages for the pupils in using video to record their thinking and planning as opposed to other methods? Are there any disadvantages? Explore the options you have in your school for recording video and plan to use these in a science session soon and evaluate, with the pupils, the impact that this makes.

As well as using video, which is a very powerful tool in the primary classroom, mobile devices have a range of other affordances that will allow the pupils to spend more time on the investigation:

Still camera: Pupils use the camera to capture the stages of their investigation or key moments or events. These can then be annotated using an application such as 'iAnnotate' or 'Explain Everything'. As well as the built-in camera there are a number of adaptations that will allow you to use your camera to capture the big and the small and to make slideshows, animations and annotate stills.

Audio: Using the built-in recording device pupils can record their ideas and thoughts from their investigations. Again though the built-in microphone has limited capacity there is a huge range of add-ons to enhance the capacity of the device.

Dictation: Free software will allow the pupil to dictate their observations, which will then be transcribed by the device. 'Dragon Dictate©' offers free software for both iOS and Android platforms.

Using technology to capture enquiry data

Another key element of investigative science is recording data and this can be difficult and prone to error. Technology can play a vital part in this data capture and such use of technology is at the heart of every science lab in the world, and should be present in the primary classroom (Davies, Collier and Howe, 2012). There have been a number of attempts to get data logging or data-capture technologies into primary classrooms; this has included initiatives such as giving a digital microscope, which could be hooked up to a computer, to all English primary schools but without providing support or professional development – not surprisingly many of these never made it out of the box.

The 2000 English National Curriculum for Science stated that, 'all pupils should develop the key skills of using IT ... opportunities for using ICT include the use of sensors in sound, light and temperature' (DfES, NC 2000: 27). The 2013 (draft at time of writing) guidance states that pupils should 'learn how to use new equipment, such as data loggers' (NC 2013: 16). While some primary schools are using data logging equipment that can be connected to laptops or desktop computers this is rare as this equipment is expensive and fairly complex.

Table 8.2 Data capture via applications

Area of the curriculum	Examples of data to be captured	Equipment needed[1]
Life processes and living things	Pulse rate	Timer (built in) Pulse monitor Heart rate
	Plant recognition	Leafsnap Application TreeID Application
	Micro-organisms	Proscope© microscope for iPad
	Humidity	Humidity probe
	Variation	Camera
Materials and their properties	Temperature/Heat flow	Celsius temperature probe
	Reflectivity	Light senor
Physical processes	Sound	Recording app on deviceoScope
	Light	Light sensor (built in)
	Forces	Accelerometer (built in) Inclinomter
	Earth and Space	Camera (built in)
	Movement and time	Ilab timer Accelerometer (built in) Stopwatch (built in)

Mobile technologies come with a range of applications that can be used to capture data. Some of these will use the affordances of the device while others utilise a range of accessories.

There is also a growing range of sensor devices that will interface with a tablet device. While these are not cheap they can offer an amazing range of opportunities for primary science, giving children the opportunity to carry out more sophisticated scientific enquiries such as measuring the humidity levels around their classroom to determine the best place to grow plants, or exploring temperature change around the school. This information can be used to consider the heat absorptive properties of different materials, or more accurately capture the speed of a car as it travels down an inclined plane in order to explore the relationship between gravity and acceleration.

Two to consider are Globisens Labdisc (www.globisens.net), which contains a range of internal sensors, and PASCO SparkLinkAir (www.pasco.com), which allows you to connect the range of over seventy external sensors to your iPad. Both of these work via a Bluetooth connection.

Task 8.3 The affordances of the tablet in the classroom

Explore the affordances of the mobile device to see what capabilities it has for the recording of data in your classroom. Explore also how these can be enhanced with inexpensive add-ons. If you already have mobile devices in your school do an audit of the applications for science and explore what you could add for a relatively low cost.

Using technology to analyse and evaluate data

Capturing data is, of course, only the beginning of the process. Once you have captured data it can be very difficult for the primary pupil to analyse the data in order to make the link between their hypotheses and then to draw both specific and more general causal links between the independent (the variable that is to be changed) and dependent variables (the variable that is being tested). This is where having easy and immediate access to a range of technologies can bring great benefit.

There are a number of ways in which the pupils in your class can analyse and evaluate data using spreadsheets, graphing programmes and databases.

Case study 8.2 Using a spreadsheet when investigating friction

A Year 5 teacher is exploring the concept of friction as a force that opposes motion in moving objects. The pupils have devised their experiment using an inclined plain, a range of materials and some toy cars. They intend to time the cars going from a fixed point on the slope and then, across a fixed amount of the material, they will then calculate the speed of the cars. The teacher has also been talking to them about the importance of eliminating errors and how this can be helped by repeated measurements. In order to help them with their calculations they have programmed a spreadsheet to work on the speed of the vehicle and also to work out the mean of their measurements using the following calculations:

Speed = distance/time

Mean = (Test 1 + Test 2 . . . / Number of tests)

This allows the pupils to concentrate on the design of their investigation and once they have measured the time taken (using a stopwatch app on their device) they are able to enter this time into their spreadsheet, which quickly calculates the speed. As they enter repeated measurements the spreadsheet calculates the mean time for their set of measurements, thus improving the reliability of the investigation. The application is also able to present their data in a range of graphical formats, allowing them to choose the best option in order to present their data.

The technology allows children to access more easily the analysis of the data – thus they can explore the accuracy of their hypotheses and in changing the values of variables, model different situations. This allows them to do science in ways that professional scientists do.

a

b

Figures 8.2a and b Year 5 children investigate friction.

Task 8.4 It's more than just recording the data

Consider this use of technology using the enhancement and transformation framework in Table 8.1. What are the advantages for the pupils in using the spreadsheet to analyse their data as opposed to other methods? Are there any disadvantages? Working with other teachers in your Key Stage, or with the IT co-ordinator, explore what spreadsheets you could write, or adapt from ones found online, for your science curriculum.

Using technology to present and assess their findings

Having planned and carried out the investigation and analysed the data the final stage for the pupils is to be able to present their data, a requirement of the draft National Curriculum in England for Science, where pupils should be engaged in, 'a range of activities including collecting, presenting and analysing data' (NC, 2013: 3). Traditionally this might have been an oral report to the class or as a piece of written work for marking by the class teacher.

The mobile device allows the pupil to present their investigation in a more creative and dynamic way. There is a large and growing range of inexpensive tools that can be used by the pupil to present the multi-modal data they have collected in the planning, recording and data-gathering parts of their investigation (see www.mmiweb.org.uk/hull/ipad/index_0.html for more details). These include video-editing software, animation software, e-book creation software, as well as presentation or desktop publishing software.

Once an artefact has been constructed there is also now a range of tools that will allow the teacher or other pupils to comment, critique and explore further developments for the work – drawing the pupil, the teacher and their peers into a collaborative learning cycle (Kolb, 1984). As well as developing the range of presentation styles, giving pupils choice encourages them to think about audience and purpose, a beneficial learning outcome in itself.

Using technology to develop and extend knowledge

Perhaps the most widely used affordance of technology is in individual research. Assuming that the school has a robust wi-fi network the mobile device becomes the 'more knowledgeable other' (MKO) (Vygotsky, 1978), giving the pupil access to a wide range of support materials. These may be directly from the Internet or, more suitably, from a range of support materials chosen by you to which the pupil has access. There is a huge range of support materials and the nature of this material is such that any list will soon be out of date. One of the roles and skills of the twenty-first century teacher is in being able to use appropriate Web 2.0 tools to curate resources for their pupils to use (see Barber and Cooper, 2012). This role of MKO is developing as the software becomes more sophisticated and more interactive teaching and learning interactions take place; this could be in the form of assessment activity that adjusts depending on the answers given, access via video sites to expertise (e.g., the Khan Academy model –www.khanacademy.org), or the developing use of interrogative algorithms that allow the user to interface with the software. This is being developed in tools such as Siri (the Mac iOS interface) and the Wolfram Alpha search engine (www.wolframalpha.com).

However, as well as access to the Internet via a browser, or even to your school's Virtual Learning Environment, there is a large and growing number of applications that help enhance subject knowledge. These include applications that will recognise the songs of different birds (Birdsong ID), allow you to explore the elements (Elements) or identify trees from their leaves (TreeID). There are also science dictionary, glossary and encyclopaedia apps (both general and specialist), most of which are multi-modal in format (e.g., Video Science), as well as apps that will allow you to identify the stars and other heavenly bodies (GoSkyWatch).

There are also applications that offer simulations to explore scientific ideas and models. Again a growing range of these can be found that allow the pupils to change the parameters of an investigation and explore how this impacts on the process – this modelling is a core part of the science taking place in laboratories all over the world and brings real-world context into the primary classroom.

Teachers' use of technology

> Any teacher who can be replaced by a machine, should be.
> (Arthur C. Clarke, *Electronic Tutors*, 1980)

In this section we are going to explore a number of ways in which you can use technology to extend and transform your teaching, and hence the learning, in your classroom. As you will have seen from the first part of this chapter the opportunities for pupils offered by mobile devices are huge and this should change the way we as teachers will operate in the classroom. This should move us away from the need to give information and much more to situate and contextualise it and to make sure that the learning is individualised for the differing needs of the pupils. As the technology takes on some of the roles that we might have had as teachers (knowledge store, skills tutor) we become learning architects and personalised learning facilitators, developing learning pathways for our students and situating and setting challenges so that the maximum learning can take place. Fullan and Langworthy (2014) explore these ideas in their report *A rich seam how new pedagogies find deep learning*.

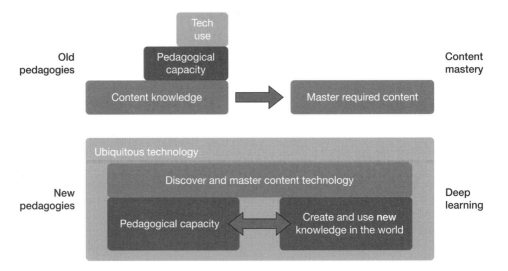

Figure 8.3 Deep learning (from Fullan and Langworthy (2014: 3)).

Using technology to present and demonstrate

A core role of technology for the teacher is using it to present information to the pupils. The danger in presenting information disassociated from the investigation is that the information is de-contextualised and outside of the pupils' experiences (Eshach, 2006; Murphy and Beggs, 2003) and this can lead to boredom and disengagement.

So, information transfer should be kept to a minimum and driven by the need from the pupils. The use of mobile devices allows the information, curated by the teacher, to be available to the pupils when they demand it. This information can then be accessed by and presented to the pupils, in a variety of creative ways.

The lack of facilities in the primary classroom can make access difficult to some areas of the curriculum, and again this is where the use of the mobile technologies can be of great use to the teacher with the added affordances of portability and touch-screen adding to the affordances of the desktop machine.

Collaboration and virtual visits and visitors

'Beaming in' visitors via videoconference software (e.g., Skype, Facetime) is relativity easy, and this can be to the whole class or to smaller groups or individuals. This can allow you to develop links to scientists working in local industry and allow them to give you virtual tours of their facilities where access would be difficult, time-consuming or too dangerous. It also allows your pupils to work in collaboration with pupils from other schools locally, nationally or even internationally. A number of projects have used this approach such as 'Toys in Space'[2] (where the children go to explore how objects move in zero and microgravity environments); 'Food for Thought'[3] (where the children go to think about the requirements for food on a long space mission to Mars) (both NASA); the 'Osprey Flyaway project[4]' (where a bird migration expert was 'brought into' the classroom (Leicester and Rutland Wildlife Trust)); and the benefits of Euglena[5] (an algae that is 0.5mm but contains most of the nutrition needed for humans to live (Japan)).

Simulations

The use of technology for simulations is an important area for the science teacher, allowing the pupils to have some experiences that would otherwise be impossible (for example visiting the Sun!). There is a growing number of websites that have simulations on this but also a number of applications that allow the teacher to demonstrate, and then the pupils to explore these. An exciting one is Frog Dissection[6], which allows you to, as the name suggests, dissect a frog – a difficult thing to do in the primary classroom.

The ability of the technology to bring into the classroom experiments that otherwise would not be possible due to time, health and safety or cost allows an enrichment of curriculum and applications offer low-cost solutions. For example, when looking at sound the application Sound Generator[7] puts a signal generator in the hands of the teacher, or the pupils, for a few pence rather than a piece of equipment that would cost hundreds of pounds and might only be used once or twice a year.

Modelling change

In the case study above we saw how technology allowed the pupils to model ideas using a spreadsheet. The teacher could build on this by using the spreadsheet to model how changing the incline of the slope could impact on both the speed of the vehicle and the resultant frictional forces, using a model either they had developed or one that they had sourced online. The way in which the technology enables the 'dull calculation' to happen in the background allows the pupils to explore the relationships between dependent and independent variables without the barrier of mathematical skills; it is not that these skills are not important but, as we have seen above, if the skills are a barrier to the investigative work the children are more likely to get bored.

Demonstration and sharing of practice

Most mobile devices are equipped with a camera and the ability to send images, via a wireless network, to the screen in the room. Thus your mobile device with a simple stand (often constructed 'Heath Robinson like' from a couple of piles of books!) becomes a visualiser[8] for teacher demonstrations and also a portable visualiser to allow pupils to see, and share, in the work of others in the classroom. The added affordance is that it is also easy to capture video of these occurrences, providing differentiated support, opportunities for re-use and assessment possibilities (see below).

Technology that supports professional practice

In this final section we explore a number of ways in which you can use technology to develop your own subject knowledge and to aid in planning and assessment, as well as the development of Personal Learning Networks (PLNs).

Lack of teacher confidence and subject knowledge is identified as one of the major issues in the teaching of primary science (Murphy *et al.*, 2007). The technology can help with this as it allows the teacher access to resources, as well as giving them more confidence to set research tasks for their students.

The technology also gives them access to a number of support networks within both the teaching and the scientific community. Easy access to social media makes the setting up of PLNs a reasonably simple task. Technologies such as Facebook or Twitter allow the less confident primary school teacher to develop networks with both more confident and/or experienced colleagues, but also with the scientific community and, as we have seen above, the possibility to bring those people into their classroom. The TES is one of the largest of these international communities (www.tes.co.uk/teaching-resources/) and some of the developing communities on Twitter include @theASE, @tesScience and @ITEfaraday.[9]

Assessment in science with mobile technologies

The mobile device provides great opportunities for the teacher to both gather evidence of achievement and provide feedback on this. The still camera, video and audio recording affordances allow the teacher to capture data as pupils undertake investigations, to record conversations with the pupils and to capture evidence from their written work – all of which can then be used for formative and summative feedback and assessment (see, for example, the app 'ExplainEverything').

During lessons data-capture tools such as 'SurveyTools' or 'NearPod' allow more interactivity, allowing you to gather live data to use to inform and develop practice. Additionally it enables you to, discreetly, gather formative assessment on the pupils in real time, making a demonstrable impact on the teaching and learning in the classroom. Gathering data in this way allows the teacher to target specific pupils, or specific groups of pupils, based on real-time data for focused feedback and improvement – a key factor in individual pupil progress (Hattie, 2009). Access to the tablets also allows the teacher to direct the pupils to previously curated resources, allowing for independent or peer learning.

Summary and key points

> If we teach today as we taught yesterday, we rob our children of tomorrow.
>
> (John Dewey, educational philosopher, 1916)

While such a short chapter is limiting I hope that this chapter has opened your eyes, or perhaps only opened them wider, to the immense possibilities that the adoption of mobile technologies can offer to the primary science teacher. The use of the tablet device allows the teacher to get closer to my defined 'core principles' for excellent primary science.

It promotes the idea of children doing *real science* – tablet technologies are more and more prevalent in professional science labs and so children undertake science that is more like science outside the classroom.

It encourages *practical, enquiry-based investigative* work as the transmission of information can be done via curated or specially written resources, which the children can access 'just in time' rather than 'just in case', giving the teacher more time to work with the children on investigative science.

It allows, using simulations and other tools, the children to explore a range of *models of science* and allows them to adapt and develop these models as their own understanding becomes more sophisticated.

It may be that your school is still considering the introduction of tablet/mobile technologies, that you are thinking about the efficacy of BYOT (bring your own technology), that you have a small number of devices you can book out or that you have larger scale plans in place (a growing number of schools are exploring how they can organise 1:1 ownership of devices that remain with the pupils (see Burden, Hopkins and Male (2012) for examples of these in Scotland). Wherever you are I hope that you are now more excited and informed about how these devices can impact on learning and teaching in science.

If you are a student teacher check which requirements for you course you have addressed through this chapter.

Notes

1 All the apps mentioned in this table, and others, can be found at www.mmiweb.org.uk/hull/ipad
2 https://education.skype.com/projects/4610-nasa-digital-learning-network-toys-in-space
3 https://education.skype.com/projects/4609-food-for-thought
4 www.ospreys.org.uk
5 https://education.skype.com/projects/4027-euglena-discover-more-about-euglena-a-microscopic-organism-005
6 Information about apps can be found at www.mmiweb.org.uk/hull/ipad/index_0.html
7 Ibid.
8 www.learningexchange.nsw.edu.au/_resources/ipadasvisualiser.pdf
9 Search for these Twitter accounts at www.twitter.com

Further reading

Meadows, J. (2004) *Science and ICT in the classroom*. London: Fulton.

This explores in more depth the uses of technology in the primary classroom using existing rather than tablet technologies – useful if you have not yet ventured into tablets.

Barber, D. and Cooper, L. (2012) *Using Web 2.0 tools in the primary classroom*. London: Routledge. This explores the use of tools such as blogs, wikis and other social tools, including some good ideas for the science teacher.

Fullan, M. and Langworthy, M. (2014) *A rich seam: How new pedagogies find deep learning*. Pearson. Retrieved from www.michaelfullan.ca/wp-content/uploads/2014/01/3897.Rich_Seam_web.pdf.
This publication explores why the technology is not enough, but should instigate both pedagogic and personal change.

Additional texts, resources and websites

ASE/BECTA (2009) *Primary science with ICT: Pupils' entitlement to ICT in primary science*. Coventry: Becta.
Bryne, J. and Sharp, J. (2002) *Using ICT in primary science teaching*. London: Learning Matters.
Osborne, J. and Hennessey, S. (2003) *Futurelab report 6: Literature review in science education and the role of ICT: Promise, problems and future directions*. Bristol: Futurelab.
For more support on apps and tablets see the iPad project at the University of Hull – www.mmiweb.org.uk/hull/ipad/index_0.html

References

ASE/BECTa (2009) *Primary Science with ICT: Pupils' entitlement to ICT in primary science*. Coventry: Becta
Barber, D. and Cooper, L. (2012) *Using new web tools in the primary classroom*. London: Routledge.
Bryne, J. and Sharp, J. (2002) *Using ICT in primary science teaching*. London: Learning Matters.
Burden, K., Hopkins, P., Male, T., Martin, S. and Trala, C. (2012). *iPadScotland evaluation report*. Hull: The University of Hull. Retrieved from https://xmascotland.wufoo.eu/forms/scottish-mobile-personal-device-evaluation-2012/. Accessed on 25 January 2014.
Clarke, A.C. (1980) 'Electronic tutors'. In B. Bova and R. Sheckley (eds) *Omni*, pp. 77–80, Omni Publications.
Davies, D., Collier, C. and Howe, A. (2012) 'A matter of interpretation: Developing primary pupils' enquiry skills using position-linked datalogging'. *Research in Science and Technological Education*, 30(3): 311–25.
Dewey, J. (1916) *Democracy and education*. New York: Free Press
DfES (2000) *The National Curriculum for England and Wales*. London: DfES.
DfES (2013) *The National Curriculum for England*. London: DfES.
Eshach, H. (2006) *Science literacy in primary schools and pre-schools*. Dordrecht: Springer.
Fullan, M. and Langworthy, M. (2014) *A rich seam: How new pedagogies find deep learning*. Pearson. Retrieved from www.michaelfullan.ca/wp-content/uploads/2014/01/3897.Rich_Seam_web.pdf. Accessed on 1 February 2014.
Harlen, W. (2010) *Principles and big ideas about science*. Hatfield, UK: ASE.
Harlen, W. and Qualter, A. (2009) *The teaching of science in primary schools* (5th edn). London: David Fulton.
Hattie, J. (2009) *Visible learning: A synthesis of over 200 meta-analyses relating to achievement*. London: Routledge.
Kearney, M. and Treagust, D. (2001) 'Constructivism as a referent in the design and development of a computer program using interactive digital video to enhance learning in physics'. *Australian Journal of Educational Technology*, 17(1): 64–79.
Kolb, D.A. (1984) *Experiential learning experience as a source of learning and development*. Upper Saddle River, NJ: Prentice Hall.
McCormick, R. and Scrimshaw, P. (2001) 'Information and communications technology, knowledge and pedagogy'. *Education, Communication and Information*, 1(1): 37–57.

Mishra, P. and Koehler, M.J. (2009) 'Technological Pedagogical Content Knowledge: A framework for teacher knowledge'. *Contemporary Issues in Technology and Teacher Education*, 91(6): 60–70.

Murphy, C. and Beggs, J. (2003) 'Children's perceptions of school science'. *School Science Review*, 84(308). Hatfield: ASE.

Murphy, C., Neil, P. and Beggs, J. (2007) 'Primary science teacher confidence revisited: Ten years on'. *Educational Research*, 49(4): 415–30.

Murphy, C. (2003) *Futurelab report 5: Literature review in primacy science and ICT*. Bristol, Futurelab. Retrieved from http://archive.futurelab.org.uk/resources/documents/lit_reviews/Primary_Science_Review.pdf. Accessed on 1 February 2014.

NACCCE (1999) *All our futures, creativity, culture and education*. Retrieved from http://sirken robinson.com/pdf/allourfutures.pdf. Accessed on 31 May 2013.

Ofsted (2011) *Successful science: An evaluation of science education in England 2007–2010*. London: Ofsted Publications. Retrieved from www.ofsted.gov.uk/resources/successful-science. Accessed on 31 May 2013.

Osborne, J. and Hennessey, S. (2003) *Futurelab Report 6: Literature review in science education and the role of ICT: Promise, problems and future directions*. Futurelab, Bristol.

Prensky, M. (2001) 'Digital natives, digital immigrants Part 1', *On the Horizon*, 9: 1–6.

Puentedura, R. (2011) 'SAMR and TPACK in action'. Retrieved from www.hippasus.com/rrpweblog/archives/2011/10/28/SAMR_TPCK_In_Action.pdf. Accessed on 31 May 2013.

Rose, J. (2008) *Independent review of the primary curriculum: Final report*. London, HMSO.

SCORE (2013) *Resourcing Practical Work in Primary Schools*. London: SCORE.

Traxler, J. (2007) 'Defining, discussing and evaluating mobile education'. *International Review of Research in Open and Distance Learning*, 8(2). Retrieved from www.irrodl.org/index.php/irrodl/article/view/346. Accessed on 31 May 2013.

Veen, W. (2004) *Homo Zappiens: Growing up in a digital age*. New York: Network Continuum Education.

Vygotsky, L.S. (1978) *Mind in society: The development of higher psychological processes*. Cambridge, MA: Harvard University Press.

Webb, J. (2012) 'The iPad as tool for education – A case study'. Naace. Retrieved from www.naace.co.uk/publications/longfieldipadresearch. Accessed on 31 May 2013.

9 ICT in Modern Foreign Language teaching

Monika Pazio (with additional case study from Patrick Carroll)

Introduction

As a famous Chinese proverb says: 'Do not confine your children to your own learning, for they were born in another time.' Children nowadays are born into a digitalized world, grow up with it and learn through it. Technology has a lot to offer to language teachers. Its importance has been emphasized in *Languages for all: Languages for life, a strategy for England* (DfES, 2002). Recent research (Wade, Marshall and O'Donnell, 2009) shows that the number of teachers who are inclined to incorporate ICT resources for language learning is increasing; this integration, however, is quite often technologically rather than pedagogically driven.

   The aim of this chapter is to present creative and innovative ways in which technology can be used in the classroom in individual, group and whole class activities. The chapter starts with the discussion of pedagogical and theoretical principles and looks at different projects or activities that to a large extent incorporate those principles. Since ICT adoption is divided across the country, mostly due to the diversity of available equipment, the examples and case studies presented below will be suitable for some contexts but inappropriate for others. However, the examples are meant to serve as an inspiration and illustration of what teachers do around the country and how they adapt technology to benefit language learners

Objectives

By the end of this chapter you should be able to:

*   identify the links between ICT and Modern Foreign Language (MFL);
*   understand the concept of normalized ICT use and effective integration;
*   look at and evaluate the examples of innovative practice;
*   determine when it is appropriate to use ICT to enhance learning.

The link between ICT and MFL

Other chapters in the book focus on how technology can aid learning in other curriculum subjects. The benefits that are universal relate to motivation and engagement through the introduction of an element of fun and play, using the world so familiar to young learners. However, educational technology has much more to offer to language learners and teachers. As it is pointed out in Dearing's report (DES, 2007) it is the access to target language and culture that makes it such a valuable tool:

> Young people's familiarity with ICT offers a great opportunity to language teachers. It seems to us that a determined commitment to use this world, which is so familiar to young people, is a key to increasing the engagement of young people of all ages with languages. New technologies can facilitate real contacts with schools and young people in other countries. They can also provide stimulus for creative and interactive work.
>
> (DES, 2007: Online)

The use of technology to teach languages is not a new idea. ICT integration in MFL education dates back to 1960s and has been traditionally referred to as Computer Assisted Language Learning (CALL). The term initially referred to the use of PCs; however, usage evolved along with the new technology that was introduced to education. The use of the term has been challenged and alternative acronyms have been proposed, including Blended Learning, Technology Enhanced Language Learning and recently Mobile Assisted Language Use – MALU (Jarvis and Achilleos, 2013). Nevertheless, CALL remains to be the most popular acronym and nowadays serves as an umbrella term that incorporates a variety of equipment including flip cams, Web 2.0 tools and mobile devices.

Where is 'CALL' going?

We know where we have been with CALL. Warschauer and Healy (1998), Warschauer and Meskill (2000) and recently Bax (2003) offer a typology of CALL stages. These typologies give us insight into the history of ICT integration in MFL education and additionally an indication of where we should be going, namely normalization (Bax, 2003). In Bax's words normalization is achieved:

> when computers (or other technological equipment) are used every day by language students and teachers as an integral part of every lesson, like a pen or book, without fear or inhibition, and equally without an exaggerated respect for what they can do. They will not be the centre of any lesson, but they will play a part in almost all. They will be completely integrated into all other aspects of classroom life, alongside course books, teachers and notepads. They will go almost unnoticed.
>
> (Bax, 2003: 23)

Accomplishing that stage demands fulfilling certain conditions related to attitudes, logistical solutions, training (Bax and Chambers, 2006) and, as a result, changes in pedagogy. Those changes lead to effective, normalized teaching, which maximizes learning.

Effective teaching with ICT

The discussion of normalisation and what it entails leads us to the question – what is effective language teaching with ICT? Just like ICT integration in other subjects, ICT for MFL education has been technologically rather than pedagogically driven. The quote from Scott Thornbury best describes this situation as 'a technological tail is wagging a pedagogical dog' (2009: Online). This creates obstacles to effective teaching where technology is not used to aid learning but rather to 'tick an ICT box'. In order to answer the question about what effective MFL teaching is we need to consider two aspects, namely what effective integration entails and what effective early language learning is.

Task 9.1 Reflecting upon effective MFL teaching

Think about your own practice and beliefs about teaching languages to young learners or primary teaching in general if you are a generalist. Create a table with two columns. In one column write down what makes effective MFL teaching in the primary classroom. In the second column think about how ICT can enhance that. Discuss your ideas with others; think of examples of activities you use in class.

When discussing effective teaching with ICT it is important to consider when to use it. Generally, if the same outcome can be achieved without the technology then there is no need to force it into the lesson. Technology should be able to transform learning and the teacher and his/her planning is the main agent in executing that change. The SAMR model (Substitution, Augmentation, Modification, Redefinition) offers an examination of levels of integration and guidance as to what integrated technology should be able to help the teacher achieve (see Figure 9.1).

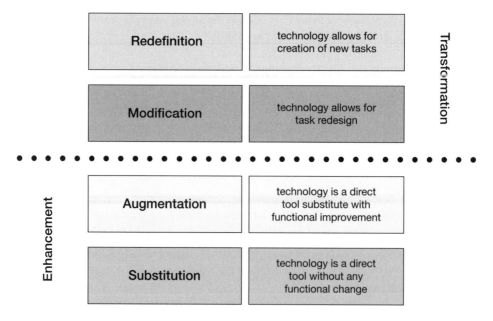

Figure 9.1 Adapted from the SAMR model (Puentedura, 2009).

The SAMR model shows technology integration as a series of steps, starting at a mere substitution, for example replacing flashcards with PowerPoint and then augmentation and moving towards modification and finally redefinition. It serves as guidance for effective ICT integration in general. The goal is to aim for task redefinition, at which stage technology offers a completely different learning experience that otherwise could not be possible.

Task 9.2 Understanding the SAMR model

Study Figure 9.1 and research The SAMR model (use 'Google Scholar' to type in SAMR Puntedura). Think about an activity that you do with your students that involves ICT integration. Where would you place your activity on the SAMR scale? How would you amend the activity at each level of the model? Discuss your ideas with colleagues.

When considering how ICT can support language teaching we need to consider what is essential for successful primary FL in general. Sharpe (1992, 2001) proposes four key ideas of primary MFL that are important for the success of primary teaching, and they focus on four Cs:

- communication
- culture
- context
- confidence.

Even though those ideas were expressed some time ago they still pertain as guidelines for good practice and are in line with principles identified by other sources (Cameron, 2001; Pinter 2006). Four Cs will be examined closer in relation to examples of projects or case studies.

Reinforcing the 'C' in ICT

In the area of predominance of Communicative Language Teaching (CLT) the emphasis is placed first and foremost on the ability to communicate. This is emphasized in England in the draft curriculum 2013/2014 for Key Stage 2 languages as expressed in the teaching aims, i.e., pupils should:

- engage in conversations; ask and answer questions; express opinions and respond to those of others; seek clarification and help
- speak in sentences, using familiar vocabulary, phrases and basic language structures
- write phrases from memory, and adapt these to create new sentences, to express ideas clearly
- present ideas and information orally to a range of audiences
- describe people, places, things and actions orally and in writing.

(DFE, 2013: 213)

Task 9.3 Reinforcing communication and developing speaking skills

Think about how you reinforce communication in your classroom/how you support development of speaking skills, and write down some examples of tasks. Do your examples involve technology? Now think about your use of technology and whether and how it promotes communication and interaction in both written and spoken form.

There is a common misbelief coming from anecdotal reports from the teachers, but also views expressed by academics (Thornbury, 2009), that technology in fact impedes communication. This is related to the use of 'Interactive Whiteboard' when used as a substitute for discussion, which places the teacher as the central point in the classroom interaction. These views should be and will be challenged here.

The most popular projects that involve and focus on communication are eTwinning projects, but these will be discussed in relation to culture. The examples chosen to illustrate teaching communication, written or spoken, and reinforcing speaking skills are less obvious and more innovative in nature.

A lot of schools are investing in iPads/tablets and piloting their learning potential. An interesting and innovative way of introducing communication in the classroom with iPads is using the Comic Life app (Dempster, 2012a). Teachers use dialogue as a form of practising speaking with a very common warmer at the beginning of the lesson, i.e., 'talk to a partner' activity. Linaker Primary School took on board this simple tested pedagogic approach and turned it into a talk to a partner-written activity, reinforcing written communication in the classroom.

Comic Life app

The activity was used with Y6 students learning Spanish. The teacher asked the children to create comic strips of their conversation using Comic Life app on iPads. Some children used pictures of themselves they took with iPad cameras; others searched for photos on the Internet or used images from their photo libraries to create a conversation.

This activity is an interesting way of reinforcing literacy skills in a foreign language, is suitable for absolute beginners and can be treated as a follow up to the spoken task. It is also a more productive take on dialogues, which in the traditional form model spoken language and in this case may serve as an assessment or for further practice.

Another example from Linaker Primary is 'Mi Familia' project (Dempster, 2012a). As it was pointed out earlier, one of the descriptors of attainment in the English Curriculum at Key Stage 2 suggests that students should be able to describe people and places orally and in writing, as well as present ideas and information orally to a range of audiences. The final result of the project is an oral description with children having an opportunity to practise all skills throughout.

Mi Familia project

About the app – Aurasma is a free app that can be downloaded on an iPad or iPhone. It allows the user to blend real-world images with interactive content such as videos and other animations, referred to as auras.

Lesson objective – to reinforce the use of vocabulary and structures for talking about my family both in speaking and writing.

The children were discussing the topic of 'My Family' in Spanish. In the first stage of the project the children focused on vocabulary that would be useful in the further part of the project – describing their families. The Aurasma app gives an opportunity to deliver key vocabulary in a more creative way. First a vocabulary page with covered vocabulary was created, which was later transformed with Aurasma into a piece of augmented reality[1].

Sad	_____	Worried	_____
Happy	_____	Crazy	_____
Nervous	_____	Energetic	_____
Angry	_____	Confused	_____
Calm	_____		

Figure 9.2 Aurasma vocabulary activity (Dempster, 2012a).

The first stage of the project used the blank worksheet as a trigger image with the keywords typed in as an overlay. After discussing the relevant vocabulary the next step was writing a paragraph in Spanish about their families. Each child emailed a photo of their families to the teacher for printing and was recorded speaking about their families. The printed photo was set as a trigger and the video of them talking about their families served as an overlay (aura). Just as in the first stage the trigger was again a sheet/image, but when the device was held over the trigger, a video was shown instead.

The activities involving the use of Aurasma evoked enthusiasm in the children and encouraged them to be creative. The children were motivated to complete the task and had greater opportunities to practise pronunciation and develop both writing and speaking skills.

Both projects/activities described above presented an original application of new technology to reinforce written and spoken communication. In both cases the use of technology reinforced communication rather than created obstacles to it. This can be done with any technology but teacher planning and task design is crucial in achieving the lesson objective.

The case study, which is an annex to this chapter, provides another example of the use of Aurasma.

Culture

Although the 2013/14 draft of the English curriculum seems to relate mostly to linguistic gains the importance of culture should not be omitted. Culture is embedded within language teaching. The goal of Early Language Learning (ELL) is as much to develop linguistic knowledge as to instil positive attitudes towards cultures (Tinsley and Comfort 2012). This is also emphasized by Ofsted (2013a) which relates to culture through the following inspection criteria for MFL:

- all pupils are provided with first-hand experience of the culture of the country where the language is spoken through visits or visitors or through the use of ICT;
- resources, including new technology, are used imaginatively to develop pupils' cultural awareness and their ability in all four skills.

The two projects described below aim to do that – they use different technology in each case in order to deepen children's understanding of different cultures.

eTwinning project 1: citizenship and MFL (British Council, 2008)

The two partner schools exchanged mascots – a Scottish teddy and French cockerel. The mascots' experience of life in the other country was recorded by pupils through use of digital camera/blog/email. Both sets of children made puzzles in their own language for others to solve. Both groups made storybooks on local history/geography.

A novel was written between the schools with one chapter in French and one in English alternately, along with illustrations. It tackled comparisons between school lunches, playground games and cultures.

The pupils were inspired and motivated. They had a great deal of fun working collaboratively on the many different projects. More importantly, they gained increased confidence in speaking a foreign language.

The second project also aims at cultural understanding through exchanges; however, it is more creative when it comes to technology use. QR codes have been in use for quite a long time, mostly for marketing, but also have been adopted to use for educational purposes. The most common uses involve creating QR treasure hunts or QR posters. The codes are extremely easy to create and read. To create them you just need to copy and paste the link to the video or document that you want to link the code to into a QR generator, such as KAYWA, and to read them download a reader app, such as i-nigma.

eTwinning project 2: culture outside the box – an example of the use of QR codes

The aim of the project is to raise cultural awareness and teach children greater appreciation of their own region and understand how technology can reinforce that. The project involves sending to each partner school (Romania, Turkey, Finland, UK) things that represent their cities, details about the regions or states and finally objects that represent our countries. Each object that we send is a QR code so that our partners can scan them to find out more information. After receiving a description or item the children blog about what they have got and share what they have learnt through discussion and photos. As a result the students gain greater cultural understanding of each other and greater understanding of how technology can support achieving that understanding.

(British Council, 2012: online)

The aim of both projects was raising cultural awareness and cultural understanding, and through this instilling positive attitudes in the learners. However, when participating in exchanges we should always have language learning in mind. Again, teacher planning is crucial here. Evaluate both projects, bearing in mind what you have read in the previous sections of this chapter, using the activity below.

Task 9.4 Evaluating eTwinning projects

Go to the British Council web links (listed at the end of this chapter) and read the more detailed descriptions of the two projects available on the website. Which one did you think was more beneficial for the students and why? What criteria did you take into account to evaluate it? How would you adapt the project that you didn't choose to increase the learning potential?

Go to the eTwinning website, browse through the projects and choose one that would be suitable for your school to be involved in. What activities would you add to maximise the learning?

Context

The use of meaningful context plays an important role in early language learning. It is through flashcards, pictures and gestures that children make the meaning by drawing on clues. A useful pedagogical approach, which presents language in context, is digital story telling. Apart from contextualising the language, digital stories:

- give the teacher more opportunities to refer to the structure of the language;
- predict the meaning and draw on comparisons between languages that are already known;
- develop accurate pronunciation and intonation;
- appreciate stories, songs, poems and rhymes in the language.

All of these points have been included as success criteria in the draft English Curriculum for KS2 Children (2013/14).

Northwood Primary School – Wing Chariot digital stories

Northwood Primary use Scruffy Kitty to explore different languages. The language is presented in context and offers opportunities to refer to the language structures and analyse them. Additionally the sentences are read aloud so the pronunciation is modelled for the students. The children are encouraged to try to translate the sentence using the pictures and words they have already encountered, so they build on their own understanding. The children are then allowed to explore the stories in small groups on iPads and further analyse the language and practise repeating single words or full sentences (Hoare, 2012). Watch the video on YouTube: www.youtube.com/watch?v=t4HLf5ipRO4

All the examples discussed previously in the other sections of this chapter presented language in context; however, the technology used is not easily available to every teacher. IWB are accessible to anybody and everybody and the use of digital stories is one of the easiest but equally beneficial ways of developing MFL skills. Digital stories have a lot to offer also from the teacher's point of view. The Wing Chariot example serves as a springboard for discussing the issues related to confidence.

Confidence

In the case of languages and their non-statutory nature it is important to look at confidence from two viewpoints – the teacher's and the children's.

As Sharpe (2001) points out teacher's confidence is an important factor, which contributes to the success of language provision. The statutory nature of MFL KS2 in force from 2014 and its ambitious expectations will deepen the staffing issues primarily related to linguistic competence, and to some degree pedagogic skills. A recent survey by Tinsley and Comfort (2012) showed this theme to be reoccurring across other countries. It is generally recommended in other European countries that the teachers should have a minimum of intermediate command of the foreign language and good working knowledge of the target culture. Very basic knowledge of the language and the culture causes low confidence in a teacher's ability to teach the language. Technology can by and large help to overcome that. Those fears were expressed by a teacher contributing to the research underpinning this chapter, who admitted he found it very difficult to teach pronunciation since it was new to him as well. Availability of a resource such as digital stories gives the teacher more confidence that what he teaches is correct and makes him feel more confident in his new role as a language teacher.

Apart from improving linguistic competence, the primary MFL teacher's job is creating a relaxed atmosphere in the classroom to foster children's confidence in using the target language. One of the arguments for early language learning is lack of inhibitions and the embarrassment that sometimes accompanies older learners. However, children still need constant reassurance that there is nothing to be afraid of or embarrassed about, and a great deal of pleasure and satisfaction can be gained from learning a language. The fun factor plays an important role here.

An example of a fun and linguistically beneficial project that took on a cross-curricular approach was Nine Acres Primary School podcasting day. The project helped students to develop their confidence to speak and at the same time gave them an opportunity to publish their work.

Nine Acres Primary School podcasting day

Led by Joe Dale, Year 3 students worked on a podcast that was later placed on a website to show to a wider audience. The idea of the project was to imaginatively build on what they had been learning in class and featured the pupils speaking, singing and rapping in French. The project was collaboration between music coordinators and language teachers. The recording took three hours to complete from start to finish and about the same time to edit in 'Audacity'. The children took the lead in the project, creating the music and choosing the language.

The project delivered the learning objectives and pupils improved their pronunciation and confidence in the process. The children enjoyed speaking French and learning new words in a fun, motivating environment. As one of the coordinating teachers said:

> Today we have achieved in three and a quarter hours what I think to be a very splendid project which the children have really enjoyed to no end. We started from a plan which the adults put together but then we discussed it with the pupils. We used their ideas and their creativity.
>
> We were impressed especially with their pronunciation which in the short space of time has improved greatly, not only for the children but also for us teachers as well. Working not only with the music but also with French we created a wonderful collaborative project which has stimulated the children to learn more French through music and dialogue.
>
> (Dale, 2007: online)

The project was also well received by the families, who were proud to hear their children speaking French and commented on the podcasts placed on the school's website (Two Stars and a Wish, 2007).

Speaking is the skill with which language learners need a lot of encouragement and need to feel comfortable to undertake. To help children break the barrier of public speaking and boost their confidence the teachers quite often use such apps as 'Morfo' or 'Tellagami'. Morfo and Tellagami are also quite often a perfect solution for including in projects those children who are not allowed to be filmed.

Using Morfo and Tellagami

Both are free apps that enable shy students to record themselves speaking in the target language. The outcomes are then displayed as animation without the need for video recording. Tellagami additionally gives a possibility of inputting the text, which is then read aloud for students who are extremely shy. Linaker Primary School use Morfo for Year 6 Spanish, for example, to make celebrities speak. An example of an activity was when teaching about sport – the children made Cristiano Ronaldo say he hates football and loves ballet and dance (Dempster, 2012a).

The last example again comes from Linaker Primary – an interesting way of using an iPod Shuffle to revise vocabulary with Year 6 students learning Spanish. The activity motivated the learners and also gave them more confidence with pronunciation. There follows the activity described in the words of the teacher, Nick Dempster:

iPod Shuffle

The children were learning about Las Comidas (food). Here's what I did:

1   Once I had undertaken the initial language acquisition session with the children, I asked pupils to record themselves saying one of the phrases. This was completed on an Apple Mac recording into audacity (it could just as easily be done using audacity and a microphone on any computer).
2   I used the effects in audacity to remove background noise and ensure the children's recordings were as clear as possible. I then exported the recordings as MP3s.
3   The MP3s were then uploaded onto the iPod shuffle.
4   In the following session, we used the recordings to play lotto with the words. Nothing ground breaking, the children choose 6 of the words from the list they had learnt in the first session. I then plugged the iPod shuffle into a speaker system, and let the technology decide which phrases were said, and in what order!

The children absolutely loved the fact that their friends were the ones saying each of the words. It meant that they listened more carefully, and were translating the words with more interest and enthusiasm. It also offered self-assessment for the children that had recorded themselves, both in terms of clarity and pronunciation.

(Dempster, 2012b: online)

All the examples presented above aimed at developing learners' confidence to speak in a foreign language through creating engaging tasks. The aim wasn't to wow the children with technology but rather to use the technology in an engaging way to serve learning. The same applies to all the examples described in this chapter. The technology transformed the task as opposed to being a substitute for something already in use.

Task 9.5 Evaluating projects and their learning potential

Look at all the examples or case studies presented in the chapter and analyse them in relation to the SAMR model and the learning potential they have. Which SAMR level would you say these achieve, in which learning gains are the greatest?

Think about your learners and the equipment available to you. Plan a lesson that would incorporate one of the activities discussed in the chapter.

Summary and key points

Our perception of what technology is changes according to the saying: 'technology is everything that was invented after we were born'. The examples in the chapter included different type of technologies – some just introduced to education and others that have been present for longer. No matter what equipment or software is used we need to remember that effective teaching incorporates both pedagogical principles about teaching young learners and knowledge of how technology should be integrated. The focus should be on the target language and learning and 'ICT in the MFL lesson should be a support medium rather than an end in itself' (Jones and Coffey, 2013: 119).

Annex: case study: improving MFL for 10-year-olds using augmented reality

Patrick Carroll

Overview of study

Shaw Wood Academy in Armthorpe, Doncaster, is a large primary school in a former mining village. The Year 6 children had been experimenting with the augmented reality app 'Aurasma' within writing so they wanted to see whether or not it could be used to support other subjects.

In class we were creating role-play situations in French about activities that we did at home. For example, looking after our pets, or mentioning some of the different sports activities that we took part in outside of school. Many of the children were wanting to improve sentences by listing all of the activities that they completed at home but were not able to remember all the vocabulary they needed.

What happened? To support the children to recall the words and phrases that they were wanting to use I put up a display with the names of the activities that we had talked about, such as swimming or playing football, as well as the names of the different pets that they were wanting to mention, such as taking the dog for a walk or feeding the rabbits. Next, I linked up some of the free animations from Aurasma to each picture through the iPad (each word had been written in a distinctive font so that the app would differentiate between fonts, so that it would play the correct animation with the matching word).

Consequently, when the children were in groups putting together sentences for their role play if they were stuck on a word they could check what the word was in French by holding up an iPad to the words on the display to see the animation. The technology had an impact because after a few views of the animations many of the children did not have to check the display as they were able to link the word to the animation instinctively. Therefore, instead of me having to repeat the words many times the children would automatically remember the word as the majority of the class had made a connection through a colourful animation. The children were then eager to use Aurasma to record their group work. So on their sheet they placed a picture of an animal or activity that they had mentioned alongside their sentences that were in English. They then recorded themselves on the iPad and linked the picture on their sheet to Aurasma so that if anyone wanted to listen to them translating the English text into French they could by simply using an iPad.

Task 9.6 Developing your skills in using augmented reality software

Find a photograph of yourself. Then record a description of yourself in another language using a mobile device that will download the free app Aurasma. Using Aurasma link the video to the photograph so that when you hold up your mobile device to the picture it changes from a picture of you to your video description. Create a channel so that others can subscribe to it, meaning that they will be able to use their own device to see your video.

Note

1   To see how Aurasma works on this activity either download the free app on your iPad or iPhone, search for and follow Linaker Primary school and scan the image above with your phone. Alternatively go to YouTube by entering the address below: www.youtube.com/watch?v=Va_WX96Da-A

References and further reading

Aurasma (n.d.) Available online at: www.aurasma.com. Accessed on 27 May 2014.

Bax, S. (2003) 'CALL – past, present and future'. *System*, 31(*1*): 13–28.

Bax, S. and Chambers, A. (2006) 'Making CALL work: Towards normalisation'. *System*, 34(*4*): 465–79.

British Council (2012) *E-twinning: Culture outside the box.* Available online at: www.etwinning.net/tr/pub/connect/browse_people_schools_and_pro/profile.cfm?f=2&l=en&n=81097#process. Accessed on 4 January 2014.

British Council (2008) *E-twinning: Citizenship and MFL.* Available online at: www.britishcouncil.org/etwinning-quality-label-calder-primary-school-scotland.htm. Accessed on 4 January 2014.

Cameron, L. (2001) *Teaching languages to young learners.* Cambridge: Cambridge Language Teaching Library, Cambridge University Press.

Dale, J. (2007) *Nine Acres Primary podcasting day* (14 March 2007). Available online at: http://joedale.typepad.com/integrating_ict_into_the_/2007/03/nine_acres_prim.html. Accessed on 1 January 2012.

Dempster, N. (2012a) *Other iPad apps to use in MFL lessons* (6 December 2012). Available online at: http://linakerict.blogspot.co.uk/2012/12/other-ipad-apps-to-use-in-mfl-lessons.html.

Dempster, N. (2012b) 'Using an iPod Shuffle in language lessons' (7 March, 2012). Available online at: http://linakerict.blogspot.co.uk/2012/03/using-ipod-shuffle-in-language-lessons.html. Accessed on 10 March 2013.

DES (Department of Education and Skills) (2007) *Languages review.* Available online at: www.teachernet.gov.uk/_doc/11124/LanguageReview.pdf. Accessed on 28 October 2007.

DFE (2013) *The National Curriculum in England. The framework document.* Available online at: www.gov.uk/government/uploads/system/uploads/attachment_data/file/210969/NC_framework_document_-_FINAL.pdf. Accessed on 21 July 2013.

DfES (2002) *Languages for all: Languages for life, a strategy for England.* Nottingham: DfES Publications.

Hoare, S. (2012) *Teaching languages with stories to touch* (2 January 2012). Available online at: www.youtube.com/watch?v=t4HLf5ipRO4. Accessed on 19 January 2013.

Jarvis, H. and Achilleos, M. (2013) 'From computer assisted language learning (CALL) to mobile assisted language use'. *TESL-EJ*, 16(*4*): 1–18.

Jones, J. and Coffey, S. (2013) *Modern languages*, 5–11. Routledge: London.

Ofsted (2013a) *Modern languages survey visits*. Available online at: www.ofsted.gov.uk/resources/ generic-grade-descriptors-and-supplementary-subject-specific-guidance-for-inspectors-making-judgemen. Accessed on 6 March 2013.

Pinter, A. (2006) *Teaching young language learners*. Oxford: Oxford University Press.

Puentedura, R. (2009) *As we may teach: Educational technology, from theory into practice*. Available online at: https://itunes.apple.com/itunes-u/as-we-may-teach-educational/id380294 705?mt=10. Accessed on 20 February 2013.

Sharpe, K. (2001) *Modern Foreign Languages in the primary school: The what, why and how of early language teaching*. London: Kogan Page.

Sharpe, K. (1992) 'Communication, culture, context and confidence: The four Cs in primary modern language teaching'. *Language Learning Journal*, 12: 40–2.

Shaw Wood Primary School use of aurasma – www.youtube.com/watch?v=5qRcIek4NY0

Thornbury, S. (2009) 'On interactive whiteboards (again!)'. (7 June 2009). Available online at: www.teachingenglish.org.uk/blogs/scott-thornbury/interactive-whiteboardsagain. Accessed on 10 December 2010.

Tinsley, T. and Comfort, T. (2012) 'Lessons from abroad: International review of primary languages'. Research report. London: CfBT. Available online at: www.cfbt.com/evidencefor education/pdf/Lessons%20from%20abroad_International%20review%20of%20primary%20langu ages.pdf. Accessed on 15 July 2012.

Two Stars and a Wish (2007) *Nodehill French*. Available online at: http://nodehillfrench.typepad. com/two_stars_and_a_wish/2007/03/nine_acres_prim.html. Accessed on 12 April 2013.

Wade, P., Marshall, H. and O'Donnell, S. (2009) 'Primary Modern Foreign Languages: Longitudinal survey of implementation of national entitlement to language learning at Key Stage 2'. Final Report. DCSF. Available online at: www.nfer.ac.uk/nfer/publications/. Accessed on 1 October 2009.

Warschauer M. and Healey D. (1998) 'Computers and language learning: an overview'. *Language Teaching*, 31: 57–71.

Warschauer, M. and Meskill, C. (2000) 'Technology and second language learning'. In J. Rosenthal (ed.) *Handbook of undergraduate second language education*. New Jersey: Lawrence Erlbaum, pp. 303–18.

Useful websites

Joe Dale's Professional Blog http://joedale.typepad.com/

MFL Sunderland teacher training podcasts www.sunderlandschools.org/mfl-sunderland/resources-pr-fr-podcasts.htm

eTwinning projects www.etwinning.net/en/pub/index.htm

10 Nurturing the developing musician through the use of technology

Jon Audain

Introduction

The process of making music is one of the few activities to engage both sides of the human brain. When introduced from an early age, music education has the tools to develop a young person in all aspects of their development. The UK DfE report (2011: 42) on the importance of music education in schools states that, 'Music can make a powerful contribution to the education and development of children, having benefits which range from those that are largely academic to the growth of social skills and contribution to overall development.' Technology can be used to support teaching, and to enable pupils to compose, make, record and perform music. It can also remove barriers for groups who might not otherwise be able to access music (DfE 2011: 36).

However, the skills of music must be taught, experienced and nurtured, and space must be given for creative potential to develop. Music education involves the areas of composing, performing, listening and appraising, and singing. Through the different disciplines, a child develops confidence in their music making, composing and group work skills, ultimately leading to better performance and a rise in a child's self-esteem.

Objectives

By the end of this chapter you should:

- have a range of ideas about how you might use technologies in music education in your classroom in performing, singing, composition, listening and appraising;
- understand how hardware can support music making;
- understand how to use software tools to support composition.

What does the use of technology in music involve?

The use of technology should enhance the music-making process. Not all activities can be considered as music. Making a musical instrument is not music, though playing it may be (Mills, 2009: 2). At the core of all activities provided should be the consideration of how the technology supports the music making (see Table 10.1).

Developing rhythm work, singing and composing using the interactive whiteboard

With its large visual display, the interactive whiteboard is useful for supporting whole class teaching. Images can be used to stimulate composition work; notation is made easier

Table 10.1 How technology can support music making

Technology	How it supports music making
iPods/MP3 player	Music can be downloaded and played during lessons to support steady pulse work, singing using backing tracks or within the use of listening and appraising activities.
Keyboards	Music can be composed using the instrument as well as different voices and rhythms to support composing and performing activities.
Microphones and video camera	Can be used to record compositions as formative or summative assessment. Video evidence can also support the practitioner in assessing practical skills, as well as how children react to each other during group work.
Mobile technology	The use of apps can develop new aspects to composition and performance. Some apps represent the factual elements of music and music theory.
Desktop software	Software can support the composing curriculum, usually in the form of sequencing or music making through exploratory play.
Interactive whiteboard	The use of the web and specialist music services (i.e., 'Singup', 'Charanga') during whole class and group work to model musical concepts through the use of the interactive board as well as specific whiteboard tools.

using manuscript paper, and the use of tools to create shapes and lines can be used to structure rhythm activities. This enables all children to use the large display and be guided in their music making, as a whole class, instead of looking down at a paper copy.

The 'shape' tools on the whiteboard provide a useful structure for developing rhythm work and flashcards. Create grids to indicate bars then use the circle tool to create rhythmic beats that the children then need to clap back (see Figure 10.1).

Select the 'Drag a copy' or 'Clone' function to make it easier to replicate different rhythms and drag these up on the board.

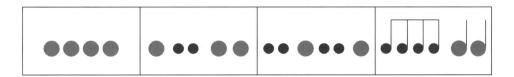

Figure 10.1 Developing rhythm patterns using the shape and line tools.

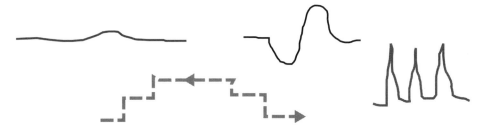

Figure 10.2 Four examples of taking a line on a walk.

Encourage children to warm up their singing voices by producing a 'sirening' sound while taking a 'line on a walk' (see Figure 10.2).

Select a different colour, or if you are using the SMARTBoard one of its special pen effects, and draw a continuous line, varying the line from top to bottom of the board. Encourage the children to copy the line with their voices so they exercise their full vocal range. Experiment with different lines and shapes to challenge the children.

The interactive whiteboard can be used to develop graphic scores to support composition work. Insert abstract shapes or images relating to a curriculum topic, such as weather, across a timeline; the children have to use the images from start to finish to compose music to (see Figure 10.3).

Figure 10.3 An example of a graphic score created using the interactive whiteboard shapes and lines.

The use of YouTube in music education

Since the introduction of YouTube there have been many clips available to show to develop discussions with children. For example, ask: 'Why do people listen to music and how does it affect their lives?' Use '500 Miles' by The Proclaimers and 'The Streets of London' as examples. Discuss how they make the children feel. Do they want to learn how to play an instrument or watch examples of music from around the world? The likelihood is that YouTube will have an example of what they choose.

Remember to screen the clips to check that there are no inappropriate surprises. When watching YouTube clips, you may want to start the clip at a certain point in the video. A quick tip is to click the 'Share' tab under the video and then find the exact place in the clip. Then copy the URL web link and paste it into your whiteboard flipchart. That way when you click on the link it will take you to that exact point, therefore not affecting the flow of your lesson.

Composing

Practical activities to develop musical composition offer unique opportunities for children to experiment with instruments, rhythms, patterns and ideas. Although technology does not replace the physical experience it can offer different ways for children to compose either through the perspective of using different digital instruments to create new compositions or by sequencing, organising or interacting with sound.

Task 10.1 Using technology to support assessment in music

Technology can support the process of assessment in music education and can be combined with traditional methods of recording. Modern technology means that capturing, recording, saving and archiving audio is now very straightforward (Fautley, 2010: 33). In the midst of music making, learners can struggle to stand back objectively and reflect on the overall impression. Good primary music teaching encourages regular opportunities to use formative assessment to develop dialogue, musical ideas and skills. Formative assessment needs to be provided in such a way that enables learners to be able to work independently and develop critical skills so they can reflect on and evaluate their work objectively, identifying areas for improvement, while also recognizing achievements (Papageorgi and Hallam, 2010: 142).

- Provide the children with an individual digital recorder for each group. Ask the group to record aspects of the composition process, i.e., their musical ideas of their entire compositions.
- Encourage children to record *both* the rough musical ideas and to reflect on the positives and negatives, as well as performances of the entire composition, ensuring all the group members are involved at different stages.
- Design an ongoing assessment sheet for children to use when performing their work at the end of the lesson. Provide a space for children to record thoughts from peers as well as their own personal 'two stars and a wish' reflection for the next lesson. For a useful starting point, explore Major and Cottle's (2010) article which examines the significance of teacher questioning during compositional work and how it can enhance children's dialogue.

Task 10.2 Building a portfolio of musical composition

Collect excellent pieces of pupil work as samples to play to the subsequent year groups during the same topic. Final compositions can be uploaded to an online space, virtual learning environment or embedded in a blog post for parents to listen to or download onto an mp3 player.

Composing using ICT used to be limited and in some ways developed a narrow sense of composition.

Older software titles worked on organising samples of music to support the composition process. Advances in technology and the introduction of mobile devices have made composition much more creative and inventive. The work of Hugill (2012) and Partti (2012) for example, investigate the understanding of the 'Digital Musician'. Hugill explains that '. . . good music can be made at any stage, with any equipment and using any technique' (2012: xvi) and the combination can lead to some interesting examples of music making.

Table 10.2 Mobile apps to support composition work (Audain, J., 2014: 174)

Musyc is a really interesting app. Sounds are made by musical objects bouncing off the lines you have drawn as well as the objects you have placed within the screen. It is great fun and certainly an interesting way to compose.

Isle of Tune (the mobile app and the web application) is a novel way of looking at composition. The Isle of Tune lets you compose a piece of music by building your own land. Each building piece makes a particular sound. The house makes a low xylophone sound; the flowers are the sound of keyboards and the lamp posts are different percussion beats. All of these can be customised by pitch and you have the ability to change the different sounds. You are given a piece of field where you can put down a road and then musically decorate it with the different objects. Finally you place up to three different cars on the road. As the car passes the object it triggers the sound. Isle of Tune is a great resource open to everyone.

There are many examples on Isle of Tune for you to consider. Search for 'Don't Stop Believing' and you will see the talent of some people. However, inherent in the notion that the resources are open to everyone does raise one potential e-safety dilemma (see Chapter 19). Anyone can upload an island they have created. Unfortunately some people choose to name these islands in inappropriate ways. This either becomes a programme that you do not use or a teaching point about etiquette and how you should name files appropriately. You can talk through how the children create their own island and explain the dangers and sanctions if children are found searching during school times. This certainly does lead to a good discussion; it is just a shame people find it difficult to behave and act appropriately.

Madpad presents you with a four-by-three grid. Each square comprises a sound. You can record your own or use a grid that other people have produced. Due to the multi-touch nature of the iPad it means that more than one sound can be combined together. Take two fingers and slide your fingers up and it speeds the sound up, while the opposite way will slow things down. You can record your own signing, instruments, rhythms and sounds and then use these to make your own compositions.

Try some of the apps (shown in Table 10.2) and explore some of the curriculum software (shown in Table 10.3) that support composition work. Further software to support general music education is listed in Table 10.4.

Developing performance skills through the use of mobile technology

The following case study provides an example of how you can develop performance skills using the iPod or iPad.

Case study 10.1 Developing iPod/iPad bands to foster performance and group work

There are now many different devices that can generate sound and music. Why not create your own mini-band. The North Point iBand (www.youtube.com/watch?v=F9XN fWNooz4) provides an example for inspiration.

There is a number of different instruments available on iPad and iPod that can be combined together. Search for different instruments in the app store and spend time exploring different options as the quality of instrument apps varies. Look for how responsive

Table 10.3 Curriculum software to support composition work (Audain, J., 2014: 167–186)

2 Simple Music toolkit is a suite of different programmes to develop different musical elements. The children can record and play sounds by clicking different musical instruments. They can organise different musical sounds into a sequence as well as begin to explore different things.

Compose World is a software title that has been available for a long time in schools. It presents different musical building blocks to the user. Behind each one is a musical pattern. The children drag down the different musical blocks to create a tune.

Dance eJay allows children to build up music by stringing together samples of dance music to create a music track.

Musical Monsters and *Mini-Musical Monsters* is a colourful piece of software for composing. The main screen has a blank grid in which the monsters are placed. At the bottom of the screen is the control box where the children select the monster they would like to hear. Behind each one is a different musical sound played by an instrument. You can adjust the pitch so it sounds higher or lower and you can change the tempo of the whole piece so the music is played more quickly or at a slower speed. Mini-Musical Monsters relies just on pictures for children to create their music and allows very young children to explore musical sound.

O-Generator takes an alternative look at composing music using software. It presents a musical bar that would normally be read in a linear way and converts it into a circle, so the beats in a bar go round in the same way a clock hand does as it counts time. You choose the combination of musical instruments and then you turn on and off different 'pads' to make the music. Set your drum, set your guitar rift and then as the counter arm rolls over the pad it will play all the sounds. A different but exciting way to compose more modern pieces of music.

Table 10.4 Software to support general music education

The Dums allows children to explore different instruments. It introduces them to the sound of different instruments and the children select them to find out more information. There is also an international version in which children can learn about gamelan, Indian Raga and African music, among other styles.

Rhythm Maker presents a number of percussion instruments down the left-hand side of the screen. By entering different beats by clicking on the timeline, the children can create rhythms. This can be played together, creating a percussion background that can be exported.

Audacity (free) is not really a dedicated piece of music software but it can be used within the classroom. Use it to record compositions, singing or instrumental backing tracks that can then be played in class and used to support colleagues who are not so confident. Audacity provides tools for editing your track and cutting out sections. There are also a number of special effects, such as being able to speed tracks up. This software is useful for creating podcasts as the tracks can then be exported as mp3 tracks.

Sibelius if you run a school orchestra or instrumental groups, then *Sibelius* is notation software that will allow you to quickly write out scores and transpose them. This does save endless amounts of time for your music coordinator if they have to rewrite music or transpose it for the clarinets or trumpet players in your school.

they are under your fingertips; quality apps have a higher response rate. Each instrument will need an amplifier. There are some cheap but portable speakers that can plug into the iPad/iPod just using a 3.5 mm headphone jack.

The rock band configuration listed below provides a useful starting point:

- iAmGuitar (https://itunes.apple.com/en/app/iamguitar/id407752080?mt=8)
- Six Strings (https://itunes.apple.com/gb/app/six-strings/id374226640?mt=8). This app will let you adapt the chords as well.
- NLog MIDI Synth (https://itunes.apple.com/gb/app/nlog-midi-synth/id391268291?mt=8).
- BaDaBing (https://itunes.apple.com/gb/app/badabing/id395952688?mt=8).

Use the Ultimate Guitar Tabs app (https://itunes.apple.com/gb/app/ultimate-guitar-tabs-largest/id357828853?mt=8). Songs are submitted here with the chord symbols and the lyrics. By using this app, you then know the correct chords to give to your guitars and chords or notes to give to your keyboard players. There are a range of modern tunes that are updated regularly; so finding something current that children will really enjoy playing is relatively easy. Next, write out the lyrics on the board and copy the chords just above the words.

For keyboard players, I use the idea of an ICT concept keyboard. Find a sheet of clear acetate film (as you would use on an overhead projector) and place it over the iPad. A small amount of sticky tack at the top of the iPad prevents the acetate from slipping. Load up the keyboard app and note the chords in the song. Cut squares of address labels to the same size as the keys and then label just the chords you need.

Practise each separate part at a time and then piece together the tune, inviting individual children or the whole group to sing the melody.

Producing your own iPad/iPod band can be a great experience, especially for the children when collectively they are playing songs from Adele through to The Beatles!

(Adapted from Audain, J., 2014: 170–171)

Opportunities to use ICT to develop listening and appraising skills

Music provides a wealth of listening opportunities. Listening is a fundamental part of the music process. It is useful for reviewing work composed, motivating a person as they work, as well as opening the listener to new musical genres by varying the listening 'diet'. Music is personal and has an emotional connection with each individual.

Vary the children's listening experience from jazz to classical to music from around the world and different times in history. Establish a classroom practice where, if the music is on when everyone is working then everyone must be able to hear it.

Establish rules for listening – Challenge the children to consider how many times they sit, listen and focus on the music. We use music a huge amount as a background sound-track. Listening to music critically involves the learned discipline of sitting still without distraction; something at first children and sometimes adults find difficult. As Mills (2009: 75) outlines, this '. . . means that music in school will be essentially different from many pupils' experience of music at home'. Ask the children to listen to certain features:

- Which instruments do they hear?
- How does the music tell a story?
- Ask them questions relating to the different musical elements of pitch, duration, dynamics, tempo, timbre, texture and structure.

Around the world challenge – Create a classroom display or insert an image of a world map on an empty interactive whiteboard flipchart. Put a challenge to your class at the beginning of the year that as a class you are going to see how many pieces of music from different countries you can listen to. As you listen to a piece of music then you place an image of a dot/shape/cat/plane (whatever you like) on the relevant country to show that you have visited. Why not have a whole-school competition to see how many different pieces of music you can listen to? That way you can swap music with colleagues.

Responding to music

Listening and responding to music connects all strands of music. The creative journey is one involving a good deal of trust and respect between teacher and pupils, teacher and other colleagues, and between the children themselves (Bunting, 2011). Valuing individual responses to music can begin this process. Below are two activities to develop these skills:

Create a listening grid – create a four-by-three grid on the interactive whiteboard. Place headings at the top of each square, such as rhythmic, percussion instruments, fast, slow, singer. Have musical word banks on the flipchart. As you listen to the pieces of music, the children come up and drag the words that fit the music. Alternatively you can get the children to use voting devices to answer questions or respond to the music with the aspects each piece has.

Sliding scales – using your interactive whiteboard software, draw a number of lines on the page and lock them into position. From the resources bank, insert an arrow, a pointer or a cartoon character. Use this to assess how much the class likes different aspects of the music. For example, under each line write a musical aspect such as singing, instruments, drums, woodwind. Then at certain points throughout listening, stop the track and slide the image from left to right, depending on how much the class liked the singing/instruments/drums and so on.

Summary and key points

This chapter has provided an overview of how you might use technologies in your classroom to develop pupils' sense of rhythm work, singing, composition and music making. The importance of developing listening skills was also highlighted. Developing your own skills requires professional commitment and is helped if you can find colleagues to share ideas with. Joining a professional association is a great way to support your ongoing professional development.

Further reading

Bray, D. (2009) *Creating a musical school.* London: Oxford University Press.
>Chapter 8 (p. 167) provides a useful reference point for using ICT and e-learning to develop musical skills and create positive attitudes. The chapter explores the considerations for schools implementing the use of technology in music.

Fautley, M. (2010) *Assessment in music education.* London: Oxford University Press.
>This text is essential reading that explores the use of assessment across areas of music education. A comprehensive guide exploring written and aural forms of assessment.

Major, A.E. and Cottle, M. (2010) 'Learning and teaching through talk: Music composing in the classroom with children aged six to seven years'. *British Journal of Music Education*, 27(3): 289–304.
>The authors of this article describe a study in which students composed in pairs and were questioned by researchers. Pupils' use of scaffolding techniques and the importance of evaluating compositions through dialogue are explored through the article.

Websites

www.singup.org
'500 Miles' by The Proclaimers – www.youtube.com/watch?v=69AvNm8zubo
The Streets of London – www.youtube.com/watch?v=DiWomXklfv8
Musyc (www.fingerlab.net/website/Fingerlab/Musyc.html)
Isle of Tune mobile app (https://itunes.apple.com/gb/app/isle-of-tune-mobile/id430845597?mt=8) and the website (www.isleoftune.com)
MadPad (www.smule.com/madpad)
2Simple Music toolkit (www.2simple.com/music)
Compose World (www.espmusic.co.uk/composeworldinfo.html)
Dance eJay (www.ejay.com/uk)
Musical Monsters and Mini-Musical Monsters (www.busythings.co.uk/cd-rom-musical.php)
O-Generator (www.o-music.tv/index.htm)
The Dums (www.espmusic.co.uk/thedums_desc.html)
Rhythm Maker (www.espmusic.co.uk/rhythmmaker_desc.html)
Audacity (http://audacity.sourceforge.net)
Sibelius (www.sibelius.com)
The Schools Music Association (www.schoolsmusic.org.uk)
International Society for Music Education (www.isme.org)

References

Audain, J. (2014) *The ultimate guide to using ICT across the curriculum for primary teachers: Web, widgets, whiteboards and beyond!* London: Bloomsbury.
Bunting, P. (2011) 'Realising creative development'. In N. Beach, J. Evans and G. Spruce (eds) *Making music in the primary school: Whole class instrumental and vocal teaching.* London: Routledge.
DfE (2011) *The importance of music: A national plan for music education.* London: Department for Education.
Fautley, M. (2010) *The assessment in music education.* United Kingdom: Oxford University Press.
Hugill, A. (2012) *The Digital Musician* (2nd edn). London: Routledge.
Major, A.E. and Cottle, M. (2010) 'Learning and teaching through talk: Music composing in the classroom with children aged six to seven years'. *British Journal of Music Education*, 27(3): 289–304.

Mills, J. (2009) *Music in the primary school* (3rd edn). London: Oxford University Press.

Papageorgi and Hallam, (2010) 'Issues of assessment and performance'. In S. Hallam and A. Creech (eds) *Music education in the 21st century in the United Kingdom: Achievements, analysis and aspirations.* London: Institute of Education.

Partti, H. (2012) 'Cosmopolitan musicianship under construction: Digital musicians illuminating emerging values in music education'. *International Journal of Music Education*, 2014, 32(*1*): 3–18.

11 Teachers and pupils incorporated

Developing a co-constructed classroom

Gina Blackberry and Deb Woods

Introduction

> I was really frustrated about the way my pupils seemed to lack any sort of engagement with the topic. They had to research an invention of some sort; a topic imposed on them ... and which I quite frankly thought was ... boring. I watched them go through the process of spending countless hours on the Internet and copying great chunks of information and producing something which in the end wasn't really their work and that they didn't really understand. Gina mentioned something about a WebQuest and I'd never heard the term before, like many terms that are coming up now and I had no idea what it was and ignored it for a little while.
>
> (Deb, 2010)

The realization that an aspect of our teaching practice is not working has the potential to function as a powerful agent of change. However, effecting that change can drive powerful cognitive and affective responses that function to either support or prevent the change from being implemented. Despite participating in 'traditional' forms of ICT professional development, Deb struggled with Information and Communication Technologies (ICT) integration for a range of reasons and this was reflected in her initial decision to ignore creating a WebQuest. Evidence suggests she is not alone in facing these struggles.

In this chapter we weave the threads of two distinct but inter-related narratives about personal and professional change: how we overcame our technology phobias and how we created a co-constructed learning environment we called 'Teachers and Pupils Incorporated'. It will also identify some of the steps we undertook to create the learning co-operative.

Objectives

At the end of this unit you should be able to:

- reflect upon your thoughts and feelings about pedagogy and ICT and how these might be functioning to prevent change in your classroom;
- understand what a co-constructed learning environment is;
- understand how a co-constructed learning environment can benefit pupils and support your own professional learning;

- consider action research as the methodology to underpin your planned change;
- implement some steps to creating your own co-constructed learning environment.

A context for our narratives

Our story took place 'Down Under' in an urban independent (private) school in Australia. Deb, a primary school teacher, was cognizant of the need to learn more about using ICT in the classroom. As a doctoral candidate, I was interested in researching teachers' cognitive and affective responses to ICT integration. For two years we worked with Deb's pupils in Years 3, 4 and 5 to investigate if, and how, ICT could be used to transform young pupils' learning. We adopted an action research approach to guide our work and to track our cognitive and affective responses to ICT integration. Action research is a methodology that encourages self-reflection and engages action cycles to plan for and effect change. This chapter is not intended to provide a review of the methodology but rather to share our narratives of change and how action research framed our work and facilitated the creation of a co-constructed learning environment using ICT.

Task 11.1 Learning about action research

Action research was the vehicle through which change, professional learning, and reflection on our practice could take place. To familiarize yourself with action research read the following papers:

www.aral.com.au/resources/aandr.html
www.alara.net.au/aral/actionresearch
www.actionlearning.com.au/Classes/ActionResearch/Books/Book-Action
    ResearchForImprovingPractice.pdf

What is a co-constructed learning environment?

A social-constructivist philosophy underpins a co-constructed learning environment. Learning is understood to be active and involves solving authentic problems in real situations in collaboration with peers and teachers. Emphasis is on the 'social, distributed and collective nature of learning' (Laferriere, Lamon and Chan, 2006: 77). In practice this means that, as appropriate, the teacher moves away from being the 'sage on the stage' and the disseminator of knowledge to a 'guide on the side', whereby careful questioning is used to identify pupils' existing knowledge about curriculum content areas and subsequently what they would like to know and learn. Thus, the teacher facilitates an enquiry-based and experiential learning process. Information and communication technologies play an integral part in a co-constructed learning environment. Applications such as the Internet, Skype, email, Twitter and Survey Monkey support pupils accessing knowledge from a variety of sources in a timely manner, while software such as Prezi, YouTube, VoiceThread, WordPress and Glogster allows pupils to transform their learning into a variety of multimodal texts and to share it with others.

The identification of pupils' prior knowledge functions to help situate learning curriculum content within personally relevant and meaningful frames of reference. This also enables the teacher to accurately differentiate learning to suit learners' styles and needs. For example, during a unit of work on philanthropy, Deb's pupils identified and researched a person or cause that was personally meaningful to them, discovered how they might support that organisation/cause and proceeded to plan and implement a range of philanthropic initiatives. ICT supported this learning in a number of ways, from researching on the web, concept mapping, sending emails and creating letters and reports, brochures, advertisements and so on.

Task 11.2 Reflecting on your current pedagogical practice

Critically examine your pedagogy and the way you currently use technology with your pupils. Is there room for improvement/change? How can you get your pupils to learn subject content without lecturing them? With a teaching colleague select a Key Learning Area (KLA) and brainstorm ways of using ICT to create a constructivist learning environment.

Teachers and change

If you have completed Task 11.2 it is likely that you have experienced uncomfortable thoughts and feelings. Maybe you think you don't have enough time to make changes or perhaps you feel incompetent using technology. Whatever your thoughts or feelings, fear not! You are not alone. An education system that embraces new technologies and constructivist pedagogies presents a myriad of possibilities, options, dilemmas and challenges for teachers. Ultimately, the extent to which new approaches will be integrated or adopted hinges on teachers' decisions about 'if, when and how this can be done' (Bate, 2010: 1042), and subsequently their ability to change their practice (Culp, Honey and Mandinach, 2003; Haydon and Barton, 2007; Somekh, 2008).

Guskey (2002) argued that change is a difficult and gradual process for teachers. Ultimately any change in pedagogy and the integration of ICT is dependent upon what teachers do, how they think, and what they feel. For us confronting and implementing change was, at times, frustrating, time-consuming and daunting. Deb also experienced tensions related to striking a balance between covering the curriculum requirements and fully embracing a co-constructed learning environment. It is possible that the move to a co-constructed learning environment may cause anxiety for those teachers who prefer an authoritarian management style and who like to be in control and have a clear understanding of the direction in which lessons will proceed. Furthermore, a co-constructed classroom values the teacher as a learner too and thus the approach challenges the entrenched view that teachers know everything.

The power of our thoughts and feelings

> Despite my uncertainty about the technology and pedagogy, I knew there had
> to be a better way (to engage and motivate pupils) and I had to find it. I could
> have left things the same and it would have been easier but so frustrating for me.
> I needed to inspire and interest the pupils.
>
> (Deb, 2011).

Like many teachers around the world, when we first began working together, Deb's
qualitative (depth of use) and quantitative (frequency of use) use of ICT in the classroom
could be described as low (Bate and Maor, 2008; Freebody, Reimann and Tui, 2008;
Ertmer and Ottenbreit-Leftwich, 2010; Auld *et al.*, 2008). A review of empirical studies
found 123 barriers that played a role in the low utilisation of ICT. Some of these barriers
relate to inaccessible equipment, hardware reliability, school culture, teacher variables
and pupil issues (Hew and Brush, 2007). Other barriers documented in the literature
testify to a link between teachers' attitudes, beliefs, and the ability to change (Ertmer
and Ottenbreit-Leftwich, 2010; Phelps and Graham, 2008). Some studies have concluded
that teachers with traditional beliefs use technology in 'low-level' ways, while teachers
with more constructivist beliefs implement more pupil-centred or 'high-level' uses
(Judson, 2006; Roehrig, Kruse and Kern, 2007).

The power of our beliefs and feelings over our professional practice suggests that to
ignore them would be folly. As Senge (1992) observed, the failure to appreciate teachers'
mental lives has undermined many efforts at reform. Action research allows teachers to
'carefully examine their own feelings and thoughts that underlie their actions [and] aims
to empower all participants by developing their awareness of all obstructive elements
within a particular context as well as the personal constraints that prevent real change'
(Koutselini, 2008: 30).

Facing our thoughts and feelings

For many of us, when we are confronted by change, our hearts and minds will often
go into overdrive. Our headspace can be overtaken by thoughts such as, 'How will I
. . . ?', 'Can I . . . ?', 'Should I . . . ?' and 'Will it work?' Affectively we may feel scared,
cautious, anxious and apprehensive.

**Task 11.3 Conduct a self-audit of your thoughts, feelings and
obstructive elements**

The suggestions we have made in this chapter so far have undoubtedly stirred
certain cognitive and affective responses in you. Using the ideas you generated in
Task 11.2 as your starting point, critically examine what you think and how you
feel about possible changes you could make to your practice. What is standing in
the way of initiating change and what can you do to drive the change? Be honest!
You may like to create your audit using a mind-mapping tool like MindMeister
(www.mindmeister.com). Talk about your thoughts and feelings with others. You
may come to realise, as we did, that you really are not alone.

As we worked through the action cycles, our conversations and reflections identified a range of barriers that Deb perceived and that were likely to prevent the successful implementation of technology in her classroom. Foremost on her mind was the amount of time and effort it would take for her, and subsequently her pupils, to learn how to use the software. Second, Deb worried about being reliant on technology to support the learning experiences. Issues of access to computers, the reliability of the hardware and software, and her perception that pupils may not have sufficient skills to use the technology were in her thoughts. Finally, she worried that she did not have the technical knowledge or competence to explicitly instruct the pupils in how to use the software. Reflecting on her initial thinking Deb said, 'I kept thinking I needed to know it all and that it was going to take up lots of my time.' We suggest Deb's lack of experience in using ICT in the classroom worked to produce these unhelpful thoughts and that, in turn, these thoughts translated into feelings of concern and anxiety. In combination these cognitions and affect worked to create avoidance behaviours (Blackberry, 2012).

However, what also emerged from our conversations was Deb's deeply held belief that her classroom could be a more productive and exciting place. This belief, and the overwhelming sense of frustration she experienced because she perceived her pupils were unmotivated and highly dependent upon her, gave us a tangible starting point for our collaboration. We argue it was the depth of her conviction that things could be better that underpinned her ability to confront her misgivings about using ICT for teaching and learning.

New knowledge doesn't always lead to change

To develop a co-constructed learning environment and fully realize the potential of ICT, many teachers need to acquire new forms of knowledge, skills (Pearson, 2003), behaviour (Fullan and Stiegelbauer, 1991), thoughts (Koutselini, 2008), attitudes and beliefs (Bowe and Pierson, 2009; Buehl and Fives, 2009). Teacher change is 'dependent on the continual transformation of a teacher's knowledge and skills' (McMeniman, 2004: 59). Fullan suggested educational change depends on 'what teachers do and think' (2007: 129).

Traditionally, teachers have attended transmissive style, professional development workshops and seminars to learn new skills and acquire knowledge. However, these types of professional learning rarely acknowledge or respond to teachers' thoughts and feelings or cognition and affect. Moreover, workshop facilitators who are positioned as 'experts' can further disenfranchise ICT novices by fueling their cognitive and affective discomfort. As Deb explained, experts often use jargon and move too quickly through explicit instructions, which means participants often lose their way. Asking for instructions to be repeated only draws attention to ineptitude and fuels feelings of inadequacy. These types of professional development fail to consider the various factors that individual teachers consider barriers to ICT integration. Nor do these types of learning opportunities support teachers back in their classrooms to implement change. We advocate a co-constructed approach to professional learning as a catalyst for change.

Very early on in our collaboration, I suggested Deb work with a group of pupils to create an animation. Her response was: 'Oh OK back to scratch. We're changing all of this now. Written work all round OK?' The laughter with which she responded to my suggestion masked a range of awkward and uncomfortable affective and cognitive responses she attached to the idea of creating an animation.

Deb's initial reaction to go back to written work highlighted how unaware and insensitive I was to how she was thinking and feeling. I had slipped back into the transmissive model of professional development. Her candid comments also enabled me to understand the need for teachers to be supported back in the classroom environment. And so began our quest to develop an authentic professional learning experience that was framed by Deb's needs, her beliefs and feelings and the educational ecosystem within which she worked.

Planning to change

Planning a change is the first step in any action research project. From the outset, Deb clearly articulated the areas for change: pupil independence, motivation and authentic, experiential learning. In addition, she was cognizant of the professional need to integrate ICT. In Australia a range of national policies has articulated 'an official discourse in support of a vision for ICT to be imbedded in our schools' (Jordan, 2011: 417).

We then examined the syllabus documents and found sources of information on the Internet that were relevant, age appropriate and contextualized to our local environment. Once these were identified, we considered pedagogical approaches. Deb investigated the concept of a WebQuest and decided that, with some modifications to the original version by Bernie Dodge (2007, see http://webquest.org), this format would be most appropriate for her young pupils. She perceived the benefits of having some control over the Internet content her young pupils could access.

The final step in the planning phase was to create an assessment task. We opted for the pupils to show their understandings by creating an animation. Deb's misgivings related to her inability to use the software, the fact that she did not know how to do it, her apprehension of the time it would take and questions of access to the computers. Left unsupported, Deb's apprehension could have resulted in avoidance. These anxieties were overcome by timetabling computer access and mentoring, guidance and support during every planning meeting and assurances that this would continue during the implementation phase. After much consideration, it was decided PowerPoint would be the software of choice. Factors such as pupils' prior experience of using PowerPoint, availability of the software on school computers and Deb's feeling of needing to learn how to use it drove this decision. Cognizant of her anxiety, we arranged some 'play time' with PowerPoint to explore its potential to create simple animations prior to the introduction of the task to pupils. In a short period of time (one and a half hours), we managed to experiment with some of the software features and how they could be used to create animation. With her newly acquired skills, Deb felt a little more comfortable about teaching the pupils how to use the software. Perhaps more importantly than the acquisition of some technical skills, however, was the realization that her knowledge was finite and her acceptance of the fact that her pedagogy would change.

It's going to be very trial and error for me this time. It's going to be making some moves because it's been a long time since I taught in this way and . . . the pupils need to venture in to learn and they should have a certain amount of choice.

(Deb, 2010)

Task 11.4 Planning your change

We used five steps in planning our change and suggest you begin by following these steps.

Step 1: Find a mentor. You may already have identified a teaching colleague that you would like to act as a mentor. Another good way to get started is to join an online community of practice, such as MirandaNet (www.mirandanet.ac.uk/).

Step 2: Prioritize change. Using the list you created in Task 11.2, prioritize issues in order of importance.

Step 3: Acknowledge, talk about and find ways of addressing your thoughts and feelings about the changes you are planning. When you are aware of what is driving your thoughts and feelings you can act on it.

Step 4: Recognize and plan for obstacles. It is possible you might meet with opposition from school colleagues, administration and parents. Issues of access can also be problematic, as can the reliability of networks.

Step 5: Once you are cognizant of the potential and possibilities, you can begin planning to make changes. Begin on a small scale and slowly. Rome was not built in a day.

Implementing change

Now you might be able to teach me some things about PowerPoint because the last time I used it was a long time ago and they've actually upgraded it since I last used it. You might know some things I don't so together we're going to come up with as much as we can know and do about PowerPoint.

(Deb, 2010)

Deb began the introduction to the animation lesson by establishing what the pupils already knew about PowerPoint and how they had used it previously. It was clear none of them knew how to create paths or transitions so she began teaching them using the pedagogy she felt most comfortable with – a very traditional, explicit instruction approach. However, very quickly her knowledge of the software evaporated and she realized that the pupils were moving ahead of her instructions. At this point, Deb drew on the model we used in the professional learning session. She altered the pedagogy from explicit instruction to facilitating learning by asking pupils authentic questions: 'Can anyone tell me how to . . . ?' 'Someone find out how you can . . .' 'I know the software will . . . who can find out how to do that?' Such questioning provoked meaningful challenges for the pupils. They became highly engaged in the problem-solving tasks and began conversations and collaborating to find solutions, sharing them with the rest of the class. During the exploration of the software, pupils also came to understand other capabilities and were excited to share these with their teacher and the class. An additional bonus to the pedagogical change was that the move away from explicit teaching freed up time for Deb to observe the pupils' capacity to work independently and collaboratively with their peers.

A co-constructed learning environment had authentically evolved because Deb was not the software expert. Deb had been placed in a position where she had to relinquish the role of 'expert' and forego explicit teaching. This allowed her to re-envision herself and accept that, along with her pupils, she was a learner too. She became a part of the collaboration and joined in the discovery process.

Participating in the process was valuable for several distinct reasons. First, Deb experienced the joy of watching the pupils' capacity to work independently and collaboratively with their peers. This facilitated meaningful formative assessment practices. Second, she began to adopt an enquiry-based learning approach to solve technical and software problems and finally, as a result of this experience, she realized she no longer had to spend copious amounts of time learning how to use the software in order to teach it. These observations and experiences provided her with evidence that contradicted her initial beliefs about needing to know everything about ICT, pupils' abilities and pedagogical approaches to learning.

> Observation and reflection allowed me to see the way pupils approached solving problems differently when technology was involved. I no longer felt the pressure to explicitly teach the skills. I realized I don't have to do this. If the pupils do it, I don't have to know this so the pressure is gone. I started to think this is going to be a lot easier than I had initially thought. Now I realize that 20 heads are better than one for problem solving! I began to see the kids as helpers.
>
> (Deb, 2010)

Creating and implementing the WebQuest followed. From a technical standpoint, software guided Deb through the creation of the learning experiences. At times this was a frustrating task as unfamiliarity with the software made for moments of anguish about whether it would indeed work or if information would be lost. Again Deb's new mantra of two heads being better than one supported her through these times.

From a pedagogical perspective, again Deb moved away from a teacher-instructed pedagogy and embraced constructivist pedagogy. Deb introduced the pupils to a computer-mediated way of working where they could use the computers to work collaboratively or independently on a range of set and optional learning tasks. Instructions were imbedded into the WebQuest and tasks were scaffolded in such a way as to alleviate the need for Deb to re-iterate instructions and give lengthy explanations. The transition to working in this way was relatively straightforward and uncomplicated. There is an extensive repository of ready-to-use, teacher-devised WebQuests at http://questgarden. com/author/examplestop.php. Alternatively, you may wish to adapt one of these or create an entirely new one.

Reflection on change

Critical reflection and self-critical reflection underpin action research. Regular reflection and conversation allowed us time to become more introspective and transparent about considering the why and how questions related to our practice. We could turn the spotlight on ourselves to examine our ICT practices (what we were doing), our cognition and affect (why we acted in certain ways) and to monitor the changes we made (how things happened). Thus, reflection played a critical role in coming to understand our inhibitions with ICT.

Our reflections were often driven by informal observations of this new approach to teaching and learning, together with feedback from the pupils.

> One thing I learnt was that you all seem not to be scared to have a go and mess around and play with the computer and discover how things work. I heard a few pupils say they didn't know how to do things but I noticed they didn't give up like they sometimes do in maths. They actually admitted they didn't know how to do it and straight away they went to find out how to do it.
>
> The pupils learnt more and much more quickly than I had expected.
>
> (Deb, 2010)

These types of observations provided evidence that this new pedagogy was highly effective and they functioned to challenge Deb's original beliefs about pupils' abilities. Greater pupil motivation and engagement was evidenced in the quality and quantity of work pupils produced while formal assessment tasks provided empirical evidence of gains in pupils' achievement levels, particularly for those pupils identified as having learning difficulties, and again these challenged original beliefs.

Critical self-reflection also enabled Deb to reappraise her original thinking:

> I've learnt so much about myself . . . I like a personal challenge and I like being able to accomplish things that I've never done before but I've also got to have a reason to do it . . . there has to be a reason to take on the next challenge. And it's reinvigorated my teaching. I'm passionate about the changes I've witnessed in the pupils' learning and they're engaged and motivated so it's working for me on so many different levels.
>
> (Deb, 2011)

The benefits of a co-constructed learning environment

Our reflection on the changes we made indicated the benefits to our pupils of a co-constructed learning environment including:

- pupils were highly engaged and motivated due to the relevance of the learning tasks for them;
- pupils became independent, self-regulated and autonomous learners who took charge of their learning;
- productive peer collaboration and communication;
- pupils' interests and learning needs were identified and incorporated into the curriculum;
- individualization of the learning programme. Pupils learned at their own level and worked in a self-paced environment. There was no obvious distinction drawn between more capable and less capable learners and that contributed to improvements in self-esteem and self-efficacy for less-able pupils;
- a community of learners developed which was characterized by peer-to-peer learning, peer-to-teacher learning and teacher-to-peer learning.

The benefits for us included:

- more time for us during class to work with individual pupils and to observe the learning taking place. This supported ongoing assessment practices;
- a reduction in our anxiety and feeling we needed to know how to use software and to explicitly teach skills;
- pupil motivation translated into productivity, which reduced the amount of time spent on tasks;
- recognizing we were self-sufficient;
- authentic professional learning that responded to our personal and environmental contexts.

Creating co-constructed professional learning

Operating on the same premise as that for the classroom, it is our experience that co-constructed professional learning allows participants to acquire the new knowledge and skills they perceive they need to learn within the regular classroom and school ecology. Thus, learning is authentic, timely and highly contextualized. Beyond supporting professional change, co-constructed professional learning allows for the expression, validation and support of personal cognitions and affect responses to change, again within the very environment where it takes place.

The development of a supportive, collegial working relationship is critical to the success of co-constructed professional learning. Our work suggests that those teachers who are able to identify areas of their practice they would like to improve, who are able to recognize and relate their thoughts and feelings to a mentor, and are supported to do this in their classroom environment are most likely to transform their practice in sustainable ways (Blackberry, 2012). The role of the mentor is critical at every stage of the action cycles. A successful mentor can assist you by:

- helping you to identify aspects of professional practice for change;
- encouraging reflection, conversation and negotiation;
- modelling enquiry-based learning;
- sensitively questioning and challenging your ideas and eliciting deeply-held and personal thoughts and feelings;
- being a good communicator and listener;
- being available to support you, physically and emotionally.

Summary and key points

It is unrealistic to expect that teachers will be able to transform their classrooms with ICT and develop a co-constructed pedagogy quickly or easily. They need to reflect on their practice, together with their thoughts and feelings about pedagogy and ICT, and be supported to make small, incremental changes. Our experience suggests that with realistic planning, the support of a mentor, and the willingness of teachers to hand over the reins of teaching in favour of enquiry, the foundations of a co-constructed classroom can be laid. Persistence and problem solving can lead to changes in pedagogy. We argue that teachers' thinking and self-determination about ICT and pedagogy are powerful predictors of their preparedness to change. Such a position implicates those concerned with raising qualitative and quantitative uses of ICT to listen to and consider teachers' thinking as an essential part of the professional learning for change equation. If you are a student teacher check which requirements for your course you have addressed through this chapter.

Further reading

Bowe, R. and Pierson, M. (2009) 'Professional development in educational technology: What have we learned so far?' In A.B.M. Pierson (ed.) *Transforming classroom practice*. Washington, DC: International Society for Technology in Education.
> This chapter offers an overview of initiatives and strategies for increasing teacher adoption of technology.

Ertmer, P.A. and Ottenbreit-Leftwich, A.T. (2010) 'Teacher technology change: How knowledge, confidence, beliefs, and culture intersect'. *Journal of Research on Technology in Education*, 42(3): 221–9.
> This paper strongly advocates for the incorporation of appropriate ICT use for effective teaching.

Finger, G., Jamieson-Proctor, R. and Watson, G. (2007) *Transforming learning with ICT*. Frenchs Forest, NSW: Pearson Education Australia.
> An easy-to-read teacher guide to the integration of ICT. While international developments and research are drawn upon, there is also lots of practical advice in this book.

Richardson, W. (2008) *Blogs, wikis, podcasts, and other powerful web tools for classrooms* (2nd edn). Moorabbin, Victoria, Australia: Hawker Brownlow Education.
> This book shows how educators can use Web 2.0 tools to create authentic and meaningful learning experiences for pupils.

Relevant websites

Partnerships in ICT in learning: www.une.edu.au/simerr/pages/projects/26ictpartnerships.php
> A range of projects investigated partnership approaches to professional learning. The partnerships aimed to transform classrooms using technology-rich approaches to teaching and learning.

QuestGarden: http://questgarden.com/

WebQuest.Org: http://webquest.org/

Zunal.com: http://zunal.com/

Each of these websites explain the principles of guided inquiry, provide examples of WebQuests that have been created by teachers and offer step-by-step guidance in creating your own.

References

Auld, G., Holkner, B., Fernando, A., Henderson, M., Romeo, G., Russell, G., Seah, W.T. and Edwards, S. (2008) *Exemplar schools using innovative learning technologies*. Retrieved from http://www.academia.edu/2578578/Exemplar_schools_using_innovative_learning_technologies. Accessed on 28 May 2014.

Bate, F. (2010) 'A bridge too far? Explaining beginning teachers' use of ICT in Australian schools'. *Australasian Journal of Educational Technology*, 26(7): 1042–61.

Bate, F. and Maor, D. (2008) *Patterns of ICT uses in Australian schools by beginning teachers: The three Rs*. Paper presented at the 7th European Conference on e-Learning, Agia Napa, Cyprus. Retrieved from http://researchrepository.murdoch.edu.au/8706/. Accessed on 28 May 2014.

Blackberry, G. (2012) *Turning teachers on to ICT: Acknowledging the place of affective constructs in professional learning*. Paper presented at the Australian Computers in Education Conference, Perth, Western Australia.

Bowe, R. and Pierson, M. (2009) 'Professional development in educational technology: What have we learned so far?' In A.B.M. Pierson (ed.) *Transforming classroom practice*. Washington, DC: International Society for Technology in Education.

Buehl, M. and Fives, H. (2009) 'Exploring teachers' beliefs about teaching knowledge: Where does it come from? Does it change?' *The Journal of Experiential Education*, 77(4): 367–408.

Culp, K., Honey, M. and Mandinach, E. (2003) *A retrospective on twenty years of education technology policy*. Retrieved from http://ocw.metu.edu.tr/file.php/118/Week12/Culp_JECR.pdf. Accessed on 6 May 2012.

Dodge, B. (2007). WebQuest.org. Retrieved from http://webquest.org

Ertmer, P.A. and Ottenbreit-Leftwich, A.T. (2010) 'Teacher technology change: How knowledge, confidence, beliefs, and culture intersect'. *Journal of Research on Technology in Education*, 42(3): 221–9.

Freebody, P., Reimann, P. and Tiu, A. (2008) *Alignment of perceptions about the uses of ICT in Australian and New Zealand schools*. Sydney: Centre for Research on Computer Supported Learning and Cognition, Faculty of Education and Social Work, The University of Sydney.

Fullan, M. and Stielgelbauer, S.M. (1991) *The new meaning of educational change*. New York: Teachers College Press.

Fullan, M. (2007) *The new meaning of educational change* (4th edn). London: Teachers College Press.

Guskey, T.R. (2002) 'Does it make a difference? Evaluating professional development'. *Educational Leadership*, 59(6): 45–51.

Haydon, T. and Barton, R. (2007) 'First do no harm: Developing teachers' ability to use ICT in subject teaching: Some lessons from the UK'. *British Journal of Educational Technology*, 38(2): 365–8.

Hew, K.F. and Brush, T. (2007) 'Integrating technology into K-12 teaching and learning: Current knowledge gaps and recommendations for future research'. *Educational Technology Research and Development*, 55(3): 223–252.

Jordan, K. (2011) 'Framing ICT, teachers and learners in Australian school education ICT policy'. *Australian Educational Researcher*, 38: 417–31.

Judson, E. (2006) 'How teachers integrate technology and their beliefs about learning'. *Journal of Technology and Teacher Education*, 14(3): 581–97.

Koutselini, M. (2008) 'Participatory teacher development at schools: Processes and issues'. *Action Research*, 6(29): 29–48.

Laferriere, T., Lamon, M. and Chan, C. (2006) 'Emerging e-trends and models in teacher education and professional development'. *Teaching Education*, 17(1): 75–90.

McMeniman, M. (2004) *Report of the review of the powers and functions of the board of teacher registration*. Available online at: www.qct.edu.au/pdf/csu/btrfinal.pdf. Accessed on 15 September 2011.

Pearson, J. (2003) 'Information and communications technologies and teacher education in Australia'. *Technology, Pedagogy and Education*, 12(1): 39–58.

Phelps, R. and Graham, A. (2008) 'Developing technology together, together: A whole-school metacognitive approach to ICT teacher professional development'. *Journal of Computing in Teacher Education*, 24(4): 125–33.

Roehrig, G.H., Kruse, R.A. and Kern, A. (2007) 'Teacher and school characteristics and their influence on curriculum implementation'. *Journal of Research in Science Teaching*, 44: 883–907.

Senge, P. (1992) 'Mental models'. *Planning Review*, 20(2).

Somekh, B. (2008) 'Action research'. In L.M. Given (ed.) *The SAGE Encyclopedia of Qualitative Research Methods*, Vol. 1. Thousand Oaks, CA: SAGE.

12 Education in an interconnected global space

Sharon Tonner

> In a world in which different peoples and traditions are coming into closer, more frequent contact than ever before, it is crucial that young people learn how to listen intently, empathize with others, acknowledge divergent opinions, and be able to resolve conflicts
>
> (Opening speech from UN Secretary General Ki-moon, 2010)

Introduction

Today's pupils live in an interconnected, globalised world where they can connect, communicate, collaborate and create with their global peers. Time and location are no longer barriers to learning with pupils in other communities and countries, due to technology providing online global spaces that enable collaborative learning. In education, the importance of pupils engaging in online collaborative learning with their global peers has two benefits: developing the necessary skills for their future employability and developing an understanding of global awareness.

Pupils need to be able to use technology to connect with others to enable them to develop their online communication and collaboration skills, which Punie and Cabrera (2006) state are of great importance if pupils are going to be able to compete and work with others around the world. They need to not only be knowledgeable of concepts and have appropriate skills, they also need to be innovative and creative if they wish to succeed in the future. More importantly, if pupils are going to be working with people from around the world, they need to have an understanding of the world that they live in, where they can explore similarities and differences between their own lives and those of their global peers, alongside engaging with complex global issues.

Education, therefore, requires a global view where pupils learn *in* and *about* global spaces. Learning *in* a global space is where pupils use online social networks to connect with their global peers and work collaboratively, whereas learning *about* global spaces focuses on pupils developing a global awareness.

This chapter will provide an introduction to the notion of what it means to learn in and about global spaces through the use of ICT. Two case studies are presented that illustrate innovative and creative examples of projects undertaken by pupils, alongside a step-by-step guide on how to create effective collaborative projects using ICT.

Objectives

At the end of this chapter you should be able to:

- demonstrate an awareness of the importance of embedding global citizenship and sustainability into education;
- discuss different ways to connect your class with other schools across the world through ICT;
- develop your skills using ICT in creative ways to connect pupils with their global peers.

If you are a student teacher check the requirements of your course to see which relate to this unit.

Learning *about* a global space

Learning about a global space is where pupils develop an 'awareness of other cultures and diversity and become socially-aware, responsible global citizens' (Hunt, 2012). The importance of pupils developing an understanding of the wider world around them and making connections with global issues is promoted by various organisations, for example Think Global, which states that education plays a vital role in preparing pupils to live, engage, interact and work in a global society. Embedding a global dimension into pupils' education provides opportunities for what the UK Department for International Development and the Department for Education and Skills (DFID/DFES, 2005) defined in their document, *Developing the global dimension in the school curriculum*, as 'exploring the world's interconnections' where they can make links with their own lives and others and explore issues from other countries in the world. The DFID/DFES (2005) also agreed that education plays a key role in helping pupils become responsible global citizens who 'make informed decisions and take responsible actions'.

Think Global defines learning *about* a global space as education that fosters:

- critical and creative thinking;
- self-awareness and open-mindedness towards difference;
- understanding of global issues and power relationships;
- optimism and action for a better world.

At the heart of learning about a global space, DFID/DFES (2005) explain that there are eight overlapping concepts:

- global citizenship;
- interdependence;
- social justice;
- diversity;
- human rights;
- sustainable development;
- values and perceptions;
- conflict and resolution.

These concepts are similar to those embedded in Scotland's Curriculum for Excellence (The Scottish Government, 2012), where global citizenship is at the centre of the curriculum (see Figure 12.1), which involves developing pupils' knowledge, understanding, skills and values of:

- learning about a globalised world;
- learning for life and work in a global society;
- learning through global contexts.

Likewise, two key educational government documents have global learning situated within the main goals: Every Child Matters (ECM) was a government initiative for England and Wales (DOE, 2003) and Getting it Right for Every Child (GIRFEC) was launched in Scotland (The Scottish Government, 2008).

It is therefore important that teachers understand how learning about a global space can have an impact on pupils' learning (Wisely *et al.*, 2010). We need to think of ways of bringing a global dimension into the classroom that provides opportunities for active and participatory learning, alongside questioning and critical thinking (Bourn, 2011;

Figure 12.1 Global citizenship at the centre of the Scottish Curriculum for Excellence.
Source: The Scottish Government, 2012: 10.

Shah and Brown, 2009). Hunt (2012) explains that opportunities for discussion are important as they allow stereotypes to be contested, to allow pupils to have an understanding of multiple perspectives and feel comfortable with ambiguity.

Research undertaken by the Development Education Research Centre (Hunt, 2012) highlights the benefits of the inclusion of a global dimension into curricular content where nearly all of the schools who completed the questionnaire agreed that it had a positive impact on pupils' learning, especially for schools who were involved in an international school link. It was also found that the greatest impact was where global learning was embedded into the school ethos. This view is supported by Oxfam and The Scottish Government (2012), who state that one of the elements of a successful school partnership is a whole school approach. Other benefits that Bocconi, Kampylis and Punie (2012) discuss are that pupils are more enthusiastic and motivated to engage in learning with an openness to new ways of thinking and a desire for positive change on a local and global scale. They also explain that teachers will be introduced to new teaching ideas, alongside the use of ICT, with opportunities for collaborative learning through real audiences and contexts.

Some of the main ways that schools are promoting a global dimension, as discussed by Holmes and Gardner (2012), are through, for example, topic work, interdisciplinary learning, collaborative projects with a linked school, cultural trips, exchanges or work with other organisations, for example the 'British Council: eTwinning, Connecting Classrooms and Comenius'. For those schools that engage in learning about a global space, recognition of their active engagement with global learning can lead to awards, for example, the UK Eco-Schools Award, the Sustainable Schools Award, the Rights Respecting Schools Award, the Fairtrade Schools Award, the eTwinning Quality Labels and National Awards, and the International Schools Award.

Learning about a global space, therefore, provides pupils with opportunities to develop as global citizens and requires a commitment by teachers to ensure that learning is not bolted on but is meaningful, relevant and active. Hunt explains that learning about a global space is 'not what is taught, but also how it is taught' (2012: 15), with The Scottish Government providing a summary of how a wider perspective of developing global citizens can be achieved (see Figure 12.2).

Task 12.1 Learning about global spaces

To develop your understanding of what it means to learn about a global space, read the following two articles and write a short reflective piece, for your professional development portfolio, that reflects upon the key messages that are being conveyed.

1   The Scottish Government (2012) *Developing global citizens within Curriculum for Excellence*. Edinburgh: Learning and Teaching Scotland. www.education scotland.gov.uk/learningteachingandassessment/learningacrossthecurriculum/ themesacrosslearning/globalcitizenship/about/developingglobalcitizens/what. asp
2   Hunt, F. (2012) *Global learning in primary schools in England: Practices and impacts*. London: Development Education Research Centre. www.ioe.ac.uk/ GlobalLearningInPrimarySchools.pdf

Developing global citizens …	
… is not only …	**It's all about**
… a task for a single practitioner, co-ordinator or champion, eg the school 'eco-warrior'…	**a whole school vision and approach embedded in policy and practice, underpinned by distributed leadership**
… yet another initiative, something else to do …	**a context to deliver the experiences and outcomes at the heart of *Curriculum for Excellence***
… about issues in far-off countries – 'somewhere else'…	**the ways in which local and global issues are connected and relevant to the lives of children and young people – 'here and now'**
… knowing about and understanding worldwide issues …	**the knowledge, skills, values, attitudes and attributes required for children and young people to participate and contribute actively and successfully as global citizens**
… one-off projects or 'bolt-on', isolated initiatives …	**'built-in' day-to-day active learning opportunities permeating – and joining up – the curriculum**
… having an international link …	**a global perspective, where partnerships support the curriculum and help sustain a whole school vision**
… about fundraising …	**a deep commitment to social justice both locally and globally**
… having a pupil council …	**ensuring meaningful learner voice and genuine participation of children and young people in decision-making processes about learning**
… about establishing a fair trade campaign …	**establishing a wider approach and commitment to equality and social justice**
… about learning across subjects …	**learning across curriculum areas which taps into the rich contexts offered by global issues and allows children and young people to connect their learning and transfer skills**
… about learning content …	**active learning in real and relevant contexts, collaborative learning which models democracy and engages children and young people as responsible citizens now, not just in preparation for the future**

Figure 12.2 The Scottish Government's wider perspective to developing global citizens.

Source: The Scottish Government, 2012: 20.

Learning *in* a global space

Learning about a global space can be achieved through using technology to learn in a global space; for example, you can use online social networks to connect your pupils with their global peers and enable collaborative learning. The importance of extending the collaborative aspect of learning to a wider audience beyond the local environment to a global one was advocated by Friedman (2006), who previously warned that technology was flattening the world. Where locality used to dictate a job's location, many jobs are now globalised due to technology enabling people around the world to work together. Friedman (2006) provides an excellent example of collaborative working across locations when he described how Disney™ made an animated movie: the script was created in one country, the animation in another, the voice-over and music in another location and the final production in Disney studios. Location, culture, language and time zones are no longer barriers to collaboration as technology enables people to work together anytime, anyplace, anywhere. Web 2.0 enables this as it changes the nature of the web from distributed to participatory, where 'people control the tools of production and publication and use them to collaborate' (Solomon and Schrum, 2007: 46).

The use of social media in the form of virtual 'spaces' or 'studios', as Loveless (2007) called them, enables pupils to create and share work and, more importantly, it enables learning from one another and with one another. These benefits are also applicable to teachers. As Bacigalupo and Cachia (2011) explain, working with other teachers enhances our teaching through learning different pedagogical approaches and content knowledge. This social constructivist approach to learning using social media was advocated by Howe (2008) through his term 'Crowdsourcing', where he stated that crowds contain more knowledge than the individual. Leadbeater was of a similar view; however, he warned that 'Crowds are not automatically wise and mobs are not necessarily smart. It depends on how they are made up and come together' (2008: 61). If left unsupervised, he claimed that the collaborative dialogue could result in 'a deafening babble', just like in the primary classroom if pupils are left to voice their thoughts and opinions without a teacher facilitating the communication. Online communication is no different. Leadbeater (2008) suggested that the organisational recipe for success lies in the three ingredients: participation, recognition and collaboration. Tapscott (2008) provided two additional ingredients where rules for cooperation and a facilitator were also required to ensure successful collaboration using Web 2.0 tools with learners. We can, therefore, use social media to extend the boundaries of the classroom to create an online global learning space, where we are mindful of the key ingredients that will ensure that learning in a global space is as productive as the learning that takes place beyond a global space.

Global spaces afford opportunities for creative learning through using a range of multimedia tools to communicate shared learning experiences. There are many examples on the Internet of teachers using ICT creatively and innovatively to enable pupils to learn about a global issues. Some projects are organised and managed on a small scale as a one-to-one project using one or two ICT tools, while others are more ambitious on a larger scale where multiple schools are involved and a wide range of ICT tools are incorporated into the project.

It should be noted that working collaboratively with schools around the world can sometimes not run as smoothly as a lesson in the classroom due to various factors:

- communication barriers;
- lack of communication;

- time differences;
- available time;
- limited participation from partner school;
- expectations not being the same;
- ICT level of competence of partner teacher;
- ICT resources available;
- different ways of teaching;
- cultural misunderstandings.

For learning in a global space to be successful it therefore requires three further ingredients: patience, understanding and simplicity.

The following case studies exemplify innovative and creative ways of learning in a global space to develop pupils' knowledge and understanding about a global space.

Task 12.2 Examples of global projects

Over the past eight years I have been involved in small- and large-scale projects while working as a primary teacher and through my role as an Ambassador for the eTwinning programme. In Table 12.1 there is a small selection of projects that use a range of ICT tools in a creative way to enable pupils to learn in and about a global space. These projects were successful due to incorporating the five ingredients of success for collaborative projects:

1   Participation of all pupils and teachers involved;
2   Recognition through publishing content online;
3   Collaboration through working together on a common goal;
4   Rules for cooperation agreed by all members of the project;
5   A facilitator who organised, managed, supported and motivated everyone to be active participants.

Read each project to develop an understanding of how technology can be used to enable learning in a global space. Next look at the different ICT tools that were used each month for the 'Voices of the World' project and select one tool and activity to teach your class. Create a lesson plan to accompany this activity where the learning intention focuses on ICT skills. Share your lesson plan with your ICT lecturer or a teacher at school to discuss the content of the lesson.

Case study 12.1 Schoolovision

Website: http://schoolovision.eu/
Project type: eTwinning www.etwinning.net
Lead practitioner: Michael Purves primary teacher at Yester Primary School, Scotland, UK
Schools involved: primary schools from 38 different countries across Europe: from Iceland in the north-west to Azerbaijan in the south-east. Schools are from different socio-economic settings and comprise mainstream and rural schools.
Age: five–eleven years.

Table 12.1 Examples of learning in a global space

Project & link	Description	Technology
Bear Exchange http://tecnoteddy.blogspot.co.uk	Student teachers learn about other cultures through a bear exchange.	Blog Digital camera
Ted Bear Travels the World http://hsd-juniors.blogspot.co.uk/ search/label/ted%20bear	Ted Bear accompanied the famous adventurer Mark Beaumont on his challenge to cycle around the world in 194 days. The upper stage pupils read Mark's daily blog then they created their own weekly blog post to tell the story of Ted's adventures for the rest of the school to read or listen to.	Blog Voki Digital microphone

Voices of the World
http://votw.wikispaces.com/
	Schools from all over the world participated in a monthly task that used a different online ICT tool to connect schools together using images and voice. The aim of the project was to provide pupils with an awareness of languages and dialects.	Social network
		  Ning for
		  teachers
		Wiki
		Voki
		Animoto
		Voice thread
		Slideshare

Overview of the project

Schoolovision is an annual eTwinning project for primary schools based on the Eurovision Song Contest. All teachers involved are members of the eTwinning network. eTwinning is the European Commission's partner finding and collaboration website and is a part of the Comenius programme. Made up of over 200,000 individual teachers from across Europe, it offers teachers an online platform on which to find partners, develop projects and share best practice in a safe learning environment.

Schoolovision was created by a Scottish primary school teacher, Michael Purves, in 2009 as a way to engage with European schools. Since the project started, it has won many highly acclaimed awards, for example, first place in the 2009 Global Junior Challenge, the eLearning Awards 2009 and the 2010 European eTwinning Awards to note a few. In a recent award, by the MEDEA Awards (MEDEA, 2013), the judges commented very highly on the creative aspect of the project through the use of ICT. The following comments are illustrative of the judges' views:

> The pupils clearly enjoy the experience and gather some interesting insights into different European cultures ... Very good choice of media – video for what it is good at and a blog site to support – it is easy and can be done by everybody ... it shows that song can connect people in all Europe ... and it develops creativity of students.
>
> (MEDEA, 2013: n.p.)

At the heart of the project is creativity and collaborative working. The pupils needed to work together and be creative to ensure the end product is representative of their school and country and captures the imaginations of others. Prior to the project commencing each teacher plans how they will embed the project into their teaching and learning. This will be different in each country, however, all schools are required to submit a video of their chosen song. Over the duration of the project schools meet virtually online to develop their understanding of different cultures, geography skills and practise their language skills.

What happened

The project had over 1000 pupils from primary schools across Europe in the 2013 Schoolovision contest. The requirements of the project are for participating schools to upload a video to the Schoolovision blog of pupils singing a song that represents their country. Schools then attend an online virtual meeting where participating pupils can cast their votes for their favourite songs. The following provides a step-by-step guide to how this project could be organised and managed.

Step 1: The facilitator of the project creates the online blog where all videos will be uploaded then communicates with schools involved using a variety of social network platforms, ranging from the eTwinning collaborative area, to Facebook, Google chat, Google Hangouts and other video-conferencing tools such as FlashMeeting. Throughout the project the facilitator manages this community.

Step 2: The facilitator will place the rules of participation in the teacher online community and on the blog. Each partner must agree to these rules each year.

Step 3: The pupils in each school choose a song to represent their country and incorporate into their music curriculum where they practise the vocals: this could be solos, small groups and choirs and in some cases accompanying music. Auditions are held in many of the participating countries!

Step 4: The pupils then discuss how the song will be filmed. This requires a collaborative whole class or school effort to ensure that the song is representative of everyone involved. For some schools this might be as simple as all pupils being filmed singing their chosen song in their classroom or, on a more creative level, pupils plan their video with regards to the setting, costumes, who will be involved, camera angles, etc., and the song recorded separately and added to the video. This is an opportunity for the pupils and the teachers to be innovative and creative.

Step 5: Videos are edited using video-editing software then uploaded to the Schoolovision blog, which only participating schools have upload access to; the blog can, however, be viewed by anyone.

Step 6: All schools then view all contributions to decide which countries they will cast their votes for.

Step 7: On the day before the Eurovision Song Contest, every participating school from each country meets online at an agreed time using the video-conferencing tool FlashMeeting. They then take turns to cast their votes for the songs that were their favourites. All scores are collated and displayed live during the video conference with winners announced once the final votes have been cast. In order to ensure that the winning country can always be announced on the final day of the project, all partners also have to email their results to the facilitator by the night before the live vote, so that they can be collated. Thus, in the event of a failure of the ICT network at the time of the live vote, the winners can still be notified via the blog.

Step 8: The Schoolovision trophy is then engraved with the new winners' details and sent to the winning country.

Task 12.3 Reviewing eTwinning projects

Spend a little time viewing the interesting entries from the previous years, for example Iceland in 2009, Czech Republic in 2009 and 2011, Belgium in 2010 and 2011: www.medea-awards.com/showcase/schoolovision. Next, with your class create a short video, using some form of mobile technology, that is representative of their country. Use video-editing software, for example Windows Movie Maker Live or iMovie, to edit the video. Depending on the ICT skills of the class, you could teach your pupils to edit the video in small groups, thus developing their collaborative skills and enabling personalisation and choice.

If you wish to find out more about how to join eTwinning and find a partner school to create a project go to: www.etwinning.net/en/pub/discover/how_to_get_involved.htm.

Case study 12.2 Digital diary dialogues

Website: www.slideshare.net/nfalk/creating-a-world-class-learning-environment
Lead practitioners: George Glass, Nick Falk, Anne Jenkins and Pasi Siltakorpi
Project type: connecting classrooms and eTwinning: http://schoolsonline.british council.org/programmes-and-funding/linking-programmes-worldwide/connecting-classrooms
Schools involved: Cauldeen Primary School, Scotland (inner city mainstream primary school), Pääskytie School, Finland (special needs school), Sackville Secondary School, England (urban inner city comprehensive school)
Age: 5–16 years

Overview of study

Digital Diary Dialogues was a Connecting Classrooms project that connected the pupils in Scotland, Finland, England and a guest school in Afghanistan, in an exchange of their daily lives and activities. Connecting Classrooms is managed by the British Council and provides school partnerships with over 50 countries in the world; for example, partnerships with schools in Sub-Saharan Africa and South Asia can be funded by the UK government through the Department for International Development. The main aim of Connecting Classrooms is to:

'equip students with a deeper understanding of:

- other countries and cultures;
- their rights and responsibilities as global citizens;
- the skills needed to work in a global economy and build a fairer, more sustainable world.'

(British Council, 2014)

The project was based on using mobile phone technology to communicate daily activities through digital imaging, video, text and audio. Emotional responses to the activities of the pupils' daily lives were also included to communicate feelings. This approach was highly effective and motivational for all the pupils involved, utilising and extending the existing student knowledge and skills base and harnessing the potential of communication technology as a highly effective motivating learning tool involving 24/7 anywhere, any time learning opportunities. Each school used the information and materials to meet the curricular and cultural needs of their classes. The wide range of ages demonstrated the cross-sector, cross-curriculum, collaborative approach needed to engage at the different levels of language skills, providing peer-to-peer support.

What happened

Each day, each group of pupils in each country at given points of their day and at their local time transmitted their activities and feelings to all the other participants using the text message feature of the mobile phone. The pupils then compared, contrasted and used the information in ways that address their individual curriculum needs, such as PSD, citizenship, social sciences, etc. The staff and pupils developed new mobile phone pedagogies, creating learning objects throughout the project to address the issues of lack of infrastructure and technology in the Afghan partner's school. The staff in the partnership interacted and planned the detail of the project activities prior to each week of action. Pedagogical exchange ensured maximum benefit for all the pupils involved. A trial run to test the mobile technology and any communication issues took place the week before the project started. Each day of the series of week-long activities, which included Saturday and Sunday to accommodate the different cultures involved, pupils recorded their activities and their feelings using their mobile phones. A video, digital photograph, text using plain language, a text using their own text shorthand, and an audio exchange were the actions each pupil carried out.

Adaptions to the mobile technologies to address learning needs came from the students themselves. The boys created football coaching learning objects using the mobile phone video facilities, following their school training to share with their Afghan peers in response to the unstructured street football images sent to them. The pupils, while recording their emotional response to spring, created Haikus to accompany the digital images of spring in order to match the text lengths appropriate to the technology. The pupils were creative, highly motivated and fully engaged in taking home the technology to continue their work at home and at weekends, recording, analysing and exchanging their daily lives and those of their partners. The pupils quickly realised that what they had seen as a communication tool at the outset became a highly effective learning and teaching tool, available to them 24/7. Mobile and online safety issues were discussed and exchanged, heightening the pupils' awareness of the issues that could affect them in this online environment.

The following provides a step-by-step guide to how this project can be organised and managed.

Step 1: Register with Connecting Classrooms and create a partnership with other schools.
Step 2: Discuss with partner schools the rules of participation and the project's learning outcomes.
Step 3: Create a timeline for participation and what themes/questions will be addressed.

Step 4: Test mobile technology to ensure that it is successful. The technology is not restricted to mobile phones and text messaging, it could be tablet devices and communication tools that use an Internet connection (please note that this could restrict the anytime, anyplace aspect due to requiring an Internet/wifi connection).

Step 5: Share with pupils the learning objective for the week and discuss possible contributions.

Step 6: The pupils take pictures of learning objects. If the technology allows, they can edit the picture to ensure that the learning object is recognisable.

Step 7: The pupils attach the chosen picture to a text message and compose a relevant message to accompany the learning object. This will then be sent to the relevant school.

Step 8: The pupils then discuss the learning objects with their peers and provide an appropriate response or question, resulting in a digital dialogue.

Step 9: There are various options for presenting and sharing the learning objects for the week. One way of doing this is to use the online tool Animoto (see websites below). Depending on the mobile device that is being used, if the device supports flash or apps the presentation can be created using the device. If the mobile device does not support these options then the images can be uploaded to a computer and the Animoto presentation can be created online.

Step 10: The Animoto presentations can then be shared by placing them on a collaborative blog.

Task 12.4: Explaining your culture project using Animoto

With your class, create small groups and provide each with a mobile device. Each group is required to take images of key learning objects that represent an aspect of their culture. These images, with an accompanying message explaining the object, will be sent to another member of the group. A digital dialogue can then pursue to extract further information. Each group can then create an Animoto presentation to share what they have learned. Before your pupils create an Animoto presentation you will need to create an education account and teach your pupils how to use the online tool.

Summary and key points

Learning in a global space online enables collaborative and participatory learning with a global audience, rather than the confined nature of learning in a physical classroom or geographical location. These spaces provide opportunities for rich learning to take place that is relevant and in a real-life context. As McLuhan stated, 'technological environments are not merely passive containers of people but are active processes that reshape people and other technologies alike' (1962: 7). This chapter has provided a small insight into how ICT can facilitate learning about a global space through innovative projects that use a range of simple ICT tools. Our job as teachers is to prepare our pupils for the future where they will need the skills to navigate an interconnected world, and an understanding of their role as a global citizen. Learning in and about a global space is about making your pupils mindful of their actions and how it will affect others locally and globally. It is therefore worth remembering one of Albert Einstein's quotes: 'The world we have created is a product of our thinking; it cannot be changed without changing our thinking.'

If you are a student teacher check which requirements for your course you have addressed through this chapter

Further reading

The following documents provide a deeper insight into learning in and about a global space:

Bacigalupo, M. and Cachia, R. (2011) *Teacher collaboration networks in 2025. What is the role of teacher networks for professional development in Europe?* Luxembourg: Publications Office of the European Union.
DFID/DFES (2005) *Developing the global dimension in the school curriculum.* London: DfES.
eTwinning (2008) *Adventures in language and culture.* Available online at: http://ec.europa.eu/dgs/education_culture/documents/publications/handbook_en.pdf. Accessed on 28 June 2013.
Loveless, A.M. (2007) *Creativity, technology and learning: A review of recent literature.* Bristol: Futurelab.

Relevant websites

Learning about a global space

Oxfam: www.oxfam.org.uk/~/media/Files/Education/Teacher%20Support/Free%20Guides/oxfam_gc_guide_building_successful_school_partnerships.ashx
Think Global: www.think-global.org.uk/pages/?p=3857 and http://globaldimension.org.uk/

Learning in a global space

Animoto: http://animoto.com/education/classroom
British Council: www.britishcouncil.org/schools
Edublogs: http://edublogs.org/
eTwinning: www.etwinning.net/en/pub/index.htm
Voki: http://voki.com/

References

Bacigalupo, M. and Cachia, R. (2011) *Teacher collaboration networks in 2025. What is the role of teacher networks for professional development in Europe?* Luxembourg: Publications Office of the European Union.
Bocconi, S., Kampylis, P. and Punie, Y. (2012) *Innovating teaching and learning practices: Key elements for developing creative classrooms in Europe.* Available online at: www.elearningeuropa.info/sites/default/files/asset/In-depth_30_1.pdf. Accessed on 28 June 2013.
Bourn, D. (2011) 'Discourses and practices around development education: From learning about development to critical global pedagogy'. *Policy & Practice: A Development Education Review*, 13: 11–29.
British Council (2014) *Connecting classrooms.* Available online at: http://schoolsonline.british council.org/programmes-and-funding/linking-programmes-worldwide/connecting-classrooms. Accessed on 22 May 2014.

DFID/DFES (2005) *Developing the global dimension in the school curriculum*. London: DfES.

DOE (2003) 'Every Child Matters'. Presented to Parliament by the Chief Secretary to the Treasury by Command of Her Majesty, September 2003, Cm 5860, London: Stationery Office.

Freidman, T. (2006) *The world is flat*. Washington: Picador Publishers.

Holmes, B. and Gardner, J. (2012) *e-Learning: Concepts and practice*. London: Sage Publishers.

Howe, J. (2008) *Crowdsourcing: Why the power of the crowd is driving the future of business*. New York: Three Rivers Press.

Hunt, F. (2012) *Global learning in primary schools in England: Practices and impacts*. London: Development Education Research Centre.

Leadbeater, C. (2008) *We think: Mass innovation not mass production*. Washington, DC: Profile Books.

Loveless, A.M. (2007) *Creativity, technology and learning: A review of recent literature*. Bristol: Futurelab.

McLuhan (1962) *The Gutenberg galaxy: The making of typographic man*. New York: Signet.

MEDEA (2013) *MEDEA Awards*. Available online at: www.medea-awards.com/home. Accessed on 28 June 2013.

Punie, Y. and Cabrera, M. (2006) *The future of ICT and learning in the knowledge society*. Luxembourg: European Commission.

Shah, H. and Brown, K. (2009) *Critical thinking in the context of global learning*. London: DEA.

Solomon, L. and Schrum, G. (2007) *Web 2.0. New Tools, New Schools*. Washington, DC: ISTE.

Tapscott, D. (2008) *Growing up digital: How the Net Generation are changing the world*. London: McGraw-Hill Publications.

The Scottish Government (2008) *A guide to Getting it Right for Every Child*. Edinburgh: The Scottish Government.

The Scottish Government (2012) *Developing global citizens within Curriculum for Excellence*. Edinburgh: Learning and Teaching Scotland.

UN Secretary General Ki-moon, B. (2010) 'Secretary-General's Message for 2010'. Available online at: www.un.org/en/events/youthday/2010/sg.shtml. Accessed on 28 April 2013.

Wisely, T.L.K, Barr I.M., Britton, A. and King, B. (2010) *In a global space – Research and practice in Initial Teacher Education*. Edinburgh: Scottish Development Education Centre.

13 Special educational needs and technology

Christina Kuegel

Introduction

This chapter outlines how new technologies can be used to develop inclusive practices and argues the case for a social rather than medical model through which to view learning needs. The chapter begins with a discussion surrounding key terminology and proceeds by examining how technology supports the particular needs of pupils with special needs and disabilities.

Objectives

At the end of this chapter you should be able to:

- consider the potential for technology to enable learning for pupils with special educational needs and disability (SEND);
- select appropriate technology based tools to support the needs of the pupils;
- identify resources to keep up to date in the field of SEND and technology.

Background: definitions and statutory requirements

The term 'inclusive education' or 'inclusion' continues to hold diverse definitions and characteristics throughout government policy and the current research literature.[1] In England government guidance establishes statutory measures for schools and sets out three principles for developing an inclusive curriculum (DfES, 2001).

1. Setting suitable learning challenges.
2. Responding to pupils' diverse learning needs.
3. Overcoming potential barriers to learning and assessment for individuals and groups of pupils.

Although the definition of 'inclusion' often encompasses those with English as an additional language (EAL), gifted and talented (G&T), looked after children (LAC), transient population and other minority groups, this chapter focuses on pupils with SEND who have a learning difficulty that calls for a special educational provision to be made for them. Pupils have a learning difficulty if they:

(a) have a significantly greater difficulty in learning than the majority of children of the same age;

(b) have a disability which prevents or hinders them from making use of educational facilities of a kind generally provided for children of the same age in schools within the area of the local education authority;

(c) are under compulsory school age and fall within the definition at (a) or (b) above or would so do if special educational provision was not made for them.
(Department for Education and Skills (DfES), 2001, p. 6)

As 'inclusion', 'inclusive practice', 'SEND' and 'learning difficulties' hold different meanings for different people it is therefore important for you to explore your interpretation of the terms.

Task 13.1 Defining inclusion

Ask a range of peers and professionals for their definition of inclusion. Browse some of the government guidance, academic literature and support organisation websites (see Additional resources and websites at the end of this chapter) and develop your own personal definition of inclusion.

Breaking down barriers

According to the British Educational Communications and Technology Agency's (BECTA) (2003) literature review, technology can benefit pupils, teachers and parents/carers. Some specific benefits identified by BECTA (2003, 2007, 2009) include greater learner autonomy, communication support, personalised learning opportunities, attainment, motivation and engagement with learning. This is extended by Florian and Hegarty (2004) who suggest six ways in which technology can be used to meet the needs of pupils with a SEND:

- used as a tutor;
- used for exploration;
- applied as a tool;
- used to communicate;
- used for assessment purposes; and
- used as a management tool.

These can be accomplished through 'specialised assistive technologies or mainstream technologies' (BECTA, 2007, p. 6).

Attitudes and beliefs

e-Inclusion or digital inclusion (European Commission: Ministerial Declaration, Riga, June 2006) can be accomplished by addressing attitudes and beliefs (Glazzard, 2011; Sze, 2009) and clearly addressing the needs of individual pupils by selecting the appropriate technology. The two main ideological frameworks used in this field are the medical and the social model of disability.

The medical model of disability (also referred to as individual tragedy, within-child, or deficit model) views disability or persons with a disability as 'faulty' and in need of 'fixing' from their limitations (Barnes, Oliver and Barton, 2002). This viewpoint does not see a need to adapt the environment or personal views of practitioners and wider society but implies the problems and responsibilities lie with the person with the disability. This model seeks to return the person to 'normal' on the basis of identification of symptoms, diagnosis and cure (Johnstone, 2001).

In the UK the medical model was originally challenged by the disabled people's movement through the proclamation from the Union of Physically Impaired Against Segregation (UPIAS) in 1976, which states that 'it is society which disables physically impaired people. Disability is something imposed on top of our impairments by the way we are unnecessarily isolated and excluded from full participation in society'(UPIAS, 1976, p. 14). This counter argument is now known as the social model of disability (Barnes and Oliver, 1997). The social model of disability proposes that disability is constructed by those who are non-disabled who create environmental barriers, socially stigmatizing attitudes and discriminatory behaviour.

Task 13.2 Understanding your views

Reflect on the following questions:

1   What are your personal views on special education and disability?
2   Are your views similar to those around you?
3   Are there advantages and/or disadvantages to differing views?

Addressing the needs of the individual pupil

The use of technology can support the identification of needs. This may include designing assessment materials, researching SEND or computer-based assessment (CBA). One example of CBA is Lucid Ability – a computerised system for assessing verbal and non-verbal abilities. (Many of the pre-made CBA used for the identification of a SEND should not be used independently without a thorough evaluation of the whole pupil.) In addition, merely using ready-made online resources or CBA does not create an enabling environment. The tools must be individualized to assess the needs of the pupil and then support and create personalized learning opportunities during whole-class instruction, independent work and social activities. However, as Bower, Hedberg and Kuswara (2010) state, the intricate relationship between technology, content and pedagogical knowledge is complex.[2]

The SEN Code of Practice for England identifies four principal areas of need: communication and interaction; cognition and learning needs; behaviour, emotional and social development; and sensory and/or physical needs (DfES, 2001, p. 52). Each of these areas is now addressed individually in relation to supporting the pupil's needs with technology. The areas are of course inter-related.

Communication and interaction (autistic spectrum conditions, speech language and communication needs)

Technology creates opportunities to aid, develop, or teach communication, e.g., in the form of augmentative and alternative communication (AAC), which includes all forms of communication except oral speech and provides pupils with a means of communicating or interacting with others. This may be in the form of gestures, signs, symbols, or written words and includes but is not limited to single-message devices, static multi-message devices, text-based devices and voice amplifiers (Hodge, 2007).

The ability to adapt personal mobile devices to suit the needs of individuals is expanding. The number of applications (apps) to support pupils with SEND has flour-ished and specific programmes such as MyChoicePad developed in conjunction with MAKATON (a language programme that uses sign and symbols to help communication) can provide the user with the ability to learn signs, make choices and express them-selves. The programme can save time and energy, aid listening, grab attention, promote sharing, develop vocabulary, help users make requests and aid communication partners (MyChoicePad, 2012). Similar programmes to support communication include Proloquo2Go, a text-to-speech programme with supporting images. This programme claims to 'bring natural sounding text-to-speech voices, close to 8000 up-to-date symbols, powerful automatic conjugations, a large default vocabulary, full expandability and extreme ease of use to the iPhone, iPod touch and iPad' (Proloquo2Go, 2012).

There are limitations to implementing ACC, including the ability of pupils to operate effectively, technical problems, slowness, attitudes from others towards ACC, com-munication limitation of the equipment and complexity of the device (Hodge, 2007). When selecting communication tools considerations must be given first to the physical and cognitive abilities of the pupil, the capability of the technology and the types of communication that will occur (Blackstone, Williams and Wilkins, 2007). Each selected AAC tool should be easy to operate, require limited training, limited cost and should be personalised or adaptable. The challenge here is not to replace current methods of communication but to use technology alongside other communication systems (Hodge, 2007). This can reduce or possibly eliminate the communication barriers faced by pupils and begin to place the pupil and not the learning difficulty at the forefront of education.

Furthermore, technology has the potential to teach and aid the development of social skills for pupils who may find it difficult to socialise with peers or adults. For example, apps such as Quickcues (www.quickcues.com) and Hidden Curriculum for Kids (www.aapcpublishing.net) teach specific social skills, remind students of social behaviours and encourage or develop social interactions. Apps can allow the student to easily use reference material without feeling alienated from their peers and can promote greater inclusion.

Some applications are preloaded with stories to teach social skills but they may not address the immediate needs of the pupil. However, apps such as Stories2Learn (www.stories2learn.com) allow you or parents to create individualized programmes.

Cognition and learning needs (specific learning difficulties, moderate learning difficulties, severe learning difficulties, profound and multiple learning difficulties)

Cognition and learning refers to a continuum of needs ranging from pupils who occasionally need one-to-one support to pupils who may need twenty-four hours of constant one-to-one support. This section briefly examines some key design features that you should consider when using online learning for pupils with cognition and leaning needs. The Web Accessibility Initiative (WAI) provides in-depth guidance on creating and ensuring accessibility for all (see www.w3.org/WAI/demos/bad/). See also Kuegel (2013) for further details.

Augmented reality (AR) can connect the pupils' virtual worlds and the real world through the use of a webcam with GPS, compass and object recognition, and create occasions to develop authentic individualized learning. In addition, AR can provide pupils with some control of the pace at which their learning occurs and create possibilities to engage, stimulate and motivate pupils (Yuen, Yaoyuneyong and Johnson, 2011). A few tools currently available include StreetMuseum (free iPhone app that allows the user to blend history and reality while on the streets of London), and Googlesky map (free for android and lets the users interact with the stars in the sky). See also the AR tools from String (www.poweredbystring.com/) or Magma Studios (www.magma-studios. com/augmented-reality-applications).

Behaviour, emotional and social difficulties (BESD)

The SEN Code of Practice defines BESD as 'Children and young people who demonstrate features of emotional and behavioural difficulties, who are withdrawn or isolated, disruptive and disturbing, hyperactive and lack concentration; those with immature social skills; and those presenting challenging behaviours arising from other complex special needs' (DfES, 2001, p. 87). However, specific characteristics associated with behaviour are well contested among the literature (Frederickson and Cline, 2010). Strategies to support pupils with BESD include, but are not limited to, teaching pupil behaviour, positive reinforcement, matching curriculum and ability, ensuring high rates of success, structured transition between activities, and self-regulation (Sugai and Horner, 2002).

Self-regulation can be quickly and inexpensively supported by technology. It is about encouraging students to take control of their learning (Cooper, Heron and Heward, 2007, as cited in Joseph and Konrad, 2009, p. 246). e-Tools include reminder and organisational tools, such as Iprompts developed by handholdadaptive (www.handhold adaptive.com/iprompts.html), which provide picture schedules, visual countdown timers and choices between images. Many silent reminder/stopwatch/clock functions or specific apps (Motiv(r)Aider) on a mobile phone can be set to vibrate at given intervals to remind students to complete a self-regulation task. Organisational tools such as Evernote can be used for setting goals, graphing performance or recording written information regarding behaviour. Verbal recordings on apps such as Voice Notes or iTalk Recorder can help students to make verbal records of their on-task and off-task behaviour. These are a starting point for you to examine methods to support the specific needs of pupils with BESD.

Sensory and/or physical needs (visual impairment, hearing impairment, multi-sensory impairment and physical disability)

There are a plethora of assistive technologies that create enabling environments to support pupils with additional sensory or physical needs . The majority are free to download or are built into many websites, PDAs and apps. Examples include large keyboards, a simple-to-operate computer mouse, a virtual magnifying glass, text-to-speech programmes and speech-to-text programmes. However, with so many different resources available, all of them in a state of constant change and development, there is understandably a limited body of literature evaluating the 'success and performance' of assistive technologies (Jutai, Strong and Russell-Minda, 2009, p. 219).

Teachers must also take into consideration the possibility that technology can also become a barrier to accessing the curriculum and create further tensions. Slobodzian (2009) explains how the use of YouTube in the classroom has been seen as one method to bring the larger world into the classroom. However, teachers must realise that many aspects may not be accessible to students with visual or hearing impairments. YouTube has made closed captioning an option for those creating videos and in the search options teachers can filter results that include videos with closed captioning. For full details see www.youtube.com/t/captions_about.

To keep up to date, you can follow disability support organisations such as Autism Speaks at https://twitter.com/autismspeaks or British Dyslexia at https://twitter.com/BDAdyslexia.

e-Safety and SEND

Online safety for SEND pupils has to be explicitly addressed. In a survey of over 2000 secondary schools conducted by BeatBullying, the charity suggests that overall incidents of cyberbullying are not different among those with and without statements of SEN. However, pupils with SEN are 16 per cent more likely to be persistently cyberbullied. The charity defines persistent as 'happening day in, day out, over a period of months or sometimes years' (Cross *et al.*, 2009, p. 5). Incidents reported included hoax mobile calls, hurtful texts or emails, and unkind messages on social networking profiles (Cross *et al.*, 2009). Furthermore, Childnet International describes specific risks for pupils with SEND and these include difficulties with terminology due to language delays, interpretation of content or interactions, understanding of safe and acceptable information to share, or some children may not realise that their behaviour online might be viewed differently by the receiver and therefore may be interpreted as bullying or even sexual harassment. See also Chapter 19.

Summary

This chapter has outlined how enabling environments can be created by addressing attitudes, clearly identifying the needs of the individual pupils, and using appropriate technologies to meet their needs.

Acknowledgements

The contributions of Yota Dimitriadi and Nick Peacey to earlier editions are acknowledged.

Notes

1 For further discussion see Chapter 5 in Hodkinson, A. and Vickerman, P. (2009) *Key issues in special educational needs and inclusion.* London: SAGE.
2 For further information visit TPACK – Technological Pedagogical and Content Knowledge at www.tpck.org/

Further reading

Florian, L. and Hegarty, J. (2004) *ICT and special educational needs.* Maidenhead: Open University Press.

> A key text on SEND and ICT including staff development, virtual learning environments, computer-based assessment, historical information, management of special education and whole school approaches.

Loreman,T., Deppeler, J. and Harvey, D. (2010) Inclusive education: Supporting diversity in the classroom. Oxon: Routledge.

> This book provides research-based practical methods to support mainstream inclusive practice and provides an overview of creating enabling environments.

Hodkinson, A. and Vickerman, P. (2009) Key issues in special educational needs and inclusion. London: SAGE.

> This book provides a solid foundation on SEND and numerous case study examples.

Recommended websites

www.jisctechdis.ac.uk/

> The UK advisory service on technology and special education. This site provides current research initiatives in SEND and ICT and links to online courses, events and news.

www.ed.gov/

> The US Department of Education website provides a starting place for further information on best practices in teaching, current news and government guidelines.

www.futurelab.org.uk/home

> Futurelab is an independent not-for-profit organisation that supports innovative approaches to education with technology. The site has a wide range of resources to support classroom practices through the use of technology.

www.education.gov.uk/

> The Department for Education is responsible for education and children's services in England. Resources on current research, polices and statutory guidance are available.

www.disability.gov/technology

> This site provides general information on assistive technologies and has an in-depth section on creating accessible documents.

References

Barnes, C. and Oliver, M. (1997) *Disability studies: Past present and future.* Leeds: The Disability Press.

Barnes, C., Oliver, M. and Barton, L. (2002) *Disability studies today.* Cambridge: Polity Press.

BECTA (2003) *What the research says about ICT supporting special educational needs and inclusion.* Available online at: www.mmiweb.org.uk/publications/ict/Research_Barriers_TandL.pdf. Accessed on 9 September 2010.

BECTA (2007) *The impact of ICT in schools – A landscape review.* Available online at: http://dera.ioe.ac.uk/1627/. Accessed on 18 March 2011.

BECTA (2009) *Harnessing technology schools survey: Analysis report.* Available online at: http://dera.ioe.ac.uk/1546/1/becta_2009_htssreport_report.pdf/. Accessed on 4 February 2012.

Blackstone, S., Williams, M. and Wilkins, D. (2007) 'Key principles underlying research and practice in AAC'. *AAC: Augmentative & Alternative Communication*, 23: 191–203.

Bower, M., Hedberg, J. and Kuswara, A. (2010) 'Framework for Web 2.0 learning design'. *Educational Media International*, 47(3):177–98.

Cross, E., Richardson, B., Douglas, T. and Vonkaenel-Flatt, J. (2009) *Virtual violence: Protecting children from bullying*. London: Beatbullying.

DfES (2001) *Special education needs: Code of practice*. Available online at: www.education. gov.uk/publications/standard/publicationDetail/Page1/DfES%200581%202001. Accessed 10 November 2011.

European Commission: Ministerial Declaration. Riga, Latvia (11 June 2006). Available online at: http://ec.europa.eu/information_society/activities/einclusion/events/riga_2006/index_en. htm. Accessed on 29 August 2012.

Florian, L. and Hegarty, J. (2004) *ICT and special educational needs*. Maidenhead: Open University Press.

Frederickson, N. and Cline, T. (2010) *Special educational needs, inclusion and diversity*. Maidenhead: Open University Press.

Glazzard, J. (2011) 'Perceptions of the barriers to effective inclusion in one primary school: Voices of teachers and teaching assistants'. *Support for Learning*, 26(2): 56–63.

Hodge, S. (2007) 'Why is the potential of augmentative and alternative communication not being realized? Exploring the experiences of people who use communication aids'. *Disability & Society*, 22: 457–71.

Hodkinson, A. and Vickerman, P. (2009) *Key issues in special educational needs and inclusion*. London: SAGE.

Iprompts (2012) Online. Available online at: www.handholdadaptive.com/iprompts.html. Accessed on 6 February 2012.

Johnstone, D. (2001) *An introduction to disability studies*. London: David Fulton.

Joseph, L. and Konrad, M. (2009) 'Help students self-manage their academic performance'. *Intervention in School & Clinic*, 44(4): 246–9.

Jutai, J.W., Strong, J.G. and Russell-Minda, E. (2009) 'Effectiveness of assistive technologies for low vision rehabilitation: A systematic review'. *Journal of Visual Impairment & Blindness*, 103(4): 210–22.

Kuegel, C. (2013) 'Special educational needs and technology'. In M. Leask and N. Pachler (eds) *Learning to teach using ICT in the secondary school*. Abingdon: Taylor & Francis.

Magma Studios (2012) Online. Available online at: www.magma-studios.com/augmented-reality-applications. Accessed on 9 January 2012.

MyChoicePad (2012) Available online at: www.mychoicepad.com. Accessed on 9 January 2012.

Proloquo2Go (2012) Available online at: www.proloquo2go.com. Accessed on 9 January 2012.

Slobodzian, J.T. (2009) 'Film and video technology: Issues of access for hard of hearing and deaf students'. *Journal of Special Education Technology*, 24(4): 54–9.

Stories2Learn (2012) Available online at: www.stories2learn.com/about.php. Accessed on 6 February 2012.

String (2012) Available online at: www.poweredbystring.com/. Accessed on 6 February 2012.

Sugai, G. and Horner, R. (2002) 'The evolution of discipline practices: School-wide positive behavior supports'. *Child & Family Behavior Therapy*, 24(1/2): 23–50.

Sze, S. (Fall 2009) 'A literature review: Pre-service teachers' attitudes toward students with disabilities'. *Education*, 130(1): 53–6.

UPIAS (1976) *Fundamental principles of disability*. London: Union of the Physically Impaired Against Segregation.

Web Accessibility Initiative (WAI) (2011) Available online at: www.w3.org/WAI/. Accessed on 6 February 2012.

Yuen, S., Yaoyuneyong, G. and Johnson, E. (2011) 'Augmented Reality: An overview and five directions for AR in education'. *Journal of Educational Technology Development & Exchange*, 4(1): 119–40.

14 Games and learning

Using multi-play digital games and online virtual worlds

Nic Crowe and Sara Flynn

Introduction

James Paul Gee (2003) observes, somewhat controversially, that while much of technology-based learning has a reputation for being dull and ineffective, games have developed a reputation for being fun, engaging and immersive, requiring deep thinking and complex problem solving. In the primary school, pupils' experience of games will be hugely varied. This chapter uses material drawn from research about young people's use of digital spaces to explore some of the education possibilities provided by computer/console-based game arenas (such as *Call of Duty Modern Warfare*, *Arkham City* and *The Eldar Scrolls*) and digital game worlds (for example, *World of Warcraft*, *Eve* and *Runescape*).

Chapter 17 of this title introduces the use of games for learning programming; other chapters outline opportunities for games to support learning in a range of subjects. Chapter 20 outlines the use of gaming in the early years. This chapter focuses on psychological aspects of gaming and the multi-player and online games generally played by older children and is adapted from Crowe and Flynn (2013).

It has long been recognised that education is more than the mere transfer of information or knowledge (Mezirow, 2000). As you will have read elsewhere in this book, successful learning is often based on how engaged your pupils actually are. This in turn raises questions as to the personalized nature of learning tasks and activities Multi-play gaming (playing alongside other gamers via an Internet or LAN connection) is a highly interactive experience incorporating complex layers of co-operative and competitive play and problem solving. It is perhaps surprising then that more hasn't been made of the opportunities offered by these texts to many areas of the curriculum. e-Safety is a concern for some educators and parents – see Chapter 19.

Objectives

By the end of this chapter you should:

- have an understanding of the educational possibilities offered by digital games and virtual worlds;
- be able to identify the range of digital gaming spaces that could be used to support teaching and learning;
- have considered some examples of teaching strategies that could be used or adapted to your own teaching and learning scenarios.

Why digital games?

Young people have always been early adopters of this type of technology (Raine and Horrigan, 2005) and digital games are undeniably popular. By early 2011 the digital games market was estimated to be worth US$48.9 billions, exceeding the sales of both books and popular music (PricewaterhouseCoopers, 2010). Digital games are now an important aspect of young people's leisure. The research project 'UK Children Go Online' (UKCGO) (Livingstone and Bober, 2005) aimed to offer a rigorous and timely investigation of 9–19-year-olds' use of computers and the Internet. The authors highlighted that 82 per cent of this age group have at least one games console, and that 70 per cent play digital games online. This survey also acknowledged that most young people spend nearly as much time playing video/computer games as they do engaged with homework (Livingstone and Bober, 2005). By 2010, regular game usage had risen to 91 per cent in the 12–15-year-olds age bracket (OFCOM, 2011).

The government-commissioned Byron Review follow up (2010) recognised that engaging with digital technology – including digital gaming – was becoming an ordinary aspect of childhood. Yet despite this apparent 'domesticity', computer games have been largely absent from the curriculum. We find this resistance puzzling. Prensky (2001) accuses teaching professionals of being reluctant to engage with any form of digital technology that is relatively recent and unfamiliar. Of course, such fears are not new: popular technology has always been criticised for imposing 'entertainment modality' on learning environments (see Postman, 1996; Greenwald and Rosner, 2003) but as Taylor (2006) observes, digital worlds provide users with a chance to live, and through that living, play. We would further observe that it is through this act of virtual 'play' that opportunities for learning arise (Squire, 2005). While there are a great many 'proprietary' ('educational') games out there, we suggest that more satisfying and effective learning takes place when teachers use 'commercial' (leisure-based) digital games that their pupils are already engaged with. The unique opportunity that this can offer you, is that the games are so well embedded into the everyday lives of your pupils. As Davies (2005) acknowledges, the most effective education practitioner starts from where young people 'are' – their contemporary experiences – and then seeks to move them beyond this position. Some companies, for example, Zondle, are working with neuroscientists (Dr Paul Howard-Jones) to develop games that are designed to maximise learning.

Computer games in your classroom?

What we want you to consider in this chapter then is the idea that, as with any other form of 'play', digital gaming can form the basis of effective and purposeful education-based interventions. One of the central themes of curriculum-based ICT is that it encourages problem solving and independent learning. Problem solving is regarded as a key skill for life-long learning (Hoskins and Frediksson, 2008). Writing in America, both Gee (2007; Gee and Hayes, 2009) and Squire (2005) have been leading exponents of the idea that digital games teach players to become problem solvers. In well-designed games, the player can only advance to a higher level (or unlock more desirable equipment/resources) by testing out a range of different approaches and strategies. So, for example, in the popular *Tomb Raider* series the next level is only 'unlocked' once a pre-determined set of criteria is met: *Lara Croft* must 'kill' the monster, solve the code and get to the building on the other side of the ravine. The game requires the player to ask questions such as 'What happens if I do this?' 'Where does this go?' 'What do I need to do next?' Successful completion of the game requires lateral thinking and the ability to solve increasingly complex problems. Since the game is developmental – it gets harder the further into it you get – players are required to 'learn' the skills and knowledge that they require to solve the next challenge. One of the key aspects of the most complex games is that players need to learn to cope with the rigours of the virtual world; thus one of the functions of digital games is that users are being 'taught' to 'learn'.

In narrative-driven genres, such as 'Online Role Playing Games' (often termed MMORPG[1] or MMO[2], where the emphasis is on character and skills development rather than special advancement) or popular shooters such as the *Call of Duty: Modern Warfare* series, there are opportunities for you to help your pupils explore and 'test out' a range of alternate narrative and/or character-related issues and problems. So, for example, in *Fable* or *Hard Rain* each in-game decision (for example choosing whether to be 'good' or 'bad', whether to 'assist' or 'ignore' another character) carries deep significance and real consequence as to how the future narrative unfolds. Games such as *The Sims* series, *HomeFront*, *Arkham City*, even the controversial *Grand Theft Auto* and *Saints Row* series, teach principles of representation, morality, narrative development, interactive skills and aspects of literacy, numeracy and simulation, in situated, experiential ways, that might not be possible – or as accessible – using other texts or forms. As Gee notes, good digital games will teach your pupils 'to solve problems and reflect on the intricacies of the design of imagined worlds and the design of both real and imagined social relationships and identities in the modern world' (2003, p. 48).

Task 14.1 Identifying pupils' experience of online games

Take some time to talk to your pupils about the sorts of digital games that they like to play. Can you notice any similarities and differences? Discuss with them the particular pleasures of playing different types of games. Are there different types of enjoyment? Try to include the thoughts of pupils who may not be so familiar or committed to gaming. Are there any pupils who, during the process of working with gaming technology, have developed new skills they can identify and talk about?

Learning and the psychology of digital play

In his discussions of child development the psychologist, Lev Vygotsky, describes play as 'the imaginary, illusory realization of unrealizable desires' (1933: n.p.). Play is a process through which children make sense of their world. It offers opportunities to explore some aspects of culture that might be impossible in their everyday life. It is through such fantasy that children come to develop a greater sense of meaning and purpose about their own lives (Bettelheim, 1976). So, by structuring learning in play, we are also facilitating active engagement in fantasy and activity that would not otherwise be possible. Crawford (1982) acknowledges the fundamental motivation for playing games is a desire to learn:

Games are thus the most ancient and time-honored vehicle for education. They are the original educational technology, the natural one, having received the seal of approval of natural selection. We don't see mother lions lecturing cubs at the chalkboard; we don't see senior lions writing their memoirs for posterity. In light of this, the question, 'Can games have educational value?' becomes absurd. It is not games but schools that are the newfangled notion, the untested fad, the violator of tradition. Game-playing is a vital educational function for any creature capable of learning.

(Crawford, 1982, p. 16)

Digital-based play encourages children to try new things alongside doing things that are familiar to them. In other words, they are pushing themselves forward, expanding their knowledge base and learning as a result. Very young children do this constantly and we encourage it, through speaking, reading, drawing, etc. Introducing games into the arena allows for children to reshape and transform environments. The computer or console becomes a tool that helps to produce results through activity and to develop an understanding of real-life contexts in much the same way as other forms of play.

Digital games also offer new possibilities beyond the traditional play-based contexts: 'You can't play this game on your own, you have to learn to get on with people and to develop new skills that help everyone in your group not just what is good for yourself' – Nathan (13). This quote and those following illustrate that playing digital games is a complex process involving a range of both short- and long-term strategies. Games need to be learned and for the dedicated this is a considered and deliberate process in which short-term individual and emotional responses/pleasures often need to be put aside for long-term success. In this context, learning might be conceived as social activity. It occurs not just through diegetic engagement with the game narrative but more significantly within, and through, the interaction with other players. Interactions between players is a fundamental feature of all online games (Ashton, 2009; Wright, Boria and Breidenbach, 2002) and such interpersonal communication is particularly important to child development, since 'Learning awakens a variety of internal developmental processes that are able to operate only when the child is interacting with people in his environment and in cooperation with his peers' (Vygotsky, 1978, p. 90).

Digital games and 'flow'

The popularity of digital games is a significant factor in their potential to offer learning opportunities in the classroom. Yet good digital games also represent 'microworlds' that provide immersive arenas within which play – and hence learning – can take place (de Freitas, 2006). Csikszentmihayli (1975, 1990) put forward the concept of 'flow', which he identified as the complete engagement in an activity. Flow encompasses many characteristics: a challenging activity that requires skills; clear goals and feedback; concentration, a sense of control; loss of self-consciousness. See Crowe and Flynn (2013) for more information about flow including research into thirty-two schools in Scotland linking mathematics learning and the Nintendo game 'Dr. Kawashima's brain training' for just thirty minutes a day (Miller and Robertson, 2008). They identified improvements in pupils' attitude to school: truanting and lateness dropped, children began to take a more supportive interest in the performance of peers and the pupils regarded themselves as 'smarter' as a result of using the game. However, the participants

---

Task 14.2 Ethics, barriers and educational benefits

Think about introducing digital games into an area of your curriculum. What might be the educational benefits to your students? What might be some of the obstacles to using them in class? Can you think of any ethical or safety concerns? How might these be overcome? What about pupils who have no interest in gaming?

---

in the study were already familiar with the Nintendo console and it was popular.[3] It is perhaps of little surprise then that the children responded so positively.

Using online digital games educationally

Care needs to be taken because to attempt to simulate in the classroom what is intrinsically an out-of-school leisure activity might have a de-focusing effect if tasks are over-directed. One teacher told us that he had found from bitter experience that 'game-playing is best left to the bedroom and class time better devoted to discussions and tasks that drew on pupil's game-playing experiences'.

One of the benefits of digital technology is that it affords pupils the opportunity to experience and experiment with many institutions and structures of the 'adult' world (Crowe, 2011). These are often not available elsewhere in the lives of young people. Compared with many aspects of the school environment, digital play represents a 'safe' arena in which to engage in or 'test out' 'worldly' practices, reflecting the wider ICT theme of independent learning. But they also teach interpersonal skills and teamwork.

Summary

In this chapter we have tried to show you some of the possibilities that games might offer you in terms of classroom practice and showed you how this might be supported by theories of learning and child development.

It is easy to dismiss digital games as lazy forms of popular entertainment, but to do so would be to miss out on novel modes of pupil engagement. Similarly, fears and prejudices about digital games (the digital world in general, we suspect) often get in the way of innovative practice in this area. Although many might question what game technology is doing *to* our children, a more pertinent question for you as an education practitioner might be 'What are our children doing *with* all this technology and how can I use this as a way of helping them learn?'

Notes

1 Massive Multi-player Online Role Playing Games.
2 Massive Multi-player Online.
3 Miller and Robertson acknowledge that one of the reasons that lateness dropped was that the Nintendo sessions were scheduled for first period in the morning.

References

Ashton, D. (2009) 'Interactions, delegations and online digital games players in communities of practice'. *Participations Journal of Audience and Reception Studies*, 6(*1*), May. Available online at: www.participations.org/documents/ashton.pdf. Accessed on 1 November 2011.

Bettelheim, B. (1976) *The uses of enchantment: The meaning and importance of fairy tales*. London: Thames and Hudson.

Byron, T. (2010) *Do we have safer children in a digital world? A review of progress since the 2008 Byron Review*. DCSF Publications. Available online at: www.dera.ioe.ac.uk/709/1/do%20we%20have%20safer%20children%20in%20a%20digital%20world-WEB.pdf. Accessed on 20 April 2011.

Crawford, C. (1982) *The art of computer game design*. Available online at: http://pdf.textfiles.com/books/cgd-crawford.pdf. Accessed on 1 July 2010.

Crowe, N. (2011) '"It's like my life but more, and better!" – Playing with the Cathaby Shark Girls: MMORPGs, young people and fantasy-based social play'. *International Journal of Adolescence and Youth*, 2011, Vol. 16, pp. 201–23.

Crowe, N. and Flynn, S. (2013) In M. Leask and N. Pachler (eds) *Learning to teach using ICT in the secondary school for gaming and older pupils*. Abingdon: Routledge/Taylor Francis.

Csikszentmihalyi, M. (1975) *Beyond boredom and anxiety: Experiencing flow in work and play*. San Francisco: Jossey-Bass.

Csikszentmihalyi, M. (1990) *Flow: The psychology of optimal experience*. New York: Harper and Row.

Davies, B. (2005) 'Youth work: A manifesto for our times'. *Youth and Policy*, 88(*1*): 23. Leicester: National Youth Agency.

de Freitas, S. (2006) *Learning in immersive worlds: A review of game-based learning*. JISC e-Learning Programme.

Gee, J.P. (2003) *What video games have to teach us about learning and literacy*. New York: Palgrave Macmillan.

Gee, J.P. (2007) *Good video games and good learning: Collected essays on video games, learning, and literacy*. New York: Peter Lang.

Gee, J.P. and Hayes, E. (2009) *Public pedagogy through video games*. Available online at: www.gamebasedlearning.org.uk/content/view/59/. Accessed on 3 February 2011.

Greenwald, S. and Rosner, D. (2003) 'Are we distance educating our students to death? Some reflections on the educational assumptions of distance learning'. *Radical Pedagogy*.

Hoskins, B. and Fredriksson, U. (2008) *Learning to learn: What is it and can it be measured?* IRC, European Commission Document.

Livingstone, S. and Bober, M. (2005) *UK children go online: Final report of key project findings*. London: Economic and Social Research Council.

Mezirow, J. (2000) *Learning as transformation: Critical perspectives on a theory in progress*. San Francisco: Jossey Bass.

Miller, D. and Robertson, D. (2008) *Using Dr Kawashima's brain training in primary classrooms: A randomised controlled study*. A summary for the BBC. Available online at: http://ltsblogs.org.uk/consolarium/files/2008/09/lts-dr-kawashima-trial-summary.pdf. Accessed on 1 January 2012.

OFCOM (2011) *Children and parents: Media use and attitudes report*. Available online at: http://stakeholders.ofcom.org.uk/binaries/research/media-literacy/oct2011/Children_and_parents.pdf. Accessed on 14 November 2011.

Postman, N. (1996) *The disappearance of childhood*. London: Vintage.

Prensky, M. (2001) 'Digital natives, digital immigrants'. *On the Horizon* 9(*5*). MCB University Press.

PricewaterhouseCoopers (Press-release 19 October 2010) *Social multi-player gamers named as UK technology's hottest prospect*. Available online at: www.ukmediacentre.pwc.com/News-Releases/Social-multi-player-gamers-named-as-UK-technology-s-hottest-prospect-f46.aspx. Accessed on 24 October 2010.

Raine, L. and Horrigan, J. (2005) *A decade of adoption: How the internet has woven itself into American family life*. Washington, DC: PEW Internet and Family Life.

Squire, K. (2005) 'Changing the game: What happens when video games enter the classroom'. *Innovate; Online Journal of Education*, August/September 2005. Available online at: www.innovateonline.info. Accessed on 14 September 2010.

Taylor, T.L. (2006) *Play between worlds: Exploring on-line gaming culture*. Cambridge, MA: MIT Press.

Vygotsky, L. (1933) *Play and its role in the mental development of the child*. Source: *Voprosy Psikhologii*, 1966, No. 6; translated: Catherine Mulholland; transcription/markup: Nate Schmolze; online version: Psychology and Marxism Internet Archive (marxists.org) 2002, www.marxists.org/archive/vygotsky/works/1933/play.htm. Accessed on 3 December 2011.

Vygotsky, L. (1978) 'Interaction between learning and development'. In M. Cole, V. John-Steiner, S. Scribner and E. Souberman (eds) *Mind in society: The development of higher psychological processes*. Cambridge, MA: Harvard University Press.

Wright, T., Boria, E. and Breidenbach, P. (2002) 'Creative player actions in FPS online video games: Playing counter-strike'. *International Journal of Computer Game Research*, 2(2). Available online at: www.gamestudies.org/. Accessed on 23 January 2011.

15 Mobile technologies and authentic learning in the primary school classroom

Kevin Burden and Damian Maher

Introduction

The use of mobile technologies, often referred to as m-learning, is increasing in many primary schools across the developed and developing world. In the developed world mobile devices such as iPads, tablets and smartphones are being used, while in some parts of the developing world XO computers are being rolled out. Young people are also using mobile devices in greater numbers in their personal lives. In the United States, for example, research conducted by Pew Research Centre found that in 2012, 37 per cent of all youth aged between twelve and seventeen years had a smartphone, which is up from just 23 per cent in 2011. Approximately 25 per cent own a tablet device (Madden *et al.*, 2013). Younger children are also increasingly being provided with smartphones and tablets.

The significance of using mobile technologies lies in the new and unique affordances they offer learners beyond what is possible with traditional 'tethered' technologies, such as the desktop computer (Traxler, 2007). 'Mobile devices open up new opportunities for independent investigations, practical fieldwork, professional updating and on-the-spot access to knowledge' (Kukulska-Hulme and Traxler, 2005, p. 26).

The use of mobile devices allows pupils to learn in innovative and exciting ways. One of the different ways that mobile devices can support learning is the ability to provide for authentic learning experiences, which includes access to realistic settings and activities. The ability to connect to experts via mobile technologies also provides for learning experiences that are more authentic.

The focus of this chapter is to examine both literature (theory) and practice associated with the innovative use of mobile technologies in primary/elementary schools and other associated educational settings. To begin, a brief outline of the literature is presented. Next, models that have been developed as a way of conceptualising mobile learning are examined. A case study on the use of mobile technologies is presented and then the practical and pedagogical considerations associated with implementing mobile technologies into the classroom are explored. In each of the four sections a task is provided to help you develop your understanding around the focus.

Objectives

At the end of this chapter you should be able to:

*   understand the various models that underpin the use of mobile technologies;
*   be aware of some of the pedagogical and logistical considerations of using mobile technologies;
*   begin to implement the use of mobile technologies into your teaching practices.

The literature on mobile technologies

A term that is sometimes used to describe the use of mobile technology is 'ubiquitous learning'. Some of the characteristics of this include:

*   accessibility: The information is always available whenever the learners need to use it;
*   immediacy: The information can be retrieved immediately by the learners;
*   interactivity: The learners can interact with peers, teachers, and experts efficiently and effectively through different media;
*   context-awareness: The environment can adapt to the learners' real situation to provide adequate information for the learners (Yahya *et al.*, 2010, p. 121).

There are two other particular aspects to mobility, as pointed out by Kinash, Brand, Mathew, and Kordyban (2011), which are that pupils have access to lightweight portable devices but also that there is continuous access to the Internet, so pupils can learn anywhere and anytime. This latter element is what is known as untethered and ubiquitous learning. By creating opportunities to learn anywhere anytime, home–school links can be strengthened. An issue here, though, is that often homes are much better equipped than schools with technology, which can create a home–school divide which, according to Merchant (2007), is a cause for some concern.

Mobile learning technologies allow for a number of different affordances beyond those of a desktop computer. One of these affordances is personalised learning (Leadbetter, 2005; Kearney *et al.*, 2012). This allows teachers to be able to differentiate the curriculum more easily, as well as differentiate for ability, creativity and interests (Kearney and Maher, 2012). Another affordance of mobile technologies is their suitability for use in a variety of settings that traditionally have not been possible with desktop computers. Taking the mobile devices into the playground and on excursions allows students to gather information and record ideas using some of the inbuilt features of mobile technologies including cameras, audio recordings and video capture (Wishart and Triggs, 2010).

Mobile technologies can also be used effectively in more formal settings such as visits to museums or zoos, for example (Vavoula *et al.*, 2009). A further affordance of mobile technologies is that they bring together both the means of capturing data and the means to then manipulate, construct and re-represent this information. This 'convergence of activity' allows pupils to produce work in a way that is easier for them to manage and understand. An example of this is where pupils can capture still or video footage and then use the inbuilt editing software to produce a multi-modal finished text. Mobile devices can also interact with other devices to provide extra information for users, such as in the use of QR codes (see Chapters 3 and 5) and virtual environments.

Task 15.1 Surveying the pupils

Survey the pupils in your class regarding their use of mobile technologies. Ask them:

- What type of mobile technologies, if any, do they use?
- How often do they use these technologies?
- What do they use these technologies for (e.g., listening to music, using the internet, etc.)?
- What sort of restrictions, if any, do their parents put in place for their use?

Once you have this information consider how mobile devices might be effectively used in your classroom so that you can help to develop authentic learning experiences for your pupils.

Also ask your pupils what types of activities they would like to undertake using mobile technologies related to classroom learning.

One such use, which is predicted by authors of the Horizon K-12 Report in the next few years, is Augmented Reality (see Chapter 9), where information is layered onto an existing image (Johnson, Adams and Cummins, 2012). This has many educational possibilities both inside and outside the classroom.

Models available for using mobile technologies

Various models have been developed to assist researchers and teachers to understand how mobile devices, such as smartphones, can add value to the learning experience of young people (see, for example, Danaher, Moriarty and Danaher, 2009; Klopfer, Squire and Jenkins, 2002; Koole, McQuilkin and Ally, 2010; Motiwalla, 2007; Vavoula and Sharples, 2009). These models cover a number of common themes, which include the aspect of mobility itself, the opportunity for greater learner autonomy and choice and collaboration (Kearney *et al.*, 2012). Some of these models focus on the pedagogical use and application of mobile devices, while a larger number have tended to concentrate on the technical and design aspects of m-learning (Teall, Wang and Callaghan, 2011).

As the field of m-learning matures and the user base grows it will become increasingly important for teachers to be aware of the emerging issues that shape the design of pedagogically valid learning activities when mobile devices are used. Koole and her colleagues (2010) have developed a model based on this premise that identifies three converging factors, which support valid learning designs with mobile technologies. These include an awareness of the mobile device itself and its various affordances for learning (D); the characteristics of the learner, including their previous experiences with technology (L), and social aspects, which include the rules for social interaction between individuals (S). This model provides guidance for teachers who wish to design ecologically valid activities for m-learning. A similar model is currently under development in a joint Australia–UK project, which seeks to support how teachers design meaningful activities that exploit the unique affordances of mobile devices (Kearney *et al.*, 2012). In this case the authors have identified collaboration, authenticity and personalisation as macro-level affordances of m-learning, which are further subdivided into six separate strands that include agency, customisation, contextualisation, situatedness, conversation and data-sharing.

While each of these models has originally been developed with mobile phones in mind, many of the affordances and opportunities they promise are transferable to the emerging tablet technologies such as the iPad, which are being used in primary schools.

Task 15.2 Developing your own model of m-learning

Develop a model for m-learning in your classroom, drawing on the different elements of the models presented here as well as drawing on the literature. In doing this, also be guided by the information that you got from your pupils in the survey from Task 15.1 (Surveying the pupils). Consider the important elements that suit your pedagogical style. Discuss your ideas with colleagues.

The following case study highlights the use of iPads in a primary school in Australia where many of the features highlighted in the section above can be identified.

Case study 15.1 Strategies to achieve learning outcomes using mobile technologies

The research study that was conducted by Maher in 2011 examined the use of an iPad with a Year 3 class to facilitate links beyond the classroom using video conferencing. The aim of the study was to understand ways that mobile technologies, used in conjunction with video-conferencing technology (Skype), can support learning back in the classroom. The class was studying a unit on communities in the local area and being able to visit local community settings fitted in nicely with the focus of the unit. The study illustrates how mobile technologies can be used to connect to spaces beyond classrooms, museums and other traditional connected spaces and experts.

An iPad, which was connected to the Internet via 3G, was used to connect to the local council and to meals-on-wheels. An iPad was taken out to the setting and used by a staff member at each venue as a way of providing an insight into the functions of the two venues and this was then connected to a computer in the classroom, which in turn was connected to an IWB. This enabled the students, who were in the classroom, to both see the venues and talk with staff about the functions of the venue.

In talking with staff at both locations, pupils were able to experience authentic learning opportunities by looking at the activities undertaken by the experts, who they might not ordinarily have been able to talk with. The meals-on-wheels visit demonstrated how mobile technologies can facilitate new experiences as the pupils were able to experience the kitchen and surrounding areas without being there in person, which they were unable to do because of health and safety restrictions.

The results show there were successful learning opportunities as the students had access to informal authentic settings and experts who were part of the local community they belonged to. Many of the students had been to the council chambers and some students' grandparents received meals from the meals-on-wheels service. The video connection gave all students a different perspective on the venues and they collectively discussed the services, which strengthened their understanding of community services. The study illustrated how untethered learning can support learning.

There were also limitations in using the mobile device. There was a clear question–answer structure to the lessons. In this regard the lessons were not highly pupil-centred, although the pupils did have the opportunity to ask relevant questions they composed beforehand. Another difficulty encountered in the project was for the pupils to be heard by the experts using the microphone on the computer. Often the teacher had to repeat the pupils' questions, which made communication a little difficult at times. More work in the field is required to get this part of the process working satisfactorily.

Task 15.3 Developing a class-based scenario

In drawing on the ideas you developed from Tasks 15.1 and 15.2, develop your own class-based scenario and consider how you would implement the use of mobile technologies into your own teaching. Use the pupils from Task 15.1, or consider who your next class will be, and try to develop a lesson or series of lessons using the mobile technologies available in your school.

Practical implications for using and supporting mobile technologies in classrooms

Learning with others and through collaboration with mobile technologies

The opportunities to support social and collaborative forms of learning through mobile technologies build upon a considerable body of socio cultural and situated learning theories (Pachler, Cook and Bachmair, 2010), which have recently been confirmed in a number of meta-analyses of technology use in education (Higgins, Xiao and Katsipataki, 2012; Luckin *et al.*, 2012). These studies suggest that mobile technology has the potential to support many of the more social forms of learning, such as conversation (dialogical learning) and data sharing (Kearney *et al.*, 2012). The size and portability of mobile devices are ideal for collaborative activities such as group work and sharing of data between users, since they can be used spontaneously as and when the learner wishes to undertake this type of activity. A wide variety of Web 2.0-type applications such as NearPod, GoogleDocs and Twitter enable learners to work together to complete a task or activity and this can be both in face-to-face or distant contexts. In the primary/ elementary school setting it is more likely that pupils will be situated in real-time face-to-face contexts. However, applications such as these still support high levels of sharing and interaction, such as the collaborative production of a narrative in which pupils work in groups using an application such as GoogleDocs on their mobile device to draft and refine the text together. It is likely more applications and tools will emerge to support this form of collaborative learning. Early examples, such as NearPod, have already demonstrated how traditional forms of teaching (e.g., the whole-class presentation) can be extended and enhanced on a mobile device by enabling feedback from users during the presentation, which can also be undertaken remotely in non-face-to-face contexts.

Learning in authentic settings and contexts

Mobile technologies work in a variety of different contexts, which include the formal classroom, but extended into informal contexts such as museums and field trips and the playground or the home. The mobile device itself acts as a mediating technology, enabling pupils to access and organise their work seamlessly between different contexts.

In the classroom itself mobile technologies offer opportunities for making both the setting and the tasks or activities, which are designed by the teacher, more authentic and realistic. The appropriate use of games such as Minecraft, for example, have been shown to create a more realistic context for pupils when they are working on a topic about real-world problems such as environmental issues or, in the case of history, a re-creation of a disaster such as the Titanic (Burden *et al.*, 2012). Additionally, individual access to the Internet through a mobile device allows the teacher to design more realistic tasks for pupils, which approximates more closely to real-world events and situations. Once such example is the use of apps that track and collate real-time data from the world, such as earthquakes and volcanic eruptions (e.g., QuakeSpotter) enabling pupils to observe and analyse genuine data virtually in real-time.

Learning in informal settings - a mystery at the museum example

The term informal learning refers to learning that occurs outside of the school in settings that are designed for education and enjoyment. Some of the venues that this term applies to include museums, zoos and art galleries. The ways mobile devices can be used are varied. In one example called 'mystery at the museum' a small group of pupils collaborated to solve a mystery inside the museum, interacting through mobile devices (Cabrera *et al.*, 2005). The pupils each received a different piece of information via their device and then were required to come together and solve the mystery. While the findings indicated favourable learning outcomes one of the concerns of the project authors was that they were designing an activity that focused pupils' attention on the interactivity with each other rather than the museum exhibits. While the pupils in the project were high-school pupils this activity could be easily adapted for primary-school pupils.

One of the liberating features of mobile technologies is their portability, which allows them to be taken into the field to support pupils' gathering of data that can then be used back in the classroom to further their understanding of the focus of the investigation. In this way the devices support pupils' learning in authentic settings. In one example pupils used handheld computers to facilitate their learning on environmental issues using the 3Rs ('Reduce, Reuse and Recycle') in a Singapore primary school. Using handheld computers throughout a field trip, the Year 4 pupils investigated 'how wastes are produced and what impact 3Rs can have on protecting the environment. The handheld computers were used to support, guide, and extend pupil thinking process within and out of classroom' (Chen *et al.*, 2008, p. 321).

While one of the affordances of mobile technologies allows pupils to collect the data, edit it and combine it to create final projects on the one device, this is not always possible or desirable. Pupils should, where it is appropriate, 'be able to create, access and manipulate their field data across a range of computer systems' (Stewart *et al.*, 2009). The increase of online spaces and the ease of sharing content between devices is much increased with cloud computing now available.

Other ways pupils can use mobile devices in informal learning settings are that they can capture images or video using a built-in camera. The use of QR codes or virtual software can provide extra information on exhibits in the form of text, speech, images, video or graphic overlays. Pupils could download interactive maps that could then be used to guide their experiences in the museum. They could also be alerted to any events that were occurring prior to the event via the mobile device. They could use them as communication tools to keep in contact with their teachers as a security measure. These are only a few of the ways that mobile devices can support learning in informal settings. What is important though, as suggested in the mystery in the museum, is that these devices enhance rather than inhibit the experience in the settings. This will require careful pedagogical consideration by both informal educators and teachers.

Learning by making and constructing with mobile devices

Knowledge construction is a powerful and motivating form of learning for primary-age pupils and mobile devices support a variety of activities that enable pupils to experience the process of knowledge production and dissemination in a number of different forms, hence supporting differentiation and variety. Until recently, for example, the opportunity to experience the production of a video or even a movie was relatively rare for primary-age pupils, requiring access to specialist equipment (e.g., video cameras, sound-recording kit, editing facilities), knowledge and understanding that was beyond the scope of most teachers and pupils, certainly on a daily or more frequent basis. The advent of mobile technologies featuring relatively sophisticated video, audio and editing capabilities has brought video production into the classroom, enabling pupils to film and edit on the device itself. Initial investigations of these technologies suggest the production of short movie trailers (e.g., iMovie trailers) based around a small number of templates are extremely popular with teachers and pupils, who produce them to summarize a particular topic or to illustrate their understanding of a particular concept or idea (Burden *et al.*, 2012). As the technology becomes more prevalent and the novelty value of using templates wane, teachers also recognise other opportunities to use these multi-modal affordances of mobile technologies to support knowledge construction. They are used, for example, to capture and describe a process or sequence, such as a performance in physical education (Maher, 2013), or dance, where pupils record their own performance to analyse later. Some teachers encourage pupils to use their mobile device to capture processes in their learning, such as an experiment in science or a particular technique in drama, which they can return to later to watch and learn from.

A wide variety of apps and tools support similar forms of multi-modal knowledge construction in which pupils take the lead in production. Animation is a good example, with a wide variety of apps such as Puppet-Pals and Toontastic, which enable pupils to construct semi-professional outputs on the device itself. The same is true for knowledge and concept maps (e.g., Popplet), which allow pupils to generate multi-modal representations to demonstrate their understanding of a topic that can then be shared or even edited with other learners.

Finally, it is also possible for pupils to record and annotate directly from their mobile device, producing a screencast or mini-video recording that combines video screenshots with additional content, such as a voice-over and annotations from the pupil. A variety of apps have emerged that support this kind of knowledge construction (e.g., Explain Everything, Show Me, etc.) and initial feedback from teachers indicates they are being used in many different and exciting ways to support learning. One of the most promising may be the use to support feedback both to and from the pupil. In one documented example a teacher has used the app Explain Everything to encourage pupils to articulate how they tackled a particular problem or question (e.g., a complex maths equation) by writing down the process and explaining their thinking verbally as they do so. The results are extremely informative for the teacher, who is able to identify any misconceptions and misunderstanding when and where they occur. However, the deeper value of such activities may lie with the pupil who is able to replay and reconsider their own thinking (and the feedback from the teacher if it is included) in a manner that makes thinking more visible (Richards, 2012).

Logistical considerations in using mobile technologies

When deciding to go down the path of using mobile technologies in schools various considerations need to be taken into account and a number of decisions need to be made. It is important that a whole-school approach is adopted so that resources are shared, which can save money and maximise learning opportunities.

If possible, one of the resources that should not be shared is the mobile device, which should 'belong' to one pupil (Burden *et al.*, 2012). The decision of who owns the device needs to be made in conjunction with the school community and will reflect, in part, the socio-economic standing of the community. In one Sydney private school (Australia) observed for a study by one of the authors, iPads were purchased by the parents and were password protected by the parents so that the pupils were unable to download games, which would potentially distract pupils in the class. The school set $100 as the maximum parents would be asked to pay for apps.

It also important to consider how to protect the devices from being damaged and what happens if they do get damaged. Having protective covers is especially important. There are a number of companies now who manufacture cases for mobile devices so if they get dropped the risk of damage is minimised. If the devices do get damaged or malfunction it is important that a system is in place so that they can be repaired and returned to the classroom quickly. It is also worth considering having insurance for the devices to cover damage.

Some suggestions put forward by Goodwin (2012), which she calls logistical considerations, include:

- If every pupil has a mobile device, how will they identify theirs?
- How will pupils personalise their devices?
- How will the devices be stored and charged?
- How often will they need to be charged?

If the devices do not need to be charged every day it is possible that charging stations can be shared, which can cut down significantly on costs.

Another important consideration is taking the devices on excursions. In a study conducted by one of the authors pupils took their iPads on a three-day camp, which included a visit to a museum. One of the findings was that while the iPads did enable a lot of learning to occur, pupils found them unwieldy when they wanted to engage in activities that required the use of both hands. A very light backpack would have allowed pupils to secure the devices when not needed. It is also worth considering the type of excursion and if the use of mobile technologies is best suited for the activities that will occur. Excursions that involve a lot of physical activity and not well suited to the use of mobiles. Finally, it should be noted that Internet-enabled mobile devices, like the iPad, raise issues relating to privacy and e-safety and younger pupils will need careful guidance and advice in order to ensure they are used in a responsible and safe manner. There is insufficient space available to explore this in any more detail in this chapter but you will find further support and advice in Chapter 19.

Task 15.4 Designing a mobile learning activity

Select one of the practical strategies for using mobile devices covered in this section and design your own activity around this strategy to use in your classroom. Try to evaluate the learning that occurred in this activity using the models explained earlier in the chapter.

Summary and key points

The use of mobile technologies, both in the classroom and beyond, repositions the role of the teacher. In a traditional classroom the teacher has generally been the sole provider of knowledge – the gate keeper. Using mobile devices, a greater number of experts can be called upon to supplement the knowledge of the pupils and to provide for different types of expertise. This expansion of experts allows new learning opportunities for both the pupils and the teacher, which allows for a community of learners to be created. Through this, teachers are able to model the learning process to pupils.

Access to mobile technologies also repositions the role of the pupil in terms of their access to sources of knowledge and their ability to act more independently. Ubiquitous access to the Internet through these devices enables pupils to locate information independently, although this raises many questions about digital literacy such as their ability to handle information in a critical manner. Pupils are potentially liberated from the physical boundaries of their own classroom when they use mobile devices that offer greater amounts of choice about where, when and at what pace learning occurs (Kearney *et al.*, 2012; Burden *et al.*, 2012).

The use of mobile devices requires that the curriculum be redefined. What constitutes the 'place of learning' is no longer the same. When learning takes place alters, so that learning out-of-school hours influences in-school learning. Who is involved in the learning process changes and new ways of collaboration are possible. These changes mean a more fluid understanding of the curriculum is required to ensure that the benefits of the devices are being realised. It is important that a whole-school approach in relation to the curriculum is set in place to ensure that staff members are being trained around their use and resources are being provided.

In considering the use of mobile technologies in the classroom, it is important that teachers have a clear understanding of how to manage the devices. Clear expectations need to be put in place for pupils, parents and the teachers. As learning requires a range of experiences it is important to consider when these devices will be used, for what subjects, and how they interplay with other ways of learning. Allowing pupils to use the devices at home is important so, when these go home, who can add apps and other content is an important issue that needs to be communicated.

Finally, the role of parents and other significant adults outside of school foregrounded when pupils use mobile devices for learning, particularly if the device is a personal one that is available to pupils beyond the school itself. Pupils can continue their work more seamlessly when it is digitised and available on a mobile device and this may help to bridge the divide between home and school, with parents taking on a more overtly educative role with their children. Some of the early case studies in mobile learning have reported interesting and potentially valuable learning gains, both for the pupil and the parent, when the device is used as a portal for sharing and explaining what the pupil is doing in school. It remains to be seen if schools will also recognise these gains as opportunities to reconceptualise where the boundaries between formal and informal education now lie in the era of pervasive and ubiquitous access to technology of this nature.

Further reading

Kukulska-Hulme, A., Sharples, M., Milrad, M., Arnedillo-S anchez, I. and Vavoula, G. (2009) 'Innovation in mobile learning: A European perspective'. *International Journal of Mobile and Blended Learning*, 1(*1*): 13–35.

Ng, W. (2011) *Mobile technologies and handheld devices for ubiquitous learning: Research and pedagogy*. Hershey, PA: IGI Global.
    This article and the book provide access to a range of ideas about how mobile technologies can enhance learning.

Additional resources and websites

Educational Technology and Mobile Learning. A resource of educational web tools and mobile apps for teachers and educators: www.educatorstechnology.com/

References

Burden, K., Hopkin, P., Male, T., Martin, S. and Trala, C. (2012) *iPad Scotland evaluation report*. Hull: The University of Hull. Available online at: www.academia.edu/3795954/iPad_Scotland_Evaluation_2012. Accessed on 8 February 2014.

Cabrera, J.S., Frutos, H.M., Stoica, A.G., Avouris, N., Dimitriadis, Y., Fiotakis, G. and Liveri, K.D. (2005) 'Mystery in the museum: Collaborative learning activities using handheld devices'. In *Proceedings of the 7th international conference on human computer interaction with mobile devices and services*, pp. 315–18. Salzburg, Austria: ACM.

Chen, W., Tan, N.Y.L., Looi, C.K., Zhang, B. and Seow, P.S.K. (2008) 'Handheld computers as cognitive tools: Technology-enhanced environmental learning'. *Research and Practice in Technology Enhanced Learning*, 3(*3*): 231–52.

Danaher, P.A., Moriarty, B. and Danaher, G. (2009) *Mobile learning communities: Creating new educational futures: 1* (1st edn). Abingdon, UK: Routledge.

Goodwin, K. (2012) *Use of tablet technology in the classroom*. State of New South Wales, Department of Education and Communities, 2012. Available online at: http://rde.nsw.edu.au/files/iPad_Evaluation_Sydney_Region_exec_sum.pdf. Accessed on 14 July 2013.

Higgins, S., Xiao, Z. and Katsipataki, M. (2012) *The impact of digital technology on learning: A summary for the Education Endowment Foundation*. London: Sutton Trust.

Johnson, L., Adams, S. and Cummins, M. (2012) *The NMC horizon report: 2012 K-12 edition*. Austin, Texas: The New Media Consortium.

Kearney, M., Aubusson, P., Schuck, S. and Burden, K. (2012) 'Viewing mobile learning from a pedagogical perspective'. *ALT-J Research in Learning Technology*, Vol. 20.

Kearney, M. and Maher, D. (2012) 'Mobile learning in maths teacher education: Driving pre-service teachers' professional development'. *Australian Educational Computing*, 27(3): 78–86.

Kinash, S., Brand, J., Mathew, T. and Kordyban, R. (2011) *Uncoupling mobility and learning: When one does not guarantee the other*. Learning and Teaching papers. Paper 25. Available online at: http://epublications.bond.edu.au/tls/25. Accessed on 15 July 2013.

Klopfer, E., Squire, K. and Jenkins, H. (2002) 'Environmental detectives: PDAs as a window into a virtual simulated world'. *Proceedings of IEEE International Workshop on Wireless and Mobile Technologies in Education*. Vaxjo, Sweden: IEEE Computer Society, 95–8.

Koole, M., McQuilkin, J. and Ally, M. (2010) 'Mobile learning in distance education: Utility or futility?' *Journal of Distance Education*, 24(2): 59–82.

Kukulska-Hulme, A. and Traxler, J. (2005) *Mobile learning: A handbook for educators and trainers*. Routledge: New York.

Leadbetter, C. (2005) *Learning about personalisation: How can we put the learner at the heart of the education system?* Available online at: www.education.gov.uk/publications/eOrdering Download/DfES-0419–2004.pdf. Accessed on 24 August 2013.

Luckin, R., Bligh, B., Manches, A., Ainsworth, S., Crook, C. and Noss, R. (2012) *Learning: The proof, promise and potential of digital education*. London: Nesta.

Madden, M., Lenhart, A., Duggan, M. and Cortesi, S. (2013) *Teens and technology*. Pew Research Center. Available online at: www.pewinternet.org/Reports/2013/Teens-and-Tech.aspx. Accessed on 25 August 2013.

Maher, D. (2013) 'Pre-service primary teachers' use of iPads to support teaching: Implications for teacher education'. *Educational Research for Social Change*, 1(3): 48–63.

Merchant, G. (2007) 'Mind the gap(s): Discourses and discontinuity in digital literacies'. *E-learning*, 4(3): 241–54.

Motiwalla, L.F. 2007 'Mobile learning: A model and evaluation'. *Computers & Education*, 49(3): 581–96.

Pachler, N., Cook, J. and Bachmair, B. (2010) 'Appropriation of mobile cultural resources for learning'. *International Journal of Mobile and Blended Learning*, 21: 1–22.

Richards, R. (2012) 'Screencasting: Exploring a middle school math teacher's beliefs and practices through the use of multimedia technology'. *International Journal of Instructional Media*, 39(1): 55–67.

Stewart, K., Thompson, K., Hedberg, J. and Wong, W. (2009) 'Using technology to support quality learning for school activities involving field studies'. *Architectures for distributed and complex m-learning systems: Applying intelligent technologies*. Hershey, PA: IGI Global.

Teall, E., Wang, M. and Callaghan, V. (2011) 'A synthesis of current mobile learning guidelines and models'. In *World conference on e-learning in corporate, government, healthcare, and higher education 2011*. Honolulu, HI: AACE, pp. 443–51. Available online at: www.editlib.org/p/38749. Accessed on 10 November 2013.

Traxler, J. (2007) 'Defining, discussing and evaluating mobile learning: The moving finger writes and having writ . . .' *The International Review of Research in Open and Distance Learning*, 8(2). Available online at: www.irrodl.org/index.php/irrodl/rt/printerFriendly/346/875oor. Accessed on 26 May 2014.

Vavoula, G. and Sharples, M. (2009) 'Meeting the challenges in evaluating mobile learning: A 3-level evaluation framework'. *International Journal of Mobile and Blended Learning*, 1(2): 54–5.

Vavoula, G., Sharples, M., Rudman, P., Meek, J. and Lonsdale, P. (2009) 'Myartspace: Design and evaluation of support for learning with multimedia phones between classrooms and museums'. *Computers & Education*, 53(2): 286–99.

Wishart, J. and Triggs, P. (2010) 'Museum scouts: Exploring how schools, museums and interactive technologies can work together to support learning'. *Computers and Education*, 54(3): 669–78.

Yahya, S., Ahmad, E.A., Jalil, K.A. and Mara, U.T. (2010) 'The definition and characteristics of ubiquitous learning: A discussion'. *International Journal of Education and Development using Information and Communication Technology (IJEDICT)*, 6(1): 117–127.

16 Web 2.0 and classrooms

Mandy Peace

Introduction

> Schools and universities should become more like hubs of learning, within the
> community, capable of extending into the community . . . more learning needs to
> be done at home, in offices and kitchens, in the contexts where knowledge is
> deployed to solve problems and add value to people's lives.
>
> (Leadbeater, 2000, p. 112)

Technology has changed the world of work and play, and has reshaped learning and
teaching in the twenty-first century. There is a vast array of digital tools available,
designed to engage and motivate learners of all ages across the curriculum. This chapter
looks at the impact the Internet, in particular the concept known as Web 2.0, is having
on classroom interactions. From the early days of the read-only web, the Internet has
shifted to a write, create, produce and interact resource. The Internet has successfully
provided an arena for collaborative opportunities, with the scope of vast audiences to
inspire and intrigue budding producers of any age or experience.

The chapter is in two parts. The first part showcases a range of ways in which student
teachers implement new technologies during school experience. The findings of the
Web 2.0 Schools Project (2008–2010), an 18-month project undertaken with trainee
and experienced teachers from two schools in South Wales, are reported. These cover
the ways in which the student teachers developed, planned, prepared and presented a
range of thematic activities using new technologies, including Web 2.0 resources. The
second part of the chapter outlines ways in which teachers can use Web 2.0 technologies
as part of their ongoing professional development.

Technology provides interactive opportunities for education, as Hargreaves (2003)
states, 'ICTs potentially provide a network structure to turn 25,000 schools and their
staff into another small world in which any two nodes can connect with each other
easily and quickly' (p. 13).

Objectives

At the end of this chapter you should be able to:

*   understand the power and the limitations of using Web2.0 for learning and teaching;
*   have an awareness of e-safety issues;
*   evaluate the use and potential of Web 2.0 and other new technologies to support teaching and learning.

Web 2.0 definitions

The term Web 2.0 (or Web 2) describes second-generation web-based services intended to facilitate collaboration and sharing. There has been a period of immense change and rapid growth of the Internet, from a text- and numbers-based research tool to the colourful, graphical world of information we have all come to know, and indeed depend on. The Internet is now a read/write tool, not simply a reference tool with one-way communication, but a collaborative communications board on which anyone can publish. Initially, to write to the web was a slow process, one that required knowledge of HTML code to make webpages work. Now, with the advent of Web 2.0 technologies, it is relatively simple for anyone, with a minimal level of expertise, to create a web space. Web 2.0 is an umbrella term used to describe the new generation of web-based communications and hosted services, such as social networking, wikis, blogs and podcasts. The term was created in 2004 by Tim O'Reilly, founder of an American media company O'Reilly Media, and was actually the name given to the conference that promoted these new technologies. Currently, the term is used worldwide to describe this read/write web that is now so much a part of our everyday lives. A key report from JISC, the Technology and Standards Watch Report (Anderson, 2007) established that Web 2.0 is more than 'just a set of cool and new technologies and services . . . it is a set of powerful ideas that are changing the way that some people interact' (p. 2).

The power of Web 2.0: why use Web 2.0?

Web 2.0 provides opportunities for pupils:

*   to be creative;
*   to have a degree of control over their own learning;
*   to solve problems;
*   to improve their personal IT capability;
*   to work cooperatively.

The 'Es' of Web 2.0

The student teachers, who took part in the Web 2.0 Schools Project (2010), were positive about the value of the project as part of their ICT development. The key benefit was the range of ideas for use of the new technologies in the classroom. They were also surprised and motivated by the pupils' ability to use the new technologies. Both these elements helped to boost their own confidence with the technology. It also made them aware that a comprehensive knowledge of specific software is not a prerequisite. In addition,

Web 2.0 technologies provide forums for discussion, informal conversations and dialogue, and can generate collaborative content. Therefore, these tools can create communities of learners who provide a vast array of ideas and representations of knowledge. The researcher found a number of beneficial factors that were termed 'Es' of Web 2.0.

These are as follows.

Enjoyable and exciting

Pupils enjoy being able to show off their work to others and, through Web 2.0, they can share their efforts with a wide audience. It can be fun to discover new ways of presenting information so that it is clear and interesting for all to read.

Energises learning

When pupils work together on an IT task there is often a buzz to their work. They exchange ideas, challenge one another's understanding and generally learn from each other, as well as from sources on the computer.

Emancipatory

Working on Web 2.0 tasks provides pupils with opportunities to take responsibility for their own learning. Using the computer they can search out information not normally available to them in the classroom.

Each year new entrants to initial teacher training courses provide fresh challenges to existing classroom practice; testing pedagogy and transforming practice. As a student teacher you may be skilled in a range of mobile and online technologies when you begin your teacher training. Your enthusiasm for technology and your ability to rapidly acquire skills is taken for granted. However, effective teaching using technologies is not just about the acquisition of a skill set, it is about developing a positive attitude and approach to learning and teaching with ICT. Haydn (2009, p. 11) says student teachers need to have 'an open mindedness and a willingness to try things out, and above all develop a critical appreciation of the potential of various ICT applications', something that you should always bear in mind.

The concerns around Web 2.0

The advent of Web 2.0 technologies into education has produced many challenges and, as a result, an increased impetus on Internet safety, due to the prospect of a diverse audience. Web 2.0 software is online and ready to access for anyone with an Internet connection, providing new avenues for collaboration and communication. It is this ease of access and speed of publication that raises schools' and parents' concerns for Internet safety. Many schools and local authorities filter Web 2.0 sites in order to protect pupils, and to keep them in a perceived 'safe' environment, without evaluating the potential value that these sites may have.

Reports such as the Byron Review (2008), Byron Progress Review (2010) and EU Kids Online, Livingstone *et al.*, (2011) discuss online safety and the needs of pupils and young people in a digital world. These reviews highlight the risks and fears that have ensued from pupils' experiences online and playing video games. Byron (2010), for example, states that her findings can help to generate a practical approach to helping our pupils manage online risks. Byron (2010) suggests that pupils need to be educated to understand, and avoid, the risks posed by the Internet, just as they would be taught about dangers in the 'offline' world. She stresses the importance of protecting young people through education, not through exclusion. See Chapter 19 for further information and tasks to support e-safety in the classroom.

The power of social collaboration

One of the most powerful aspects of Web 2.0 is the promotion of social collaboration. Many teachers would agree that communication is at the heart of the education process and Web 2.0 opens up a range of different ways of learning from each other (see Chapter 12 on ICT in global learning and Chapter 9 on Modern Foreign Languages). Sharing ideas and constructing understanding from the collaborative process is a major

Table 16.1 The power of social collaboration tools in the primary setting: examples of blogging, wikis and podcasts

Blogs
A blog is designed to be updated on a regular basis by an individual or group of users to record opinions, or collect and share information and ideas. Privacy can be set so that user details are protected; logins and passwords are required for publishing and editing.

Uses	Tasks
Journals	• Create a class journal, a collaborative piece that can be shared with other classes or parents • Group or individual journals, where pupils write their news
Creative writing	• Create a class poetry blog where the pupils are encouraged to post their creative pieces at regular intervals • Use the class or school blog as a space for pupils to publish the creative writing and where they can give feedback on the work of others • Post prompts for writing • Communicate with parents with tips on how they can help their children
Portfolio	• Pupils have their own blog page on a class blog, teachers can edit and approve posts • Build a class news broadcast using pupils' written pieces and photographs
Digital scrapbook	• Use a blog to collect images or movie clips on a theme. Pupils can evaluate and give opinions
Making connections	• Use the blog to connect with other schools • Pupils use the blog to share experiences with children from other countries • Use the blog to write to pen-pals

Wikis
A wiki is designed to be developed collaboratively by a community of users, allowing users to add and edit content. It can be password protected so that only invited or allocated users can write or edit content.

feature of Web 2.0. The potential is there for the community of pupils and teachers to learn from each other in many ways, such as co-constructing understanding or by considering different points of view. However, realising the full potential of Web 2.0 to support collaborative learning is challenging. Research into specific Web 2.0 tools, such as Walls *et al.* (2010) 'Podcasting in education' and Robertson (2008) 'Wiki technology in teacher education', suggests that there is still a way to go before education embraces these approaches. It is clear that, in addition to technical and instrumental concerns, professional development must also address the values and beliefs that underpin a teacher's practice. Using online technologies can provide opportunities to allow learners to voice their opinions on issues that are important to them.

The beauty of Web 2.0 technologies is that they allow for innovation and creativity, and that they are easily adapted to suit the needs of your classroom. Table 16.1 contains a selection of practical learning and teaching ideas for you to explore.

Table 16.1 continued

Uses	Tasks
Collaboration	• Ask pupils to write 'how to' guides, inserting images and other media • Get pupils to document local history, school, buildings, events, etc. from 'our community'. Could include interviews and podcasts from parents and relatives • Create a school brochure; include school achievement, maps and events, advertising and promoting the school and its pupils • Create a book review wiki – pupils to leave their book reviews either in writing or podcasts and encourage others to share their views • Create a school encyclopaedia – pupils to research and write about topics, news, events of interest. Encourage editing and improvement from others • Create historical wikis – topics studied in the history curriculum can be developed and discussed

Podcasts
A podcast is a multimedia digital file, usually audio in nature, that can be made available on the Internet for downloading to a portable media player or a computer. It is often embedded on blogs and wikis to create a multimedia website.

Uses	Tasks
Creating multimedia pieces	• Interview pupils about their understanding of a topic or concept. This can be done before and after the content delivery to discover misconceptions and to celebrate progression • News broadcasts, either daily or weekly broadcasts of school events that can be uploaded to the school website or the class wiki or blog • At the end of the lesson select a pair of students to record the essence of the learning. This can be a very interesting way to see what has actually been understood • Get pupils to record their music compositions. Each lesson pupils can record their progression as they explore and refine musical elements; podcast pupils' storytelling, sharing favourite stories

Managing the limitations: ensuring respectful relationships

Along with providing access to new learning and teaching opportunities, the Internet has also raised issues about privacy, online respect, safety and appropriate uses for technology, both inside and outside the classroom.

Respectful relationships are key to the functioning of all primary schools, but they may not always develop as we would wish. Learning how to behave in a classroom, and online, is something that has to be taught and developed. One way of doing this is through an online discussion of the word 'respect', followed by a classroom discussion. See Task 16.1.

Task 16.1 Developing respectful relationships

Web 2.0 tools could be used to create a totally collaborative discussion about safety online. Initiate a forum with a question such as:

> You often hear the word 'respect' used both in and out of school. What does this word mean to you and how does this relate to your online life?

Other tools, such as mind-mapping, blogging or micro-blogging, chat forums, wiki and online noticeboards, could also be used to deepen the discussion and allow for a multimedia outcome.

It is important that you develop an understanding of how children and young people use the Internet and mobile technology. You need to be aware of the implications involved with using web technologies, especially social media. Cyberbullying is something that needs to be addressed in order to ensure the safety of pupils online. There is little research to date in the UK that has examined cyberbullying among children under the age of eleven years. However, according to Monks, Robinson and Worlidge (2012), cyberbullying is used and experienced by children in this young age group. Monks *et al.* (2012) report that there is some connection between cyberbullying and traditional bullying, and that children are most likely to take the same role across the two settings. There are some excellent websites that provide insight and resources to help you deal with the issues children and young people may face in their online life. There follows a small selection of useful websites that can be used to develop an understanding of the issues involved with Internet safety. They contain useful learning resources for all ages (see also Chapter 19 on e-safety):

> www.thinkyouknow.co.uk/
> www.childnet.com/resources/kia/
> www.nspcc.org.uk
> www.learn-ict.org.uk/intsafety/

Examples of collaboration tools, e.g., in science

During science lessons children often hold misconceptions about scientific concepts. One way of enabling them to understand the concept correctly is for them to openly express their views and explain why they believe their explanations to be true. Pupils can work together in small groups to put their ideas into a form that can be shared with the class. This can be achieved using an online noticeboard tool such as Padlet, which provides the teacher with the opportunity to group together pupils' responses and hold a whole class discussion as to the validity of the statements and possibly discuss further tasks that would help in understanding the concept. A class activity that could be done in this way on the concept of floating and sinking could start with the following statements:

> I think that objects float in water because they are 'lighter' than water or sink because they are 'heavier'. Wood always floats and metal always sinks.

The teacher asks the pupils to say if they agree or disagree with the statements and asks them to provide their reasoning. See the example at http://padlet.com/wall/einkv44257

Web 2.0 in education

Haydn (2009) conducted research into the ways in which teacher training providers in England prepared student teachers to use ICT effectively in their subject teaching. The research focuses on the need for subject-specific modelling of effective ICT practices, and examines the financial aspects involved in investment of ICT in teacher training. One of the recommendations, therefore, was to exploit the use of less expensive options for ICT development, such as Web 2.0 applications and mobile technologies. Haydn (2009) suggests that future policy decisions about ICT investment need to consider how useful the different technologies are in terms of their value to learning, and how many people actually use them. Many Web 2.0 technologies are free, or inexpensive to use, and provide generic applications that can be adapted and modified to suit the users' needs. However, it is argued that Web 2.0 technologies are dynamic and that much of the content stored by these applications is of limited value. It is, therefore, of vital importance to be able to distinguish between the self-generated content and the more reliable elements. In addition, Bell (2009) suggests that these technologies help develop high-order thinking, encouraging users to apply understanding, to analyse and evaluate in order to finally create and publish. See Figure 16.1, which gives examples of what to consider.

Learning in and out of school

The impact of the learning that takes place beyond the classroom has always been recognised and developments in technology mean that we can now learn and communicate whenever and wherever we wish. Digital technologies have helped to merge the boundaries of work and play. With the use of virtual learning environments (VLEs), school websites and Web 2.0 technologies forging links between home and school, the distinction between leisure and learning have become less obvious (Banyard and Underwood, 2008). However, we need to ascertain the real value of the learning that takes place and to judge to what extent schools can, and should, capitalise on more spontaneous, unstructured learning on offer at home and harness it within the education system.

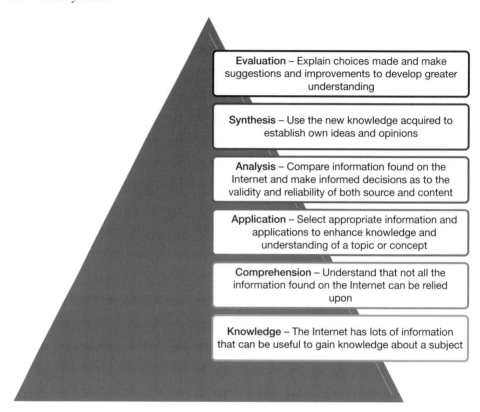

Figure 16.1 Bloom's Taxonomy in relation to acquiring information from the Internet.

Technological pedagogical content knowledge

A framework for Technological Pedagogical Content Knowledge (TPACK) developed by Mishra and Koehler (2006) extends Shulman's (1987) idea of Pedagogical Content Knowledge. The framework attempts to identify the nature of knowledge required by teachers for technology integration in their teaching. In order to effectively integrate technology into your pedagogy you need to understand the unique relationship between the components of Content Knowledge (CK), Pedagogical Knowledge (PK) and Technical Knowledge (TK) (see Figure 16.2). You need to have an understanding of the following:

- content knowledge: essential academic understanding of subjects being taught;
- pedagogical knowledge: teaching methods, thinking and learning skills, curriculum knowledge;
- technical knowledge: knowing how and what technologies best meet learning requirements.

Furthermore it is important that you understand the evolving, emerging nature of technology, and that you continue to learn, practise and appreciate how best to engage pupils in learning. Similarly, education is always changing: curriculum content, strategies for learning and teaching and assessment are all under constant review. For many student teachers, knowledge of potential technologies for use across the curriculum is limited. Student teachers tend to teach as they were taught; however, from the words of American philosopher John Dewey, 'If we teach today as we taught yesterday, then we rob our pupils of tomorrow.' Dewey (1944, p. 167). Markauskaite (2007) concurs, acknowledging that teachers' personal experiences are one of the most significant aspects affecting pedagogical beliefs, particularly in connection with the role of integrating ICT in learning and teaching.

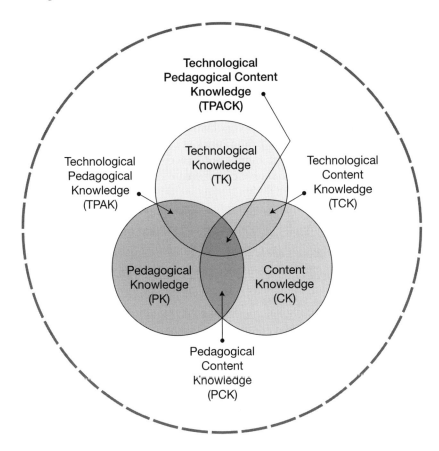

Figure 16.2 Forms of knowledge. Reproduced by permission of the publisher, © 2012 by tpack.org.

Web 2.0 and the construction of new knowledge by learners

The use of Internet-based applications, such as blogs, wikis and podcasts, supports the construction of knowledge. However, it is how this knowledge is stored, assessed and used thereafter that is of greatest importance. Gathering the information and reassembling it into material that can aid understanding is paramount. It is easy to see how media has influenced learning styles. Often text, audio and video content are linear and sequential, while web representations are frequently non-linear and multi-modal.

Today's learners are using new methods of information gathering, such as the Internet, and are processing the information in a similar way to its retrieval. Those who prefer a more sequential method of dealing with information may struggle. The analogy between brain and computer, or mind and programme, has influenced cognitive psychology (Anderson, 1990; Steyvers and Griffiths, 2008), 'In cognitive psychology the human mind is conceived of as a structured system for handling information' (Anderson, 1990, p. 56). According to most cognitive theories, information picked up by the senses is analysed, stored, recoded and subsequently used in various ways; these activities are called information processes (Steyvers and Griffiths, 2008). Some people will receive information in a sequential fashion, whereas others can build a picture from disparate sources.

In acknowledging the differences in the way we assimilate information, therefore, it is important to consider opportunities that allow pupils to produce outcomes with a similar variety. The Web 2.0 Schools Project (2010) was an opportunity for student teachers and pupils to explore these differences. In preparation for the project the student teachers explored the ideas of John Davitt's Learning Events Generator, found at www.newtools.org and as an app from iTunes or the Android store. Davitt's Random Activity Generator contains a large number of concepts and randomly combines them with a long list of ways of expressing them to create cognitively challenging tasks.

Figure 16.3 Davitt's Learning Events Generator.

The structure is simple; the challenges are separated into two sections – 'Do' (containing the concept or knowledge to express), and 'As' (defining the medium of expression or end result). From this it might be interesting to keep the 'Do' as static. See Task 16.3 as an example.

It is important that pupils are offered a range of media with which to demonstrate their understanding. So, for example, to produce an MP3 of a rap, you could use an iPod or MP3 voice recorder or you could use a software application such as Audacity and a simple microphone. The MP3 can then be uploaded to a wiki or a blog, either directly or using a hosting site such as Podbean. Creating a stop-motion animation of a role play, for example, could be carried out using a digital camera, mobile phone, video recorder, an iPad, or a webcam; the variety is essential so that pupils learn to use different technologies. The movie could be uploaded to a wiki or blog page or hosted on Youtube's schools environment, or similar hosting site. It is important that the technology is varied, so that pupils select appropriate tools for the job, and that discussion and decisions are a big part of the collaborative process. Work that pupils produce can be shared with family and friends by simply distributing a web address. Pupils can comment on each other's work, evaluate and make suggestions for improvement and celebrate each other's successes.

Task 16.3 Davitt's Learning Events Generator, e.g., learning about the heart

Choose a topic, method or learning activity, for example 'the workings of the heart', select a range of ways in which the class can present their understanding, and give each group a different method.

For example, demonstrate your understanding of how the heart works as:

- a Shakespearian sonnet;
- a rap;
- a public service announcement;
- a text message;
- a role-play activity;
- a Voki;
- a Glogster poster.

Set up a wiki using a hosting site, such as PBworks, Wikispaces or Google sites to share the pupils' work. Each group can present their work to the class, discussing the processes, difficulties and learning. They can also give feedback, or improve each other's pieces on the wiki to make a truly collaborative piece.

Try www.edutopia.org/blog/film-festival-technology-tool-tutorials. This excellent blog has multimedia tips and advice on how to use a range of Web 2.0 tools in the classroom.

Creating a learning environment for Web 2.0

Evidently, there are many variables to consider when setting up the ideal learning environment with ICT, such as the ratio of ICT equipment to pupil, the level and consistency of teacher or adult intervention and support. In primary schools pupils often work in pairs or small groups due to the constraints of the equipment rather than by design of the learning environment. However, the integration of Web 2.0 technologies puts a whole new slant on classroom management, which can open up a plethora of innovative teaching ideas. Undoubtedly the use of online technology can support communication, collaboration and knowledge building in line with constructivist principles (Smeets and Mooij, 2001; Trigg and Sutherland, 2009). A more holistic view suggests that student teachers' learning should be, in part, participation in social practices within the school environment (Korthagen, 2010). Invariably, at least part of your training programme will be an extended school placement or teaching practice, where these social interactions can be put to practical use, in a context with the learning environment for which they were intended.

Equipment reliability is another area of concern for student teachers, especially when being observed. The only rule is you must always have a backup strategy when using ICT, especially the Internet. Initially this may put you off using it in your lessons, as you may feel that you have to plan and prepare additional resources and consider alternative class management approaches. As you become a more effective teacher in general, this becomes less of an obstacle.

It is clear that it is the quality of interaction with the pupil that determines the quality of learning and teaching, and Web 2.0 technologies can have a positive impact on the quality of learning and teaching.

Summary and key points

With web technologies you can design tasks that are flexible – rather than being topic specific, they can be used across all curriculum areas. As you would expect, any work using Web 2.0 requires the first consideration to be the lesson objectives, then find a product that helps to achieve the objectives. It is important not to get mesmerised by the technology, as this would lead the way to the technology being the important aspect rather than learning through the technology. For example, giving the pupils a broad diet of technology will allow them to make informed decisions on how and what technology they chose to use.

Look at the following possible advantages and imitations of Web 2.0 and see how they apply to your practice.

Web 2.0 applications:

- are often free and/or open source;
- keep up to date and in-line with modern trends;
- is technology that is familiar to children and young people;
- promotes creativity;
- can be used to encourage independent learning;
- are beneficial for the whole curriculum;
- can be used on any platform and any device;
- provides opportunities for learning outside the classroom;
- offers opportunities for publishing to a wider audience;
- may be problematic to access due to management blocking via a firewall;
- necessitate good and reliable Internet access;
- require good Internet safety awareness.

Given the integration of technologies into our daily lives, experiential learning through and with technology from the early years needs to be part of the provision for pupils in our schools. It is important to provide rich and diverse learning environments for pupils, so that they grow up with an intuitive understanding of the world around them, including Web 2.0.

Annex: key Web 2.0 technologies

Blogs

Blogs or Weblogs refers to a simple webpage that consists of paragraphs of information, opinions, personal diary entries, news, etc., which are called posts. Some blog suggestions:

http://wordpress.org
http://blogger.com
https://edublogs.org/

Wikis

A wiki is a webpage or set of webpages that can be easily edited by anyone who has access. They can also have multimedia content with hyperlinks and comments, like a blog. Some wiki suggestions:

https://sites.google.com/
www.pbworks.com
www.wikispaces.com

Social bookmarking

Social bookmarking systems allow users to create lists of bookmarks or favourite sites and store them online so that they can be accessed remotely from any Internet point. Some social bookmarking suggestions:

http://delicious.com
http://diigo.com

Podcasting

Podcasts are audio recordings that are usually in MP3 format. They can be any type of commentary such as a radio programme, interview or lesson. To create and store podcasts try a hosting site such as:

www.podbean.com
www.apple.com/itunes/podcasts
https://archive.org/

Other useful collaboration tools

The following is a range of tools that allow for sharing ideas, files, media and alternatives to discussion forums.

http://padlet.com/ – is an online notice board maker that is ideal for making announcements, keeping notes and anything you can do with sticky notes.

https://bubbl.us – can be used to create colourful mind maps to print, embed and share ideas.

http://spicynodes.org/ – is a multimedia mind mapping tool that enables you to embed and share content.

http://edu.glogster.com/ – is a visual learning platform that can be used to create multimedia posters.

https://todaysmeet.com/ – can be used to create an instant virtual room, a little like Twitter. You can create an isolated room for a selected period of time, where you can see only what you need to see, without hash tags and other distractions.

http://edjudo.com/web-2-0-teaching-tools-links – is an online resource created by an experienced teacher to share his ideas about education and technology, giving reference to research, resources and experience. Readers can engage in conversation by leaving a comment.

www.classroom20.com/ – is a social network for those interested in Web 2.0, social media and participative technologies in the classroom. The site has great ideas to use in all areas of the primary school.

Further reading

Barber, D. and Cooper, L. (2012) *Using new web tools in the primary classroom: A practical guide for enhancing teaching and learning.* Oxon: Routledge
This is a useful book for teachers interested in the application of web-based ICTs in primary teaching.

Maloy, R.W., Verock-O'Loughlin R.E., Edwards, S.A. and Woolf, B.P. (2013) *Transforming learning with new technologies* (2nd edn). New York: Pearson.
For college students who are becoming teachers, to help develop twenty-first-century technology skills and pedagogy.

Poore, M. (2013) *Using social media in the classroom: A best practice guide.* London: Sage.
A guide to Web 2.0 sites and services, providing both an overview of different types of digital technologies and constructive guidance on how to safely use them as a tool for teaching.

References

Anderson, J. (1990) *The adaptive character of thought.* New Jersey: Hillsdale.
Anderson, P. (2007) *What is Web 2.0? Ideas, technologies and implications for education.* JISC Technology and Standards Watch. Available online at: www.jisc.ac.uk/media/documents/techwatch/tsw0701b.pdf. Accessed on 15 January 2014.
Banyard, P. and Underwood, J. (2008) *Understanding the learning space.* Available online at: eLearning Papers www.elearningpapers.eu. Accessed on 10 April 2010.
Bell, A. (2009) *Exploring Web 2.0: Second generation interactive tools.* Georgetown, DC: Katy Crossing Press.
Byron, T. (2008) *Safer children in a digital world: The report of the Byron Review.* Nottingham: DCSF Publications.
Byron, T. (2010) *Do we have safer children in a digital world? A review of progress since the 2008 Review.* Nottingham: DCSF Publications.
Dewey, J. (1944) *Democracy and education.* New York: Macmillan Company.
Hargreaves, D.H. (2003) *Working literally: How innovation networks make an education epidemic.* Nottingham: DfES Publications.
Haydn, T. (2009) *Case studies of the ways in which ITT providers in England prepare student teachers to use ICT effectively in their subject teaching.* Norwich: OECD.
Korthagen, F.A. (2010) 'Situated learning theory and the pedagogy of teacher education: Towards an intergrative view of teacher behaviour and teacher learning'. *Teaching and Teacher Education,* 26: 98–106.
Leadbeater, C. (2000) *Living on thin air: The new economy.* London: Penguin.
Livingstone, S., Haddon, L., Görzig, A. and Ólafsson, K. (2011) *Risks and safety on the internet: The perspective of European children.* London: EU Kids Online.

Markauskaite, L. (2007) 'Exploring the structure of trainee teachers' ICT literacy: The main components of, and relationships between, general cognitive and technical capabilities'. *Education Tech Research*, 55: 547–72.

Mishra, P. and Koehler, M.J. (2006) 'Technological Pedagogical Content Knowledge: A framework for teacher knowledge'. In *Teachers college record*, Vol. 108, No. 6. Michigan: Michigan State University, pp. 1017–54.

Monks, C.P., Robinson, S. and Worlidge, P. (2012) 'The emergence of cyberbullying: A survey of primary school pupils' perceptions and experiences'. *School Psychology International*, 33(5): 477–91.

Robertson, I. (2008) 'Learners' attitudes to wiki technology in problem based blended learning for vocational teachers' education'. *Australian Journal of Educational Technology*, 24(4): 425–41.

Shulman, L.S. (1987) 'Knowledge and teaching: Foundations of the new reform'. *Harvard Educational Review*, 57: 1–22.

Smeets, E. and Mooij, T. (2001) 'Pupil-centred learning, ICT and teacher behaviour: Observations in educational practice'. *British Journal of Education Technology*, 32(4): 403–17.

Steyvers, M. and Griffiths, T. (2008) 'Rational analysis as a link between human memory and information retrieval'. In N. Chater and M. Oaksford, *The probabilistic mind: Prospects from rational models of cognition*, pp. 327–47. Oxford University Press.

Trigg, P. and Sutherland, R. (2009) 'A holistic approach to understanding teaching and learning with ICT'. In R. Sutherland, S. Robertson and P. John (eds) *Improving classroom learning with ICT* (pp. 3–26). Oxon: Routledge.

Walls, S., Kucsera, J., Walker, J., Acee, T. and McVaugh, N. (2010) 'Podcasting in education: Are students as ready and eager as we think they are?' *Computers & Education*, 54: 371–8.

17 Computer programming in the primary school

An introduction

Rory McGann and Aisling Leavy

Introduction

Most pupils today are proficient at playing games on their mobile phones or communicating with their friends on social networks. So are student teachers. But what about creating an interactive game, story, or music experience? What about harnessing the power of technology to create meaningful educational challenges and in turn stimulate and develop higher-order reasoning abilities? The research underpinning this chapter involved fifty-six student teachers and in excess of 200 primary school pupils, using programming environments to provide both pupils and student teachers with experiences designed to develop skills of collaboration, communication, reasoning, analytical thinking and problem solving. This chapter initially outlines a contextual frame for programming, presenting various theoretical perspectives and an overview of supporting literature. An overview of the research coupled with case studies and sample tasks are presented to support your understanding of the potential role of programming in education.

Objectives

At the end of this chapter you should be able to:

- understand the theoretical perspectives underpinning programming;
- identify educational principles supported by the use of programming;
- consider pedagogical and methodological implications of using programming in primary education;
- carry out some introductory tasks related to programming in primary classrooms.

Theoretical perspectives of programming

A number of theoretical perspectives inform the research. These perspectives contribute to our understandings of the ways in which technology, and programming specifically, support learning. The *constructionist perspective* (Papert, 1980) is based on the premise that people construct new knowledge when they are actively engaged in constructing something meaningful. When programming and constructing artifacts, pupils are engaged in cycles of self-directed learning, which ultimately leads to the construction of new knowledge. This knowledge construction, we contend, is a by-product of the *problematizing* that occurs while pupils are constructing artifacts (in this case games/animations) in programming environments. Problematizing, the second perspective, means to 'wonder why things are, to inquire, to search for solutions and to resolve incongruities' (Hiebert *et al.*, 1996: 12). The challenge, then, is for teachers to carefully attend to instructional design and select tasks and environments that encourage pupils to grapple with key concepts and ideas. These tasks must be adequately challenging so as to stimulate learning, while concomitantly representing opportunities for success.

Overview of literature

Research on programming environments: A focus on game design

Game design is the predominant activity that pupils undertake in the programming environment. Recent research, much of it originating from *constructionist* perspectives, has focused on the educational outcomes associated from engaging young people in game design. Hayes and Games (2008) identify four goals that motivate the focus on game design. The most common motivation for game design has been for the purposes of helping pupils develop programming skills. A number of games developed at MIT (Logo, Moose Crossing, StarLogo and more recently Scratch) have advanced this research agenda. The under-representation of females in mathematics and science has stimulated interest in developing game design environments of interest to females. Third, the use of games has been shown to enhance learning in many academic domains such as science (Barab *et al.*, 2005), mathematics (Kafai 1995; Kafai *et al.*, 1998), history (Squire, 2006) and language and literacy (Gee, 2003; Robertson and Good, 2005, 2006). Finally, emphasis on the need to equip pupils with the skills to participate in a knowledge economy has precipitated the focus on 'design thinking'. Engaging pupils in game design supports the development of skills that underpin design thinking – identifying creative solutions to increasingly complex challenges.

Other positive outcomes have been associated with engaging in game design environments (See Chapter 14). Game environments are considered problematizing contexts (Kafai *et al.*, 1998), which lead to the production of ongoing learning opportunities for pupils. These environments have also been shown to support the development of computational thinking (Wing, 2006) and systems thinking, which in turn develops problem solving and design-based reasoning. Furthermore, it is through the construction of games, and problem solving and debugging along the way, that opportunities are presented for the pupil to engage in 'thinking about thinking' (diSessa, 2000). Since programming involves the creation of artifacts (i.e., games), these games serve as external representations of the pupil's problem-solving processes. Thus, programming provides the pupil with opportunities to reflect on their own thinking. Many of these outcomes are core components of and contribute to the development of twenty-first-century skills.

Specific design environments: from Logo to Scratch

The emergence of Logo into education in the 1970s stimulated research into early programming. However, despite initial interest in Logo and earlier programmes, these programmes failed to be taken up by educational systems. There is general consensus that the language and syntax were too complicated for pupils. In addition, the introductory activities were constraining and did not keep pupils motivated. The design of Scratch (scratch.mit.edu) has addressed the flaws of earlier programmes and produced an environment that is a simplified visual programming system incorporating three core design principles: more tinkerable, more meaningful and more social (Resnick *et al.*, 2009). Studies of pupils working with Scratch have found positive cognitive and affective outcomes. Programming in Scratch has made learning how to programme a positive experience and has resulted in moderate cognitive progress (Wilson and Moffat, 2012). Research also indicates the pupils using Scratch learn key programming concepts (Wilson and Moffat, 2012), such as sequencing and iteration, even in the absence of direct instruction (Hayes and Games, 2008). An analysis of 536 Scratch projects created by pupils attending a computer clubhouse over a two-year period (Maloney *et al.*, 2008) found significant increases in the use of specific programming concepts (i.e., Loops, Boolean logic, Random Numbers and Variables) from the first to the second year of the study. As might be expected, beginning Scratch users engaged in projects that required little scripting, compared to their more experienced peers. These positive outcomes, arising from working with Scratch, have been attributed to the benefits of the 'visual language' (Green and Petre, 1996) and easy-to-manipulate multimedia elements, thus reducing the cognitive load associated with mastering syntax.

Task 17.1 Developing programming in your setting

Search 'Google Scholar' using key phrases/terminology from this chapter, e.g., constructivism in education, programming and higher-order thinking skills, Scratch in education. Identify and evaluate three journal articles, jotting down key learnings that might assist you as teacher in initiating/developing a programming project in your setting.

Overview of the research underpinning this chapter

The research had three elements to its conception and subsequent design. A community organisation, 'Learning from Scratch', approached college faculty to present an initial concept of programming in primary schools. Using initial teacher educators from both the ICT and maths electives, fifty-six students (most of whom had never experienced programming) expressed an interest in supporting the initiative. These students received weekly facilitated programming sessions on campus centred around broad themes, both programming (installation, introduction to interface, scripts, syntax) and curricular application (mathematical concepts, digital storytelling, visual arts, problem solving, analytical thinking, collaboration), before carrying out placement with pupils aged ten–twelve years in eight local primary schools.

Student teachers prepared and facilitated sessions in local schools over eight weeks, with a focus on computer programming while ensuring curricular relevance. Student teachers were required to keep a reflective digital learning log (using Wordpress).

Student teachers' initial reactions to programming

The reflective blogs showed that student teachers were surprised by the ease of use and potential provided for a different way of learning and teaching. The ability to develop critical thinking skills in a logical/sequential environment, challenge higher-order

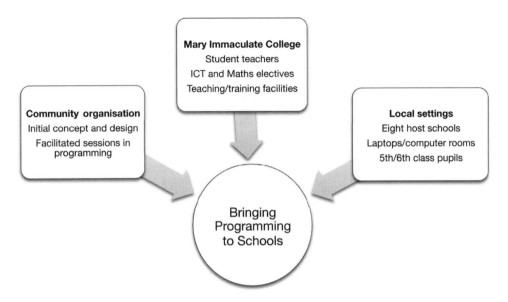

Figure 17.1 Introducing programming in schools: project overview.

cognition and problem solving, and approach problem solving through active engagement featured strongly. Reservations regarding student teachers' personal proficiencies also emerged strongly. As one student teacher put it:

'The integration of programming is something that forced me, as both teacher and learner, to move outside my comfort zone.'

(Student teacher)

Case study 17.1 Girl coding group in school 1

Isabella, Emma and Anna were three 12-year-old girls who worked together in one classroom. Their class was taught eight sessions of Scratch.

Their projects were collaborative and involved the design of multiplayer games (see Figure 17.2), narratives (see Figure 17.3) and interactive quiz environments.

Observations showed that they worked cooperatively in game design and in testing and *debugging* their games. Emma had experience of programming in a local programming club and she took on the role of expert in the initial weeks: the other two girls contributed ideas about design and game features while Emma undertook the coding. However, as the other girls became acquainted with programme features they moved to assuming more central roles in the activity.

The girls tackled key programming elements such as user *interaction* and *events*, *conditional statements* and *variables*. The group also used multimedia functions: they recorded one of the girls playing piano and used this as background music for one game.

One interesting finding is how integrating programming into the school curriculum opens a world of opportunity for some pupils. We can see in the interview transcript

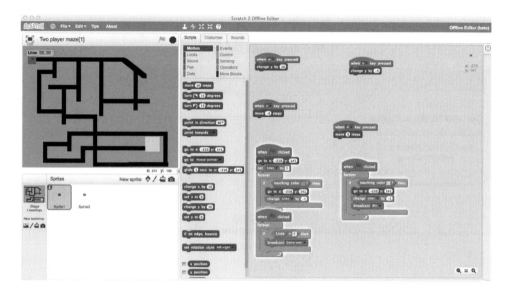

Figure 17.2 Two-player maze game.

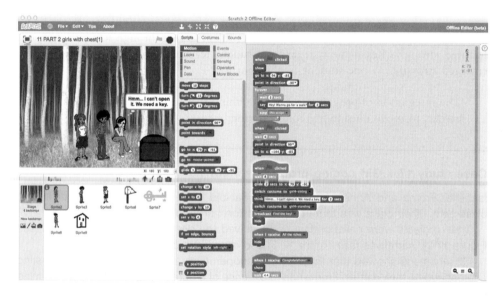

Figure 17.3 Girls find treasure.

that Isabella remarks on how she would not have considered doing programming prior to her school experience.

> *Isabella*: Scratch is really good and I like how it is really easy. I am not usually good at it (computers). Usually if I just turned on my computer I'd be proud of myself. I am just starting but I find it really easy and I like the way everything is there for you. It is very easy to do yourself. And you can teach yourself how to do it.

Another finding is the important role of the classroom community. For the more novice programmers, in this case Isabella, they draw on experts in the community for support and problem solving.

There were evident differences between novice and expert programmers in terms of what they liked about the programme (Scratch). Novice users referred to how 'easy' the game was. This was very evident in the number of times Isabella used the term 'easy' (see transcript above). In contrast, Emma referred to the flexibility of the programme in terms of the variety of activities she could design.

Task 17.2 Creating algorithms

Computers work by following lists of instructions called algorithms. Since 'computers are stupid', they will follow algorithms exactly, no matter how nonsensical. A good algorithm has a number of key components – accurate and unambiguous, the appropriate level of detail, a clear order and covers all possible outcomes with practical solutions.

With this in mind, create a simple 'algorithm' for baking a cake, buying some items (crisps and a fizzy drink) at the shop, or directions to the local post office. Jot down your initial sequence of instructions and refine to find the perfect 'algorithm'.

Programming and the curriculum

Learning principles, common across primary school curricula in many countries, include principles such as drawing on the pupil's sense of wonder and natural curiosity (DES, 1999), supporting the pupil as an active agent in learning (NCTM, 2000) and the role of collaboration (DES, 1999; NCTM, 2000; NZC, 2007) We are also acutely aware that learning is developmental in nature (DES, 1999) and uses existing knowledge and experience as the foundation. Learning can be supported by ensuring the development of higher-order thinking, problem solving and critical and creative thinking (ACARA, 2013; DES, 2002; NZC, 2007) and through ongoing formative and authentic assessment (ACARA, 2013; DES, 2002).

Computer programming using applications such as Scratch is regularly celebrated as affording learners opportunities for a 'mental workout' of cognitive and collaborative skills. With this in mind, student teachers were asked to select any three learning principles and discuss in detail (with specific examples from their school placement) how the use of programming served to support their chosen principles.

The next section draws on this work.

The pupil's sense of wonder and natural curiosity

An overwhelming majority of student teachers highlighted the potential of programming to stimulate a sense of wonder and curiosity among pupils.

The pupils were full of questions and wanted to move on to new areas of programming. 'What kind of things can you do . . . ?, will we be able to . . . ?, is there a button for . . . ?' are all examples of questions we received as we explained what the next few weeks entailed. Eagerness to learn was evident from start to finish.

They noted that programming supports the cultivation of pupil's sense of wonder.

Last week the pupils made a game which encompassed all of the programming skills learnt over the past three weeks. It was a relatively simple game which involved the user/gamer controlling a fish and trying to stay away from a shark. Although this may have been basic for some of the pupils, their natural curiosity and wonder led to questioning and experimentation as regards to programming. Some pupils decided to modify the game by including various different rules while others decided to create a completely new game. Even if some of the new ideas posed were extremely difficult to programme, it was the fact that the pupils were using their sense of wonder and natural curiosity as a creative/motivational tool. It was great to see the pupils applying their creativity and motivation to programming.

(Student teacher)

Higher-order thinking and problem-solving skills

All primary-school curricula encourage the pupil to observe, collate and evaluate evidence, to ask relevant questions, to identify essential information, to recognise the essence of a problem, to suggest solutions, and to make informed judgements. Programming in the primary classroom supports this:

If the teacher just tells the class exactly what code to use then they won't be using higher order thinking or problem solving skills as they will just do as the teacher says. If the teacher gives the class a chance to experiment with the program and get to know the commands before they start then the class should be able to start working out codes for themselves.

(Student teacher)

When pupils are using Scratch to create a game it is almost inevitable that they will encounter a challenge/problem that will result in them asking relevant questions in order to recognise the essence of the problem, thus engaging in *problematizing*. Programming activities, when structured appropriately, can challenge the pupils to suggest solutions and to make informed judgements supported by logical thinking and problem-solving skills (Clements, 1999; Marshall *et al.*, 2010).

For example, the teacher could ask them to make the dog move across the screen. The class would first need to think about how a dog would move in real life. It would take steps. Then they go look for the code to take steps, i.e., the 'move 10 steps' command. When they have found this the teacher could ask them how they would make him keep walking. The class could then go and look at all the code and find the 'forever' loop. This would make him keep walking. However, if he keeps walking he walks off the screen. The class could then be set a challenge to stop the sprite walking off the screen. The class would then find the 'if on edge bounce' command. When they have found all the code they need to put it together and add a start command, e.g., 'When space is pressed'.

(Student teacher)

These activities help to foster higher-order thinking skills, such as summarising, analysing, making inferences and deductions, and interpreting figurative language and imagery. Research suggests that pupils who have programming experience often score higher on measures of geometry knowledge and problem solving (Bitter and Pierson 2007, Papert, 1980).

Higher-order thinking involves asking questions, defining problems, analysing assumptions and considering alternative approaches. The curriculum also outlines that 'facilitating the development of higher order thinking skills can be achieved by modelling "what if . . ." processes' (NCCA, 2004). Through careful selection of pre-defined programming challenges, teachers can support and extend pupils' ability to question, analyse, investigate and think critically.

The pupil is an active agent in his or her learning

Learning is an active process of constructing knowledge, rather than simply acquiring it through transmission or osmosis. Appropriate scaffolds within a programming environment can encourage a learning journey that requires discussion, collaboration and decision making throughout. The fundamental tenet of constructivist methodologies is to provide opportunities for active engagement in a wide range of learning experiences and to encourage pupils to respond in a variety of ways to particular content and teaching strategies.

Collaborative learning should feature in the learning process

Vygotsky (1978) suggests that children working cooperatively engage in constructive discussion, share ideas and help each other. Opportunities for collaborative learning contribute significantly to a pupil's social and personal development. Collaborative work exposes pupils to the individual perceptions that others may have of a problem or a situation.

Undoubtedly, the use of programming can foster and indeed promote collaboration within the classroom. This was evident from our first week on placement, as the pupils in our class had to work in pairs while learning the art of computer programming. Such activities appeared to fuel their desire for learning while developing their ability to work in collaborative situations – communication, co-operation and listening.

(Student teacher)

Moreover, the experience of collaborative learning facilitates the pupil's social and personal development, and the practice of working with others brings pupils to an early appreciation of the benefits to be gained from cooperative effort. Carefully structuring collaborative challenges, organising pupils in pairs, promoting group work, sharing roles and responsibilities has the benefit of promoting an inclusive learning environment that values the contributions of all. This can often lead to a more positive learning outcome for all.

> By having the pupils working in pairs, however, it gave them a chance to answer questions, learn from each other, as well as praising each other's work and wanting to learn from it themselves how to do it. One of the weaker students in our class completely excelled at the task given based on working with the pen. His sprite was drawing different patterns on the screen using different pen colours. I remember the response by his partner as they watched the sprite do this: 'That is fair cool, you're class at this! How did you do that?' The pupil in return pressed stop, cleared the background and went through the process step by step.
>
> (Student teacher)

Programming: implications for teaching

As we've attempted to highlight in the previous section, the introduction of programming in any educational environment offers potential for learning affordances among pupils (and student teachers).

Teaching and learning strategies

> The time of chalk and blackboards has long gone. We have entered into a new era with technology at the heart of it. Pupils develop immensely from using computer programming at present, socially, emotionally and intellectually. Furthermore, the use of computer programming in schools allows pupil and teacher alike to develop the necessary IT skills in the changing technological society.
>
> (Student teacher)

Careful attention to lesson structure is fundamental to the use of programming. Student teachers were consistently encouraged to connect with pupils' prior knowledge, sustain pupils' interest and lead to new understanding and skills development.

> Each lesson began with some revision questions based on the content of the previous lessons. The pupils were then shown an example of a project incorporating a new function to inspire them. The new function was shown to the pupils and a challenge was set incorporating this so they could practise. When the challenge was completed, the pupils were then given the opportunity to show the others what they had made and the session ended with a review of what they had learnt. Such a lesson structure worked very well as the pupils were consolidating prior knowledge while practising the new functions.
>
> (Student teacher)

Student teachers found that some of the pedagogical competences included appropriate pacing, clear subject knowledge and effective questioning.

> The use of questioning was central in the learning process. Through question- ing, we were enabled to see what the pupils had learnt, what they found easy and

difficult, and got feedback on the lessons. The questioning also allowed the pupils to participate in self-discovery e.g. what do you think the script might be to make your sprite jump up and down?

(Student teacher)

Resource prerequisites of programming included an interactive whiteboard or digital projector, speakers and a laptop or computer preloaded with required software for each pair.

Classroom management

In implementing programming in the primary school curriculum, a balance is needed between sufficient teacher-talk, pupil engagement and structured tasks for maximum success. Areas for consideration in this regard may include communication, scanning, positive cueing and managing pupil engagement. The value of pair work, collaboration and mixed-ability grouping also warrants consideration (NCCA, 2004).

Behaviour management is often mooted as a concern for the implementation of programming in schools. While many of the student teachers acknowledge a difficulty in precise monitoring of individual/pair activities, it is suggested that effective scanning coupled with suitably engaging activities helps to ensure that class disruption is kept to a minimum.

> Despite being warned prior, we never encountered any great disruption that would affect learning . . . the pupils were totally engrossed in the programme – they took to it like a duck in water! The class teacher had informed us of the 'troublesome pupils' but this did not seem to be reflected in the programming lessons.

Task 17.3 Self-assessment

Conduct a self-assessment of your immediate learning context/environment to assess your preparedness for initiating a programming initiative. Key points to consider are:

- Will you offer the project as an out-of-school initiative or integrate it within the school day?
- Do you have access to the necessary teaching resources (teaching computer, digital projector, etc.)?
- Do you have access to the necessary pupil infrastructure (laptop computer per pair/group)?
- Do you have (or access to someone with) an introductory knowledge of a programming language (Java, Python, C++, Visual Basic or Scratch)?
- Do you have access to support materials/websites to assist with learning outcomes?
- Do you have a willingness to try something new?

Summary and key points

This chapter presents various theoretical perspectives and an overview of supporting literature in relation to programming in education. An in-depth look at pupil perspectives offers insight into how the integration of programming into the curriculum opens a world of opportunity for some pupils. Educational affordances, as experienced by student teachers, are also presented. These include using the child's sense of wonder and curiosity as a starting point for learning, developing higher-order thinking skills and availing of opportunities to ensure that the child is an active agent in their learning. Finally, some practical implications of any decision to integrate programming into education, such as planning and preparation, teaching and learning strategies, classroom management, assessment, and personal qualities and professionalism are considered. 'In learning you will teach, and in teaching you will learn.'

Further reading

O'Neill, S. and Howell, S. (2013) *Scratch from scratch: For schools and clubs.* Self-published.
Robertson, J. and Howells, C. (2008) 'Computer game design: Opportunities for successful learning'. *Computers and Education*, 50: 559–78.
Roffey, C. (2012) *Python coding club level 1–3.* New York: Cambridge University Press.

Useful websites

www.scratch.ie
www.scratch.mit.edu
www.scratched.mit.edu
www.learnscratch.org

References

ACARA (2013). *The Australian curriculum: Mathematics.* Available online at: www.australian curriculum.edu.au/Australian%20Curriculum.pdf?type=0&a=M&l=3&e=4&x=0. Accessed on 19 June 2013.
Barab, S., Thomas, M., Dodge, T., Carteaux, R. and Tuzun, H. (2005) 'Making learning fun: Quest Atlantis, A game without guns'. *Educational Technology Research and Development*, 53(*1*): 86–107.
Bitter, G. and Pierson, M. (2007) *Using technology in the classroom* (7th edn). Boston, MA: Allyn and Bacon.
Clements, D.H. (1999) 'The future of educational computing research: The case of computer programming'. *Information Technology in Childhood Education Annual*, 1999(*1*): 147–79. Available online from the EdITLib database at: www.editlib.org/p/10815/. Accessed on 12 June 2012.
Department of Education and Skills (DES) (1999) *Primary school curriculum: Introduction.* Dublin: The Stationery Office.
Department of Education and Science (DES) (2002) *Preparing teachers for the 21st century: Report of the Working Group on Primary Preservice Teacher Education.* Dublin: Stationery Office.
diSessa, A.A. (2000) *Changing minds: Computers, learning, and literacy.* Cambridge, MA: MIT Press.
Gee, J.P. (2003) *What video games have to teach us about learning and literacy* (1st edn). New York: Palgrave Macmillan.

Green, T.R.G. and Petre, M. (1996) 'Usability analysis of visual programming environments: A 'cognitive dimensions' framework'. *Journal of Visual Languages and Computing*, 7: 131–74.

Hayes, E. and Games, I. (2008) 'Learning through game design: A review of current software and research'. *Games and Culture*, 3: 309–32.

Hiebert, J., Carpenter, T.O., Fennema, E., Fuson, K., Human, P., Murray, H., Olivier, A. and Wearne, D. (1996) 'Problem solving as a basis for reform in curriculum and instruction: The case of mathematics'. *Educational Researcher*, 25(4): 12–21.

Kafai, Y.B. (1995) *Minds in play: Computer game design as a context for learning*. Hillsdale, NJ: Lawrence Erlbaum Associates.

Kafai, Y., Franke, M., Ching, C. and Shih, J. (1998) 'Game design as an interactive learning environment for fostering students' and teachers' mathematical inquiry'. *International Journal of Computers for Mathematical Learning*, 3(2): 149–84.

Maloney, J.H., Peppler, K., Kafai, Y., Resnick, M. and Rusk, N. (2008) 'Programming by choice: Urban youth learning programming with Scratch'. In *SIGCSE '08: Proceedings of the 39th SIGCSE technical symposium on computer science education*, pp. 367–71.

Marshall, A.M., Superfine, A.C. and Canty, R.S. (2010) 'Star students make connections'. *Teaching Children Mathematics*, 17(1): 38–47.

National Council of Teachers of Mathematics Commission on Standards for School Mathematics (NCTM) (2000). *Principles and standards for school mathematics*. Reston, VA: NCTM.

NCCA (2004) *Information and Communication Technology (ICT) in the primary school: Curriculum guidelines for teachers*. Dublin: NCCA. Available online at: www.ncca.ie/uploadedfiles/Publications/ICTPrimary.pdf. Accessed on 15 June 2013.

The New Zealand Curriculum (NZC) (2007) *The New Zealand Curriculum*. Available online at: http://nzcurriculum.tki.org.nz/Curriculum-documents/The-New-Zealand-Curriculum. Accessed on 24 February 2013.

Papert, S. (1980) *Mindstorms: Children, computers and powerful ideas*. New York: Basic Books.

Resnick, M., Maloney, J., Monroy-Hernandez, A., Rusk, N., Eastmond, E., Brennan, K., Millner, A., Rosenbaum, E., Silver, J., Silverman, B. and Kafai, Y. (2009) 'Scratch: Programming for all'. *Communications of the ACM*, 52(11): 60–7.

Robertson, J. and Good, J. (2005) 'Children's narrative development through computer game authoring'. *TechTrends*, 49(5): 43–59.

Robertson, J. and Good, J. (2006) 'Supporting the development of interactive storytelling skills in teenagers'. *Lecture Notes in Computer Science*, 3942, 348.

Squire, K. (2006) 'From content to context: Videogames as designed experience'. *Educational Researcher*, 35(8): 19–29.

Vygotsky, L.S. (1978) *Mind in society: The development of higher psychological processes*. Cambridge, MA: Harvard University Press.

Wilson, A. and Moffat, D.C. (2012) *Evaluating Scratch to introduce younger school children to programming*. Available online at: http://scratched.media.mit.edu/sites/default/files/wilson-moffat-ppig2010-final.pdf. Accessed on 22 February 2013.

Wing, J.M. (2006) 'Computational thinking'. *Communications of the ACM*, Viewpoint, 49(3): 33–5.

18 ICT and assessment

Gary Beauchamp

Introduction

Assessment is an integral part of the everyday life of teachers. Indeed, the main challenge facing us in this chapter is to reconsider how familiar assessment practices can be adapted, radically changed or replaced with the use of ICT. An added complication is the constant and fast-moving development of technology, allied to the fact that many pupils begin primary school as highly skilled and experienced users of technology. We need to consider how best to use these skills and experiences to allow pupils to take not only an active part in their own learning, but also in the assessment of themselves and others. In the past, assessment was often something that was done *to* pupils. Although elements of this remain in some types of summative assessments, increasingly pupils are seen as active partners in their learning, and assessment is something that is done *with* them and *for* them. Indeed, it may be argued that assessment is also done for the parents of these pupils and we need to consider how to involve them in the process and share relevant information using a variety of media to help them gain a better understanding of how their child is achieving. In this chapter we will explore how all members of the school community can benefit from using ICT in assessment.

Objectives

At the end of this chapter you should be able to:

- make the distinction between the assessment *of* ICT and assessment *with* ICT;
- recognise the potential of ICT for assessment;
- identify the affordances of ICT in supporting assessment for learning;
- perceive the potential of ICT to instigate, implement, share and provide feedback on assessments to learners and the wider school community.

In the past, most primary-school assessments were paper-based or involved verbal questioning. Any paper-based activity provided an obvious record of what the pupil had achieved, and it had always been possible to make audio recordings of group or individual discussions. What is new, for instance in written tests, is ICT's ability to facilitate a wide variety of means of undertaking and recording written tasks, being able to build them collaboratively (such as blogs and wikis), to transform the sharing of assessments (for instance by scanning and emailing, or putting on a website), or to distribute them to a potential worldwide audience. In addition, the use of sound recordings can now be enhanced by high-quality video and all recordings can be easily undertaken, edited and distributed, often from one device by pupils or teachers. Hence, as a teacher the lens you adopt to look at assessment *with*, and *of*, ICT must take account of the many advances both in technology and pupils' ability to use it. Before we consider these in more detail, however, we need to explore the essential distinction between assessment *with* and the assessment *of* ICT and why we bother using ICT in such activities.

Assessment *with* and assessment *of* ICT: why bother?

In this chapter, assessment *with* ICT is where both teachers and pupils use any ICT tool or resource to make a judgement about progress in a range of subjects or areas of learning. Assessment *of* ICT is defined as any activities when these judgements are about progress only in ICT in itself. Prior to looking at these activities in more detail, however, we need to briefly consider why we should use ICT at all in assessment. The justification provided by Becta is that 'technology can support large improvements to the efficiency and effectiveness of institution-based information and assessment processes, including setting, submission and return of work and all aspects of recording and reporting of information' (2009: 7). While this may be true, transforming this potential into practice is less straightforward, and the same report concluded that:

> Though the picture is increasingly positive in relation to classroom [ICT] use, ICT co-ordinators are less confident that teachers are making best use of technology in other ways. 23 per cent (primary) and 28 per cent (secondary) are 'quite' or 'very' confident about teachers using technology well to communicate with parents and 52 per cent (primary) and 50 per cent (secondary) are 'quite' or 'very' confident that teachers use technology well for assessment of learning.
>
> (Becta, 2009: 11)

While using technology to communicate with parents may well have improved since this time with a wider use of social media, such as Twitter, we can be less sure about changes in the use of technology in assessment. For instance, two years later, in a summary of schools from 2008 to 2011, Ofsted reported that 'the use of assessment was a considerable weakness in both the primary and secondary schools visited' (Ofsted, 2011: 6).

At this stage it is useful to consider the features of ICT use in assessment that OFSTED found as good or outstanding in English schools. They report that:

> effective tracking systems assisted teachers, pupils and parents to focus on the priorities for progress for each pupil. In a few schools the school intranet was used to store electronic profiles, making access easy for pupils and parents. Pupils were knowledgeable about their current standards and personal targets for improvement. The effective use of 'I can' statements to track pupil progress was seen in several schools. Learning objectives, set out at the start and end of lessons, included an ICT objective alongside objectives relating to other subjects.
>
> (2011: 37)

We should note here that teachers, pupils and parents are involved in the process and all gain from it. To achieve this, schools need to exploit the features of ICT to facilitate a range of activities in both formative and summative assessment.

Types of assessment

For the purposes of this chapter we will divide assessment into two types: formative and summative. The distinction between formative assessment, which explores understanding and identifies next steps, and summative assessment, a more formalised summing up, is well documented. Mansell *et al.* (2009: 9) highlight the fact that these terms should not be used as labels for different types of assessment, but rather describe how these types of assessments are used. They provide a useful list, Table 18.1, of the characteristic differences between them, which will help us to consider the use of ICT in assessment in this chapter.

Table 18.1 Characteristic differences between formative and summative assessment

Formative assessment	Summative assessment
– part of the learning process	– comes at the end
– attempts to develop learning	– assesses learning at a chosen point in time – normally by the teacher or examining board
– on-going and dynamic, between both pupil and teacher	– static and one-way, normally done by a teacher or examiner to a pupil
– 'follows the flow of spontaneous dialogue and interaction, where one action builds on (is contingent upon) an earlier one'	– 'follows a set of pre-defined questions'. (Mansell *et al.*, 2009: 9)

Black and Wiliam (2009: 8) assert that formative assessment consists of five key strategies:

1 Clarifying and sharing learning intentions and criteria for success.
2 Engineering effective classroom discussions and other learning tasks that elicit evidence of student understanding.
3 Providing feedback that moves learners forward.
4 Activating students as instructional resources for one another.
5 Activating students as the owners of their own learning.

Task 18.1 Formative assessment and the affordances of ICT

On your own, or in discussion with others, consider each of the five key strategies above in turn and identify how particular ICT resources (such as the interactive whiteboard) can be used in each.

The role of ICT in formative assessment could perhaps better be labelled as formative e-assessment, which is:

the use of ICT to support the iterative process of gathering and analysing information about student learning by teachers as well as learners and of evaluating it in relation to prior achievement and attainment of intended, as well as unintended learning outcomes, in a way that allows the teacher or student to adjust the learning trajectory.

(Pachler *et al.*, 2009: 1)

This definition establishes that pupils are equally as important in assessment as the teacher, and that this process is continual and not a one-off event. In addition, it is vital to remember that 'no assessment technology is in itself formative, but almost any technology can be used in a formative way – if the right conditions are set in place' (Pachler *et al.*, 2009: 2).

Having established these essential distinctions between formative and summative assessment, we now need to look at assessment *of* and *with* ICT.

Assessment *of* ICT

Assessment *of* ICT itself can be a problematic area. One issue of concern is that if we treat ICT as a separate 'subject', it is assessed as a set of decontextualized skills, which is at odds with its normal integration into a range of subjects.

In the past, McCormick (2004: 119) asserted that:

> This is illustrated in UK primary schools where teachers teach ICT separately from its use in numeracy, literacy, etc., exacerbated by the fact that this teaching is done in separate ICT suites. Thus the teacher takes the class down to the suite perhaps once a week for an hour for the ICT lesson. This militates both against the use of ICT to support learning across the curriculum and the development of learners' capacity to know when and how to use ICT as an everyday tool and as a support to their learning.

Even if you do not teach ICT this way now, it is important to remember that ICT is not only a skill, but also an integral part of the learning process, and with growing emphasis on pupil voice it is important that they also have a voice in when and how they should use ICT, including in assessment.

If ICT is assessed as part of subject teaching, we need to be careful that we distinguish between assessment of the subject area skills (such as history) and knowledge of the ICT component (such as creating a presentation about the history topic). This is important as Ofsted (2008: 1) states that 'schools need more help with assessing pupils' ICT capability and identifying underachievement'. Nevertheless, when assessing ICT capability

---

Task 18.2 Establishing assessment criteria

The pupils in your class produce a group PowerPoint presentation on the Romans. Discuss with other student teachers, or reflect on your own, how you would assess this. What factors do you need to assess (are you looking at the ICT skills, their historical knowledge, their punctuation or grammar, their teamwork, their presentation skills, their awareness of audience?) and how important is each factor? Perhaps you could devise a weighted set of criteria? Would this be appropriate? How would you share, or explain, these objectives with the pupils?

in an ever-changing world, a central challenge is the 'need to develop assessment practices which respond to new approaches to learning and new competencies we expect learners to develop' (Owen *et al.*, 2006: 5). This view is echoed by others, such as John and Wheeler (2008: 77), who point out that 'assessing learning within the subject of ICT can be problematic, due to the complex interplay between fine motor skills (keyboard, mouse), learning and cognition'.

Assessment *with* ICT

Earlier we defined assessment *with* ICT as where both teachers and pupils use any ICT tool or resource to make a judgement about progress in a range of subjects or area of learning. In order to make a decision about whether you should use ICT to undertake an assessment, you need to consider the special features of ICT that can be used. In doing this, you should recognise that assessment can take many forms, or modes, such as visual, sounds and text, and that ICT has the capability to work with all of these. In addition, we should also remember that many existing assessments that do not use ICT remain valid. There may be times, however, where the features of ICT mean that it is better to use ICT in assessment, or there may be ways in which ICT can enhance or even replace existing assessments. In making such decisions, we need to consider what ICT is good at and reflect on whether we should use it or not.

The affordances of ICT – what is ICT good at?

The first step in this process is to consider the affordances ICT offers. An affordance 'refers to the perceived and actual properties of a thing, primarily those functional properties that determine just how the thing could possibly be used' (Pea, 1993: 51). While the actual properties of a piece of technology, such as the pen for an interactive whiteboard, can be obvious, some are less so, but 'the affordance is there, it has always has been there, but it needs to be perceived to be realised ... The world is full of potential, not of things' (Hammond, 2010: 206). At this stage, we should note that the affordances can be seen by both pupils and teachers. To help recognise the affordances of ICT for assessment we need to consider what ICT itself is actually good at. Kennewell and Beauchamp (2007) suggest the key features of ICT are:

- *Speed*: making processes happen more quickly than other methods.
- *Automation*: making previously tedious or effortful processes happen automatically (other than changing the form of representation).
- *Capacity*: the storage and retrieval of large amounts of material.
- *Range*: access to materials in different forms and from a wider range of sources than otherwise possible.
- *Interactivity*: in this case, the ability to respond to user input repeatedly.
- *Provisionality*: the facility to change content, and change back if necessary.

Pachler *et al.* (2009) also add:

- *Communication*: the rapid sharing of ideas to a range of audiences by one person, a group, a whole class or school in a way that can be captured (for instance in a podcast).

It is these features, and others, that provide the affordances of assessment with ICT, and we should note that these features apply to all forms of ICT, ranging from classroom computers and interactive whiteboards to a range of mobile devices, from laptops to iPads. We will now consider each of these features in turn and discuss the potential they offer to help with assessment.

Speed

Before we consider the potential benefits of the speed of ICT we need to remember that 'although ICT allows things to happen quickly, the teacher remains central to the *control* of this speed, guided by the needs of the learners' (Beauchamp, 2012: 4). Nevertheless, if a pupil has produced a piece of work the ability to take a digital photograph, sound recording or movie in an instant can be vital to making a record of something that would otherwise be ephemeral, and mobile devices play an important role here. Examples of this could be the recording of spontaneous composition of a piece of music or a pupil explaining how they completed a task. Having completed an assessment quickly, however, it is also important to be able to store this somewhere that is safe and easily accessible. In this instance, the use of mobile devices linked to cloud storage solutions, or a school network, are very important. Even if a device, such as a movie camera, cannot connect wirelessly to a storage space, nearly all can either be connected directly to a computer or have removable storage cards that can be used to transfer images, movies or sound files to other devices. Again, the ability to do this quickly saves you time. This can also be important if, for instance, pupils have recorded their own sequences in a PE lesson and want to review them straightaway on the interactive whiteboard back in the classroom. Another use of speed, which has come with advances in access to the Internet, is the ability to share evidence assessment (see also 'communication' below) with a range of stakeholders almost immediately.

Automation

When using mobile devices, such as an iPad or other tablet, the fact that the device can make an automatic backup (if configured to the 'Cloud' during setup) of all images if connected to a wireless network is a good example of the benefits of automation in assessment activities and record keeping. Although there are always potential technical difficulties, this automatic and fast backup of assessment materials makes it well worth the initial effort in setting it up. Other examples of automation might include saving a mind-mapping exercise undertaken by groups or the whole class on an interactive whiteboard – which can then quickly be shared with others or emailed to you to help in future planning and assessment.

Another potential benefit of automation in assessment is the ability to search for electronic examples of a pupil's work much more quickly than if it was in a folder, in a box in a cupboard somewhere in the school. This does assume that there is an agreed policy for the format of naming electronic files (such as Y4_class 3_group 3_reversible changes) and this is something that you should consider carefully when saving assessments – a basic minimum perhaps being the pupil's name and the date of the assessment including the year.

Capacity

We have already briefly discussed the potential benefits of storing assessments, but the ability to retrieve them (quickly) from different places can be just as important. This can apply to both teachers and pupils, and indeed parents. In the past, much of the evidence of assessment took up a lot of much-needed space and was potentially hard to access. With the use of Cloud storage, school networks, virtual learning environments (VLEs), websites, blogs and so on we are only limited by our imagination and the amount of storage the school makes available. This does not mean that we need to neglect storing and moving records of work via USB pen drives or similar, but it does mean that the range of options available is now much wider, potentially more secure, and accessible to more people (including inspectors) from more places.

Range

As technology advances, there is an ever-increasing range of devices and affordances available to teachers to use in assessment with ICT. While this is important for all pupils, it can be particularly beneficial in providing a medium to interact *with* and *through* for those with particular needs, or for very young children who are not yet ready to undertake assessments that involve the ability to interpret text or respond in writing.

Using ICT as a form of assessment for those with special needs can form part of what Abbott (2007: 6) calls 'e-inclusion', which is 'the use of digital technologies to enable inclusive learning practices for people with learning difficulties'. For instance, pupils who have difficulty with writing can now make a video or audio recording of their thoughts, which is just as valid as an assessment as a written task or picture. In addition, the use of voice-recognition software can help pupils with visual impairments or other needs that make it hard to type. Furthermore, pupils whose handwriting may be hard to understand can produce legible records of their work through the use of keyboards (both real and virtual).

Another advantage of assessment *with* ICT is that it can be presented in a wide range of formats, many of which can be less intimidating than some more traditional forms of assessment. For instance, an assessment can be made much more engaging and motivating through the use of games-based assessment activities, both those produced by commercial organisations and, increasingly, assessments developed by teachers themselves – see, for example, Mr Andrews online (http://tinyurl.com/p8y563s). The latter have the advantage of allowing the teacher to personalise the assessment to their class and make it more engaging by using settings familiar to the children, such as their classroom or school.

Interactivity

The use of games-based assessments is a good example of the use of interactivity as an affordance of ICT. Although there are many different definitions of interactivity in ICT, in this context it applies to its ability to respond to user input repeatedly – without getting bored! Kennewell and Beauchamp (2007: 231) defined this type of interactivity as *feedback*, which is 'the provision of a response by the tool which is contingent on action by the user'. The response can take many forms ranging from sound effects (for right or wrong answers) to spoken feedback (but only pre-programmed responses).

Hence, ICT can be very effective if the assessment only requires the collection of scores (for example in a maths test, where results can be easily collated and shared for later use), the completion of multiple-choice-type questions, or other assessments that do not require formative feedback. We need to remember that ICT devices allow pupils 'to make the same mistake every time as, unless it is programmed to do so, ICT resources are not really able to give a response which allows for personalised formative feedback'. (Beauchamp, 2012: 7) This means we need to consider carefully how to use interactivity and assessment with ICT.

Provisionality

The ability of ICT to change content, and the way it is presented, can be very important in making assessments accessible, stimulating and relevant. Although many commercially-produced assessment materials cannot be changed, some do allow you to personalise assessment tasks, and any materials that you produce yourself can be retrieved and amended. This can take the form of editing existing assessment materials for a new class to reflect a change in curriculum requirements or using the features of ICT to create assessments in electronic formats, taking advantage of the multimodal capability of ICT.

Provisionality, in this case the ability to change the representation of materials or data, can also apply to assessment activities undertaken in the classroom. For instance, on the interactive whiteboard you can change tasks, for example an addition sum, if it proves too difficult or is presented in the wrong format. In addition, with the use of the 'undo' and 'redo' feature, you can then quickly return to the original task in its original format.

Communication

Although communication (the 'C' in ICT) has been central to ICT teaching and use, recent advances in the availability of portable devices and increased accessibility and speed of the Internet means it now occupies an even more central role. These communications can now involve the use of many media and modes, and can take place in real time (synchronous), will be recorded and accessed later (asynchronous). These communications can be saved to ensure that they provide a record of achievement (assessment), but can also be used as a potential teaching tool for future years. For example, if a group of pupils make a podcast that shows what they have learned, this not only provides a record of their achievement that can be shared with a global audience if required, but can also be used by the teacher as an example of what a podcast actually is with a future class. There are, of course, potential e-safety issues that need to be considered, but this should not prevent primary teachers making full use of the ability to communicate, and indeed celebrate, the achievements of their pupils.

Having briefly examined the features of ICT that can be used in assessment, we will now turn to consider how these can be used to instigate, implement and feedback on assessments for whole classes, groups and individuals.

Task 18.3 Audiences for assessed work

Consider Figure 18.1 below, which shows some of the potential audiences for pupils' assessments. In discussion with other students, or on your own, decide:

1　Is this list complete? If not, who needs to be added?
2　How could you share these assessments using ICT (for example, through the school website?) And who would you share them with?
3　How can you ensure that the assessments are only seen by their intended audience?

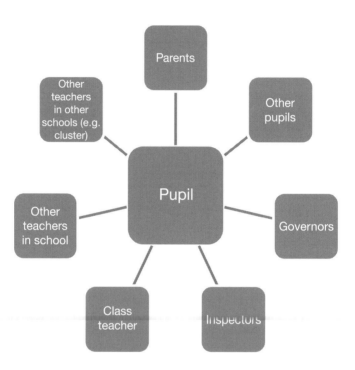

Figure 18.1 Audiences for assessed work.

Mobility

Perhaps the most significant advance in recent years is in the availability, affordability and sophistication of mobile technologies. In the case of assessment, this opens up a large number of new opportunities to set up, mark, feedback and share these assessments in a wide range of settings, both inside and especially outside of the classroom – which can be particularly useful in early years settings. While primary teachers have had the opportunity to use digital cameras (both still and moving image), sound recorders (which can now nearly all be plugged easily straight into a computer), as well as laptops and fixed PCs, in the past these were often separate devices. In addition, material from these devices needed to be transferred to a laptop or PC to be shared. Recent advances in mobile technology mean that not only are all of these facilities available in one device, but results can now be shared instantly both within the classroom and beyond. The ability to mirror these devices on other classroom technologies, such as the interactive whiteboard, opens up opportunities for peer assessment, as well as discussion of ideas, which we will return to below. This also allows opportunities to use the features of other ICT resources, such as the ability to annotate assessment work undertaken outside of the classroom on the interactive whiteboard as a means of feedback by the class teacher.

Case study 18.1 Use of iPads for assessment

An early evaluation of iPad implementation in six primary schools in Wales identified the importance of the iPad in terms of supporting assessment. Teachers in all six schools reported that the iPad was useful in terms of self-assessment and/or teacher assessment. They reported that, in terms of self-assessment, the use of high-quality video recording (in this case, iMovie) was useful to record and play back activities for pupils to evaluate their own work. The very nature of the iPad as a mobile device was regarded useful as pupils could use the iPad to record their work around different areas of the school, rather than being confined to classroom space. Teachers in one school noted that self-assessment was particularly easy, not only with the iPad but also, with the compatibility of Apple TV (which only required a basic wireless connection for instant assessment), in allowing pupils to present work to their peers. Teachers in all six schools also discussed the usefulness of the iPad for collecting alternative forms of evidence for their own assessment purposes. Teachers mentioned this was particularly valuable for pupils who were not able to create formal, written work as they could use a variety of alternative multimodal methods to record, create and store their work using a range of different integrated tools, including the camera and iMovie or specific presentation apps, including Keynote and Popplet (see Beauchamp and Hillier, 2014).

----

e-Portfolios

The ability to store and access information in a variety of formats is very significant in the use of e-portfolios and, with the growth in the use of devices connected to Cloud storage, the increased use of mobile devices and the ease with which both pupils and teachers can use these devices to record and share achievements, the construction and sharing of e-portfolios will become easier and more widespread. In fact, many schools may actually be using e-portfolios without even knowing it as they call them other things such as 'learning journeys' or even class blogs.

There are many definitions of what an e-portfolio is, but Becta (2007, p. 6) suggests that:

> e-portfolios are part of a personal online space, where learners can store their work, record their achievements (a repository function), and access personal course timetables (an organising function), digital resources relevant to their own study (personalised information) and links to other learners (for collaboration and feedback). The focus is clearly on space for learning.

In this definition it is clear that e-portfolios are both a product and a process (JISC, 2008). In other words, it is not just the ability to store and access information that is important, but also the involvement of pupils over a period of time in making decisions about what information to store that best demonstrates their achievements. This view is supported by Ultralab (2004: 9), which suggests that:

> any assessment tool or process which aims to enable the pupils to reflect on their work over time, allow them to share their thinking and the early drafts of their work, give them meaningful feedback from their teacher and their peers, empower them and provide the teacher with a variety of evidence to support their judgements surely has to be worth a consideration.

The context in which e-portfolios are used, however, is central to their success. Becta (2007: 4) advises that:

> e-portfolios benefit learning most effectively when considered as part of a joined-up teaching and learning approach, rather than as a discrete entity. The approach should include online repositories, planning and communication tools, and opportunities for both students and teachers to draw out and present e-portfolios at particular times and for particular purposes. There is then likely to be substantial impact on both learning processes and learning outcomes.

The potential for using digital portfolios in primary school is also supported by Wall *et al.* (2006: 271), who found that:

> a digital portfolio has the potential to create independent learners who are responsible for the collection of their own evidence of achievements across the curriculum and this process has an impact on the pupils and how they perceive themselves and their learning.

This potential of the use of e-portfolios in primary schools is also recognised by Estyn (Her Majesty's Chief Inspector of Education and Training in Wales), who noted that 'where assessment of ICT is good, schools ... have comprehensive portfolios or e-portfolios containing annotated examples of current pupil work for all the ICT skills' (2013: 21).

Case study 18.2 e-Portfolios

One current example of the use of e-portfolios is in primary schools in East Renfrewshire in Scotland, where a cluster of primary schools worked with their associated secondary school and a national support agency (National Glow Team) to create e-portfolios in the form of blogs. The process was that:

> Each pupil created a Glow Group in their My Glow area and into that Group they added a Glow Blog. It is the Glow Blog that is used as their e-portfolio. All staff were made members of the Glow Group where the blog lives. This membership alone, however, does not enable them to access the e-portfolio. Since no one can access another user's My Glow area, pupils additionally had to provide staff with a

link to their blog. This link to the view of the blog was added to a web links web part in a school e-portfolio Glow Group. This Group had been created ahead of time in preparation for the pupil sessions.

Pupils learned how to add content to their blog by writing posts, categorising and tagging them, adding media such as images and attaching documents. They also learned how staff can comment on the posts and where they can then access those comments from.

(http://tinyurl.com/3gcljpd)

(The above link to Glow e-portfolio's site also provides videos explaining each part of the process in detail.)

Each primary school used the pupil e-portfolios in different ways – one school links their portfolios to pupil profiles that contain:

the pupil's reflections on their learning, their progress through the curricular areas, information on achievements across learning plus a section for parental comment on their child's progress.

In ICT time, pupils add information to their e-portfolios about their weekly achievements, to build a permanent record throughout the year. This will be used at the end of the year to help pupils complete their profiles. These will then be attached to their e-portfolios.

Staff can access each pupil's e-portfolio and comment on the posts that pupils write and parents can view the e-portfolios when their child logs in to Glow at home to show them.

(http://tinyurl.com/6p73fnh)

The interactive whiteboard

Although not a mobile device, in recent years researchers have begun to focus on the role of the interactive whiteboard (IWB) as a 'digital hub' (including for mobile devices), which provides opportunities for assessment activities. This can apply to individuals, groups or even the whole class. This is particularly effective in assessing pupil's knowledge and understanding through encouraging dialogue and discussion. Mercer, Hennessy and Warwick (2010: 195) highlight how the IWB can encourage a 'dialogic pedagogy' in which pupils actively build on the contribution of other pupils and 'engages both teachers and students in generating and critically evaluating ideas, and encourages explicit reasoning and the joint construction of knowledge'. While there is not space to discuss this in more detail, the ability of the interactive whiteboard to provide a multimodal platform for pupils to make explicit their reasoning and understanding in a way that can be seen by others is an affordance for assessment that we should recognise in the IWB. As a means of assessment, this enables both other pupils and the teacher to ask questions that probe understanding, but also allows the person using the IWB to have a range of tools at their disposal to help with their explanations. Other studies have found that this can be effective in a range of subjects, including science (Murcia and Sheffield, 2010), history (Deaney, Chapman and Hennessy, 2009) and Personal, Social, Health and Citizenship Education (PSHCE) (Warwick, Hennessy and Mercer, 2011).

In all the uses of technology we have seen above, there is a need for you and your pupils to develop technical skills to make full use of assessment with ICT. Nevertheless this investment can be worth it as the affordances offered by the use of a range of technologies can considerably enhance the timeliness, quality and range of assessments that can be undertaken by both you and your pupils. Ultimately, effective use of ICT in assessment will depend on what Vanderlinde and van Braak define as the e-capacity of a school. They suggest that 'e-capacity is concerned with creating and optimising sustainable school level and teacher level conditions to foster effective change through ICT' (2010: 542). As primary schools develop their e-capacity, and teachers and pupils see the affordances of ICT in assessment, all members of the school community will benefit from more creative assessment *of* and *with* ICT, which caters for the needs of *all* learners and exploits the ever-expanding capabilities of technology.

Summary and key points

In this chapter we have explored the distinction between the assessment *of* and assessment *with* ICT in formative and summative assessment. In both these areas, the features of ICT (such as speed, range, capacity and communication) offer a range of affordances for assessment in all areas of learning, at all ages and of all abilities. We have seen that it is essential for both pupils and teachers to recognise these affordances and that this enables assessments to be shared with a wide range of stakeholders, both within the school community and beyond. In the primary school, pupils' achievements can often be spontaneous and transitory, and it is only through the use of technology that some of these can be captured and shared. It is only by recognising the potential of ICT in assessment that primary schools can use technology as a means of recording, celebrating and sharing the achievements of pupils in many forms, from annotated explanations to musical performances to creative writing, blogs and podcasts.

If you are a student teacher check which requirements for your course you have addressed through this chapter.

Additional resources and websites

Assessment with ICT

Using the IWB to support classroom dialogue

http://dialogueiwb.educ.cam.ac.uk/resources/resourcebank/: This site provides ideas for IWB activities that can be used to promote dialogue, which is central to effective formative assessment.

Assessment with ICT in early years

http://ictearlyyears.e2bn.org/planning3_35.html: This is part of a website that looks at how ICT can be used in early years settings. This particular page looks at how ICT can be used to both record and communicate assessments, including how to involve children in their own assessments.

Assessment of ICT

Using ICT – assessment tasks from Northern Ireland for KS1/2

www.nicurriculum.org.uk/key_stages_1_and_2/skills_and_capabilities/uict/tasks_and_exemplification/task_list/index.asp#top

Lancashire Grid for Learning

www.lancsngfl.ac.uk/curriculum/ict/index.php?category_id=301: This is an example local authority publication considering ICT Progression in EYFS, KS1 and KS2.

www.simonhaughton.co.uk/2011/11/my-assessment-arrangements-for-ict.html: This is one teacher's blog on his assessment arrangements for ICT.

References

Abbot, C. (2007) *e-Inclusion: Learning difficulties and digital technologies*. London: Futurelab.

Beauchamp, G. (2012) *ICT in the primary school: From pedagogy to practice*. London: Pearson.

Beauchamp, G. and Hillier, E. (2014) *An evaluation of iPad implementation across a network of primary schools in Cardiff*. Cardiff: Cardiff School of Education.

Becta (2007) *Impact study of e-portfolios on learning*. Coventry: Becta.

Becta (2009) *Harnessing technology review 2009: The role of technology in education and skills*. Coventry: Becta.

Black, P. and Wiliam, D. (2009) 'Developing the theory of formative assessment'. *Educational Assessment, Evaluation and Accountability*, 21(1): 5–31.

Deaney, R., Chapman, A. and Hennessy, S. (2009) 'A case-study of one teacher's use of an interactive whiteboard system to support knowledge co-construction in the history classroom'. *Curriculum Journal*, 20(4): 365–87.

Estyn (2013) *The impact of ICT on pupils' learning in primary schools*. Cardiff: Estyn.

Hammond, M. (2010) 'What is an affordance and can it help us understand the use of ICT in education?'. *Education and Information Technology*, 15: 205–17.

JISC (2008) *Effective practice with e-portfolios: Supporting 21st century learning*. Available online at: http://jisc.ac.uk/media/documents/publications/effectivepracticeeportfolios.pdf. Accessed on 23 May 2013.

John, P.D. and Wheeler, S. (2008) *The digital classroom: Harnessing technology for the future of learning and teaching*. London: Routledge.

Kennewell, S. and Beauchamp, G. (2007) 'The features of interactive whiteboards and their influence on learning'. *Learning, Media and Technology*, 32(3): 227–41.

McCormick, R. (2004) 'ICT and pupil assessment', *Curriculum Journal*, 15(2): 115–137.

Mansell, W., James, M. and the Assessment Reform Group (2009) *Assessment in schools. Fit for purpose? A commentary by the teaching and learning research programme*. London: Economic and Social Research Council, Teaching and Learning Research Programme.

Mercer, N., Hennessy, S. and Warwick, P. (2010) 'Using interactive whiteboards to orchestrate classroom dialogue'. *Technology, Pedagogy and Education*, 19(2): 195–209.

Murcia, K. and Sheffield, R. (2010) 'Talking about science in interactive whiteboard classrooms'. *Australasian Journal of Educational Technology*. 26(4): 417–31.

Ofsted (2008) ICT in primary and secondary schools: Ofsted's findings 2005/07. London: Ofsted.

Ofsted (2011) *ICT in schools 2008–11: An evaluation of information and communication technology education in schools in England 2008–11*. Available online at: www.ofsted.gov.uk/resources/110134. Accessed on 1 January 2014.

Owen, M., Grant, L., Sayers, S. and Facer, K. (2006) *Social software and learning*. Future lab. Available online at: http://archive.futurelab.org.uk/resources/publications-reports-articles/ opening-education-reports/Opening-Education-Report199. Accessed on 23 May 2014.

Pachler, N., Mellar, H., Daly, C., Mor, Y. and Wiliam, D. (2009) *Scoping a vision for formative e-assessment: A project report for JISC version 2.0*. London: Institute of Education.

Pea, R.D. (1993) 'Practices of distributed intelligence and designs for education'. In G. Salomon (ed.) *Distributed cognitions: Psychological and educational consideration*. Cambridge: Cambridge University Press (pp. 47–87).

Ultralab (2004) *Final report to QCA on the eVIVA project: 2002–2004*. London: Ultralab.

Vanderlinde, R. and van Braak, J. (2010) 'The e-capacity of primary schools: Development of a conceptual model and scale construction from a school improvement perspective'. *Computers and Education*, 55: 541–53.

Wall, K., Higgins, S., Miller, J. and Packard, N. (2006) 'Developing digital portfolios: Investigating how digital portfolios can facilitate pupil talk about learning'. *Technology, Pedagogy and Education*, 15(3): 261–73.

Warwick, P., Hennessy, S. and Mercer, N. (2011) 'Promoting teacher and school development through co-enquiry: Developing interactive whiteboard use in a dialogic classroom'. *Teachers and Teaching*, 17(3): 303–24.

19 Developing e-safety in the primary school

Tim Pinto and Sarah Younie

Introduction

The emergence of the Internet and mobile technologies has rapidly changed the way that people interact and communicate with others. In particular the development of Web 2.0 (2003) and the emergence of smartphones (2008) heralded a dramatic change in how the Internet became more personalised, with content specifically aimed at producing outcomes based on information provided by an individual. As the design of webpages began to change, so did concerns over the personal information that people could share with others. In 2002, the European Commission began initiatives around information and communication technology (ICT) to look at how systems could be put into place, to stop people from sharing information online with strangers.

Since the publication in the UK of the Byron reports (2008, 2010) there has been much focus on e-safety, through headlines in the media to the publication of specific standards used by OFSTED in Section 5 inspections. For primary schools, the greater use of technology by children aged between 4–11 has meant that there have been challenges for teachers in terms of educating children about risks, while keeping up to date with the latest trends in gaming, social networking and software apps. For those teaching at the primary level, there are great opportunities to empower children in supporting school structures through discussions over creating policies to utilise their digital skills to help support parents and younger pupils in the school.

Objectives

By the end of this chapter, you should be able to:

- demonstrate an understanding of e-safety and how this relates to primary-aged pupils;
- know where to locate information on e-safety for your professional practice and how to access e-safety resources specifically developed for primary-aged pupils.

Background

A major milestone in the United Kingdom was the publication of *Safer children in a digital world* (Byron, 2008), which was commissioned by the Department of Education amid fears that children could access harmful and inappropriate material via the Internet and playing computer games. The report highlighted a number of points:

- Direct contact could be made with children through the Internet and access to a range of inappropriate material through violent computer games.
- The popularity of computer games and the Internet among young people and the lack of critical evaluation skills when communicating with others online.
- The 'helplessness' of parents in being able to mange and control online access and the risks associated with sharing information.
- Corporate responsibility should be considered.

All of these concerns raised in the 2008 Bryon Report were addressed through setting up a national strategy group, called the UK Council for Child Internet Safety (UKCCIS). As Younie and Leask (2013) report, this was a seminal initiative in the UK and set 'a global precedent' (Bryon, 2010: 5) by creating a multi-stakeholder council for child Internet safety and established the UK as a world leader in children's digital safety. In order to increase awareness of how to keep safe online, UKCCIS (2009) advocate following the 'click clever, click safe code', with three simple things to remember to help keep pupils safe when online – *zip it, block it, flag it.*

Task 19.1 Understanding e-safety

- What do you understand by the terms 'e-safety' and 'safeguarding children online'?
- What do you consider to be the key issues relating to e-safety for primary aged pupils?
- How would you go about finding out more about e-safety and developing e-safety practices?

---

e-Safety policy in schools

In 2007 the Labour Government commissioned a review by child psychologist Prof. Tanya Bryon to assess the risks posed by the Internet. The Bryon Report of the following year recommended that all schools should have an 'Acceptable Use Policy', which is regularly reviewed, monitored and agreed with parents and pupils, and that all schools and local children's services use an accredited filtering service (Bryon, 2008: 9).

Following the Bryon Report in 2008, Ofsted was tasked to evaluate the extent to which schools educate pupils to adopt safe and responsible online practices (Ofsted, 2010). While the Internet offers multiple opportunities, particularly with the emergence of Web 2.0 technologies, such as social networking, online gaming, instant messaging and photo sharing, these activities can lead to risks from browsing inappropriate websites, anti-social behaviour and bullying to giving away private and personal information to unsecured sources. As other research shows, children reveal their identity to others at a far higher rate than their parents realise (Livingstone and Bober, 2005; Valcke *et al.*, 2006).

As highlighted by Younie and Leask (2013), the Bryon *Review of progress* in 2010 found that 'in Europe, 51% of teenagers use the internet without supervision from their parents and in the UK, 23% of parents with children under 11 allow their children to access the internet without supervision at home' (Bryon 2010: 10). Similarly, the Child Exploitation and Online Protection Centre (CEOP, 2007), set up to coordinate the central collection of cases for Internet-related abuse in the UK, reported that forty-nine per cent of young people surveyed have given out personal information, such as their full name, age, email address, phone number or name of their school, to someone that they met on the Internet, but, by contrast, only five per cent of parents think their child has given out such information (Livingstone and Bober, 2005: 22). Similarly, Shipton (2011) refers to a survey on young people's Internet safety by YoungPoll (Childalert, 2011), which found that the average 6–14-year-old communicates with more than 1100 people online in a year.

Consequently, a key aspect for primary schools in addressing e-safety is to create a policy for teachers, pupils and other stakeholders to follow. With the development of ICT, it is important that policies are 'living documents' and that they are incorporated into the daily workings of a school. Where they are most likely to fail is when they are not bespoke, but rather are 'badged' policies from another body, such as a local authority or other organization without thought and vision about what the school wants to gain from the document. As part of this process, it is important that the school decides who is responsible for writing an e-safety policy. Due to the size of some schools, the role can fall to the ICT coordinator to manage this and, while they do have the skillset to look at e-safety from the technology perspective, it is important that the school also looks at creating a policy that addresses the emotional aspects of using technology. The EU Kids Online project (see Hasebrink *et al.*, 2011) has highlighted that children need to be supported in terms of addressing risks and inappropriate content. The research 'In their own words: What bothers kids online?' (see Livingstone *et al.*, 2013) showed that children were alarmed by pornographic content (22%) and violent content (18%). This evidence shows that it is important that, in the creation of any policy, other members of staff, including those responsible for safeguarding and PHSE, need to be included in any policy-writing committee, as it is key that the policy reflects behaviour trends in using the technology.

Another important aspect in terms of developing an e-safety policy is to include pupils in the drafting of any document. In many ways, the policy is aimed at protecting them while using technology in school, but the principles behind any school policy will hopefully be reflected in their use of technology out of school via a robust curriculum model. Ways in which this can be done are via a school council or pupil-voice groups, but also by surveying pupils on their attitudes and behaviour online. For instance, very few policies address issues around social networking, yet many young children from the age of five use early incarnations of social media sites such as Club Penguin (www. clubpenguin.com) or Moshi Monsters (www.moshimonsters.com). As children outgrow these sites they move on to more mature sites such as Facebook (www.facebook.com/), which bring risks, especially in sharing personal information. In addressing the way that pupils behave online, the school can draft a policy that addresses attitudes and models behaviour towards ensuring that children see potential risks as they would in the same manner as road safety. Arguably, pupils can be included in the school's e-safety policy-writing group and pupils could take on the role of e-prefects and support how the school manages e-safety.

e-Prefects: pupils monitoring e-safety awareness

One key aspect in delivering the e-safety curriculum in a primary school is to look at developing peer educators, so that older pupils in school can talk to other pupils in school about online risks. There are some national initiatives such as the Anti-Bullying Ambassadors scheme (http://diana-award.org.uk/anti-bullying) that look at creating mentors, and while it is not specially focused on e-safety, it can easily be adapted to include this area.

Some schools have adopted an e-prefect system, which develops pupil ICT champions to help support the schools e-safety policy. Teacher, David Fuller suggests developing this e-prefect strategy as follows:

Schools need to consider a pupil's journey into the online world as that of a learner driver and the use of the Highway Code for their journey on a road. We invite you to think about how we can use such a strategy to help pupils 'drive' on their online road.

If we take the real world and a school environment, there are a number of layers of monitoring and safeguarding that occur daily. Some schools have prefects and they are chosen for their qualities that make them useful in this role, and they act as role models for other pupils as well as a link between the pupil body and the school. One strategy is to have e-prefects who do the same role but in the online world. Their function is to monitor and help in the smooth running of the digital playground where they are active members and can help others steer a clear path in the online world.

e-Prefect roles involve:

* receiving training on e-safety before taking up their role.
* monitoring the activities and actions of pupils of the school online, including any social networking sites; with reporting back on a regular basis to the teacher in charge of e-safety for the school.
* reporting immediately on any serious issues discovered.
* providing the school with a list of areas of concern where, in their opinion, loosening or tightening restrictions will make life easier and better for the pupil–school community as a whole.
* forming a part of the school ICT management team, rather like prefects have a voice on the school council. E-prefects should be involved in the writing of school policies on e-safety and AUP (Acceptable Use Policy).
* being given the trust to deal with minor issues in a similar manner to how a prefect deals with such issues in schools today; acting in an advisory manner.
* having some form of ownership of how the school works in the online world. This is key as, once pupils have that trust and they know there are consequences for actions (both positive and negative), then they will ensure that they look after that and be really proactive in ensuring that what is required is done.

e-Safety and data protection

Many schools focus on looking at issues based directly on technology and behaviour when drafting a policy and do not incorporate areas on information and data security. Procedures around e-safety should also include how data is managed to ensure that schools are creating a culture where great importance is put on passwords and accessing sensitive data sets. The Information Commissioner's Office (ICO) Report on Schools

(2012) showed that schools needed to address issues around data security as more schools use mobile technologies:

> We advise that procedures should be in place, and be followed, when any personal information that could be considered in any way private or confidential is taken from the school premises in electronic or paper format. For paper records, this doesn't have to be a complex procedure. Something as simple as a booking-in-and-out process could reduce risks if used in all cases and monitored. More complex procedures may be needed for personal information held on portable electronic devices.
>
> (Information Commissioner's Office, 2012: 7)

As primary schools move further to more electronic methods of accessing data via pupil management systems, it is important to ensure that procedures and good practice are an inherent part of teachers' roles and responsibilities. It is also important that, as pupils move to a more 'digital life' where passwords and biometrics will play an increasing part of their lives, they are educated on the importance of electronic security and they become more aware of how to create robust passwords.

Task 19.2 School policies on e-safety

- What is your school policy on e-safety?
- Do you know where to find your school's e-safety policy documents and have you read these? If not, please do so and once you have read the documents and this chapter, please consider if there is anything you would recommend amending in the school policy?
- Do pupils and other staff contribute to writing the e-safety and AUP (Acceptable Use Policy) for your school?
- Do you think e-prefects could be effectively deployed in your school?

ICT infrastructure in school

In 2010, OFSTED released a thematic study on e-safety (*The safe use of new technologies*), which highlighted the need for schools to install more managed networks and not lock down all Internet access:

> Pupils in the schools that had 'managed' systems had better knowledge and understanding of how to stay safe than those in schools with 'locked down' systems. Pupils were more vulnerable overall when schools used locked down systems because they were not given enough opportunities to learn how to assess and manage risk for themselves.
>
> (Ofsted, 2010: 5)

As part of their safeguarding commitments, schools need to ensure that they provide a filtering system, so pupils cannot access unsuitable or harmful material. Many primary schools use existing structures in their local authority for broadband connectivity, but in the increasing ICT marketplace, a number of schools are moving to commercial providers for online services. When schools are making decisions about protecting pupils and staff when using the Internet, they need to ensure that not only is there infrastructure in place to filter out content, but also that other services are in place to prevent pupils from downloading viruses.

Any system needs to be fit for purpose and one prevailing problem is the balance between innovation and safeguarding. Too many times, teachers are stopped from accessing particular websites or software because of the potential risk. For example, some schools do not deploy layered filtering systems, so a teacher can have access to a wider selection of sites compared to a pupil. YouTube (www.youtube.com/) is a typical example, with many service providers blocking access due to the potential access to unsuitable material. However, many teachers find the site a useful resource in delivering lessons and bemoan the fact that it is blocked by their broadband provider.

It is important that there is a layered approach to Internet access in schools, as in order to address issues around unsuitable content, schools need pupils to take risks and evaluate processes to deal with them. This is because the majority of Internet access for primary-aged pupils takes place outside of school, either in the home or using public wifi in other locations. While schools need to provide a duty of care and stop pupils accessing unsuitable sites in school, it is important that from a young age pupils are given the tools to tell a responsible adult if they stumble upon inappropriate sites. One example is the Hectors' World safety screensaver (http://bit.ly/fnGCsq), which can be installed onto computers and reduce the time in which a child has to look at an upsetting image or video. Strategies such as this are important for primary schools to address, in order that they assist in educating children (and parents) with ways in which to manage Internet use.

e-Safety and mobile devices

Over recent years, there has been a rapid increase in the use of mobile technologies in schools and many primaries have been eager to use tablets to assist with the learning process. While this is a welcome move, it is important that the infrastructure is addressed in order that pupils who use them can do so safely. Some earlier adopters have not thought about managing these systems and, in a number of cases, pupils have been able to bypass existing structures to access unsuitable content. It is important that the use of tablet devices such as the Apple iPad do not become the next 'white elephant' and that schools look at Mobile Device Management (MDM) so that they can control all sets of devices in school. Also, schools need to adapt and modify policies to reflect these changes and also ensure that if staff want to bring in their own personal device (often referred to as Bring Your Own Device – BYOD), they agree to specific stipulations about its use in school.

Curriculum resources for e-safety

As access to digital technology becomes more popular for younger children, it is growing more important for primary schools to organise a structured model of delivery to address all the potential risks associated with children's digital lives. As many children become more 'digital savvy', they need guidance and support while exploring the online world.

Over recent years, there has been a major expansion in the number of resources available through organisations such as CEOP (Child Exploitation and Online Protection Centre: http://ceop.police.uk/) and Childnet (www.childnet.com). Access to these resources is free and many include web-based games, videos and lesson plans aimed at specific year groups. It is important that the school evaluates the suitability of resources and also addresses issues that are relevant to specific pupil year groups. It is also recommended that staff receive training on the delivery of the resources, as the key message should be about empowerment and trust, rather than making children fearful about using technologies and the Internet. The review of ICT by Ofsted (2012) highlighted that the training of teachers was crucial and needed to be better implemented:

> Despite mostly good provision for e-safety, training for staff was identified as a relative weakness in the schools visited. Training did not always involve all the staff and was not provided systematically. Even the schools that organised training for all staff did not always monitor its impact thoroughly.
>
> (Ofsted, 2012: 43)

With the changes in technology and the development of the Internet, it is recommended that schools review their curriculum content in line with the National Curriculum but also with an awareness of any trends or issues that have arisen in relation to e-safety. Teachers can model the curriculum around the needs of the children through discussing concerns that they have around their online lives. A method of engaging with pupils is through the development of online questionnaires such as Surveymonkey (www.survey monkey.com). Data produced from the surveys can highlight whether pupils are using social networks at earlier ages or what types of technology they are using. This then can enable staff to design a curriculum that helps pupils deal with risks that hopefully they can use when they access the Internet outside of school. Table 19.1 provides a list of resources that you can use with pupils to highlight e-safety, which are all age appropriate.

Table 19.1 e-Safety resources to use with pupils

Year group	Content	Suggested packages
EYFS	Online stranger danger	Childnet www.childnet.com/resources/smartie-the-penguin
Year 1	Risk response strategies	Hectors World www.thinkuknow.co.uk/5_7/hectorsworld
Year 2	Sharing personal information	CEOP – 'Lee & Kim' www.thinkuknow.co.uk
Year 3	Introduction to e-safety Issues for Key Stage 2	Childnet – 'The Smart Crew' www.childnet.com/resources/the-adventures-of-kara-winston-and-the-smart-crew
Year 4	Cyberbullying	Yorkshire and Humber Grid For Learning – 'Daydreaming' www.yhgfl.net/eSafeguarding/e-safety /Cyberbullying/Curriculum-resources
Year 5	Social networking	CEOP – 'Jigsaw' www.thinkuknow.co.uk/
Year 6	Digital citizenship	www.digizen.org

We suggest the idea of 'digital citizenship' is an effective way of introducing the topic of e-safety and encouraging appropriate online behaviours. This provides a thematic approach to the e-safety curriculum and there is a growing bank of resources for teachers to use and adapt. For example, there is a range of resources from CEOP, Microsoft, ThinkUKnow, KidSmart, Digizen and Childnet International. Childnet provides materials on its website (www.childnet-int.org). 'Young People Safe Online' (Microsoft, 2007) is a set of online resources created by Microsoft aimed at teachers, pupils and parents. Specifically for primary-phase children, there is 'Welcome to Hector's World'(tm) (KS1), 'Lee and Kim's Adventure' (KS1–2) and 'Cyber Café' (KS2), which are from ThinkU Know (CEOP). Access to the CEOP resources are available through registering at: www.thinkuknow.co.uk/teachers/.

The e-safety resources outlined in this chapter are easy to access and are supported by notes for teachers. 'Staying Safe with Dongle' is from the CBBC Stay Safe website (BBC, 2010) and invites children to learn about Internet safety with Dongle the rabbit and the Stay Safe Quiz. 'The Smart Crew' is from KnowITAll by Childnet International and the 'Adventures of Captain Kara and Winston's SMART Adventure' are animations covering the five SMART rules, helping younger children understand the importance of keeping safe online. The cartoon clips are relatively short and convey the key ideas effectively, with a range of follow-up activities and lesson plans.

The 3 'Cs' conceptual framework for understanding e-safety

In preparing teacher training resources for primary pre-service teachers for the national subject association of IT in Teacher Education (ITTE), Woollard, Pickford and Younie (2010) drew on the recommendations of the Bryon Review (2008), in particular the 3 'Cs' of 'contact, content and conduct' from the *Safer children in a digital world* (www.dcsf.gov.uk/byronreview). A copy of the training resources can be found at ITTE (2010) *e-Safety in initial teacher training – Early years and primary phase* at www.itte. org.uk/node/335. Woollard *et al.* (2010) drew on Bryon's (2008) conceptual framework for understanding the complexity of e-safety, which is presented in the form of a grid. In short, there are four overarching aspects of e-safety that cover commercial, aggressive, sexual and values aspects, which are cross-referenced with the concepts of content, contact and conduct. See Table 19.2 from Byron (2008: 16).

The commercial aspects of e-safety include the negative impact of advertising, email spam, sponsorship and the way in which websites are used to gather personal information. Pupils need to be given the confidence to deal with these persistent and persuasive activities. The pupils must also receive clear guidance and instruction with regard to their conduct, including illegal downloading, hacking and gambling.

The aggressive elements identified by Byron (2008) include material of violent and hateful content, the contact aspect of being bullied, harassed or stalked and the conduct aspect of being the bully. Here, there are clear connections with the personal and social education curriculum. Byron made particular reference to the sexual nature of Internet activity and identified the importance of considering the impact of pornographic material, meeting strangers and grooming, and the child's conduct of making and uploading inappropriate material. With teenagers, this might be sexting, but with younger pupils it can involve sharing images through social networking sites with exploitative adults. The fourth aspect Byron identifies is values; here actions are often determined by the

Table 19.2 A framework for e-safety

	Commercial	Aggressive	Sexual	Values
Content (child as recipient)	– Adverts – Spam – Sponsorship – Personal info	– Violent/hateful content	– Pornographic or unwelcome sexual content	– Bias – Racist – Misleading info or advice
Contact (child as participant)	– Tracking – Harvesting – Personal info	– Being bullied, harassed or stalked	– Meeting strangers – Being groomed	– Self-harm – Unwelcome persuasions
Conduct (child as actor)	– Illegal downloading – Hacking – Gambling – Financial scams – Terrorism	– Bullying or harassing another	– Creating and uploading inappropriate material	– Providing misleading info/advice – Misuse of online info, e.g., plagiarism

Source: Byron, 2008: 16

individual's moral position. Activities include bias, racism, misleading advice/information, self-harm, misuse of information and plagiarism.

Bryon (2010) rightly highlights the importance of embedding the issue of child digital safety within a broader context of building resilience (for example, through the skills of critical evaluation, risk management and self monitoring), with a view to providing a 'clear understanding of the importance of risk experiences and their management for child learning and development' (Bryon, 2010: 2). The challenge is to empower children to manage risks and for pupils:

> to be empowered to keep themselves safe – this isn't just about a top-down approach. Children will be children – pushing boundaries and taking risks. At a public swimming pool we have gates, put up signs, have lifeguards and shallow ends, but we also teach children how to swim
>
> (Bryon, 2008: 2)

Teachers need to be aware of the threats and challenges to staying safe online and support the pupils' understanding and adoption of safe and responsible practices. This highlights the need for developing pupils 'digital wisdom', which encompasses responsible and informed use alongside an awareness of risks.

Task 19.3 e-Safety and teachers' responsibilities

Do you know where to go to locate relevant information on e-safety? Make a list for yourself now.

What are the most pertinent issues regarding e-safety for you as a teacher in your practice in terms of: a) your classroom pedagogy; and b) pastorally in your role as a form teacher?

e-Safety and parental responsibility

Data from organisations such as OFCOM show that more children are using the Internet to access games, television programmes and other media. This has been strengthened by the fact that many devices now come built in with a wifi connection, meaning that they can access the Internet from a variety of rooms in a house or in other locations using private or public connections. This has meant that parents have less control in being able to monitor their children when using devices. In addition, many feel that there is a lack of corporate responsibility by many of the large manufacturers of these products in supporting parents with controlling these devices. There are parental settings on all devices popular with children; however, they are not directly set to a 'safety' standard when purchased and on some devices they can be quite complicated to set.

Consequently, primary schools have a unique role in supporting parents during the time children begin exploring the online world. Compared to secondary schools, parents have more contact with their child's primary school through family events, such as summer fetes, and the fact that parents are more likely to collect their children at the end of the day from primary school. During these times, schools can support parents with issues around e-safety, help them to understand the risks, and help to create a dialogue of trust between parent and child. Traditional examples of this can be via holding e-safety sessions for parents, run by the school's ICT lead or a representative from the local police force or a Regional Broadband Consortia (RBC). Some primary schools have been more innovative and run sessions aimed at engaging parents and grandparents with children, so that they have explored the online world together and children have shown other generations of their family some of the knowledge they have in using the Internet. One example has been Epworth Primary School where they created 'digital champions' and followed this method (http://bit.ly/13ESlGw). Other schools have used the following projects to engage with parents:

- Running stalls at summer or Christmas fairs, giving out leaflets to parents. These stalls have usually been run by a local PCSO or member of staff who has received training on e-safety.
- Having pupil-led assemblies where pupils deliver presentations to parents on different aspects of technology and the Internet and provide information on how to keep children safe.
- Training parent ambassadors who can speak to other parents in school and develop an e-safety news board.
- Running transition events with local secondary schools looking at e-safety. This can be an effective way as usually these events are very well attended by parents.

Task 19.4 School and parent e-safety events

- Which of the above activities would work well in your school?
- What other activities like these could you do in your school to raise e-safety awareness?

Another important tool for schools is to develop a microsite from the school website to provide information and links to e-safety resources for parents. There is now a wealth of resources available to parents from organisations such as Mumsnet (www.mumsnet. com) and commercial providers such as Vodafone (www.vodafone.com/content/parents. html). They offer free resources in 'layman's terms' to help parents with specific queries and also to show how to put safe settings on popular sites such as YouTube. Yorkshire Humber Grid For Learning has produced a guide on how to develop an e-safety section of a website, which can support the ICT coordinator in a school to create a bespoke site to guide parents at home (www.yhgfl.net/content/download/15040/333704/file/ Creating%20an%20eSafeguarding%20web%20page.pdf).

Task 19.5 Developing an e-safety section on your school's website

- Read the Yorkshire Humber Grid for Learning e-safety information and consider how you could use this to inform your school on e-safety.
- Having read the Yorkshire Humber Grid for Learning information consider how you can develop an e-safety section for your school's website.

Summary and key points

The key to providing a successful e-safety programme in primary schools is to ensure that the focus is balanced between investigation and exploration of the Internet and digital technology with strategies to ensure that pupils have risk-aversion strategies to help them if they came across unwanted content or contact with others online. In the 2008 report, Byron talked about young children not having the 'wisdom' to know if something was real or not online and this is still something that needs to be addressed. With many children using more 'mature' sites such as Facebook, the challenge is to ensure they understand that an 'online friend' is different to a friend they make in the playground and schools need to explore these areas through PHSE or SEAL lessons, looking at the characteristics of what would make you suspicious of someone getting in contact with you via social networking.

The other key challenge is to begin creating digital citizenship where young people can create the sort of environment for use of the Internet where they can highlight inappropriate behaviour. It is often said that the main difference in the 'online' world is that people do not tell you off if you do something inappropriate, and this is again something that primary schools need to address. In conjunction with this, schools need to look at digital literacy as part of their overall speaking and listening skills. This used to be termed 'Netiquette' and follows the line that as we teach children to communicate in the real world, we should also look at this in the online world. Digital communication through social media will develop further and as pupils enter the workplace in years to come, they need guidance on what can or cannot be said to others online, whether it be in the workplace or at college or university. We need to raise awareness about online identity and digital footprints and highlight becoming responsible digital citizens.

A key task for primary schools is to empower children to become responsible in their online lives. The Internet brings so many opportunities and we do not want to make pupils become fearful when using the technologies of the future. As children grow, they need guidance and support and they need to have the mechanisms to inform adults (in school and out) about fears or concerns they have about the digital world. If primary schools can create these types of citizens of the future, then they will be part of the future generations that will prosper and help create a better Internet.

Further reading

BECTA, 'Signposts to safety: Teaching e-safety at Key Stages 1 and 2': www.lancsngfl.ac.uk/ curriculum/pshe/download/file/signposts_safety_ks1and2.pdf. Accessed on 9 February 2014.

Lucy Shipton, 'Improving e-safety in primary schools: a guidance document': www.shu.ac.uk/_ assets/pdf/improving-e-safety -in-primary.pdf

Websites

www.360safe.org.uk. This website provides a '360° Safe – School E-Safety Self Review Tool'.

www.thinkuknow.co.uk/teachers/. This website provides access to CEOP resources.

References

BBC (2010) *Staying safe with Dongle*. Available online at: www.bbc.co.uk/cbbc/topics/stay-safe. Accessed on 8 February 2014.

Byron, T. (2008) *Safer children in a digital world: The report of the Byron Review*. Nottingham: DCSF publications.

Byron, T. (2010) *Do we have safer children in a digital world?: Review of progress since the 2008 Byron Review*. Nottingham: DCSF publications.

CEOP (2007) *Think U Know*. Available online at: www.thinkuknow.co.uk. Accessed on 10 February 2014.

Childalert (2011) *How to keep children safe online*. Available online at: www.childalert.co.uk/ article.php?articles_id=206. Accessed on 11 February 2014.

Hasebrink, U., Görzig, A., Haddon, L., Kalmus, V. and Livingstone, S. (2011) *Patterns of risk and safety online; In-depth analyses from the EU Kids Online survey of 9 16-year-olds and their parents in 25 countries*. LSE, London: EU Kids Online.

Information Commissioner's Office (2012) *Report on the data protection guidance we gave schools in 2012*. Available online at: http://ico.org.uk/~/media/documents/library/Data_Protection/ Research_and_reports/report_dp_guidance_for_schools.pdf. Accessed on 12 February 2014.

ITTE (2010) *e-Safety in initial teacher training – Early years and primary phase*. Available online at: www.itte.org.uk/node/335. Accessed on 9 February 2014.

Livingstone, S. and Bober, M. (2005) *UK Children Go Online project*. Available online at: www.lse.ac.uk/collections/children-go-online. Accessed on 8 February 2014.

Livingstone, S., Kirwil, L., Ponte, C. and Staksrud, E. (2013) *EU Kids Online: In their own words: What bothers children online?* LSE, London: EU Kids Online. Available online at: www.lse.ac.uk/ media@lse/research/EUKidsOnline/EU%20Kids%20III/Reports/Intheirownwords020213.pdf. Accessed on 9 February 2014.

Microsoft (2007) *Young people safe on-line*. Available online at: www.youngpeoplesafeonline.com. Accessed on 8 February 2014.

Ofsted (2010) *The safe use of new technologies*. Manchester: Ofsted.

Ofsted (2012) *ICT in schools 2008–11*. Manchester: Ofsted.

Shipton, L. (2011) *Improving e-safety in primary schools: A guidance document*. Final Report. Sheffield: Sheffield Hallam University.

UK Council for Child Internet Safety (UKCCIS) (2009) *Click clever click safe: The first UK child internet safety strategy.* London: UKCCIS

Valcke, M., Schellens, T., Van Keer, H. and Gerarts, M. (2006) 'Primary school children's safe and unsafe use of the Internet at home and at school: An exploratory study'. *Computers in Human Behaviour*, 23(6): 2838–50.

Woollard, J., Pickford, T. and Younie, S. (2010) 'Evaluation of e-safety materials for initial teacher training; meeting the needs of primary phase trainees'. Proceedings of *The Association of Information Technology in Teacher Education (ITTE)* conference, Liverpool Hope University.

Yorkshire Humber Grid for Learning. Available online at: (www.yhgfl.net/content/download/15040/333704/file/Creating%20an%20eSafeguarding%20web%20page.pdf). Accessed on 9 February 2014.

Younie, S. and Leask, M. (2013) *Teaching with technologies: The essential guide.* Maidenhead: Open University Press.

20 ICT in the Early Years

Do young children need access to computers as much as they need to play with sand and water?

Christina Preston and Marion Scott Baker

Introduction

ICT has many applications in the Early Years but the Early Years setting may also pose more challenges for those introducing ICT than the older age groups, because of the need to change established customs and practices.

This chapter provides an introduction to the research that indicates that new recruits to teaching are often highly valued by the senior management because the expectation is that they will know more about digital technologies than existing staff, and be able to support initiatives in this field (Preston, 2004: Pachler *et al.*, 2011). For these this chapter outlines not only the ways ICT can benefit learning in the Early Years, but also the reasons why some members of staff may still be unconvinced about the value of computers and the need to integrate them into their work.

In this chapter we will explain how the lack of appropriate professional development opportunities has affected the attitudes and beliefs of many teachers. Information has also been included about why there is something to be learned from professionals who have reservations about the value of digital technologies in learning for primary children.

Objectives

At the end of this chapter you should:

- have an understanding of the educational advantages of using various technologies in Early Years settings;
- have enough knowledge to express your point of view in debates about the advantages and disadvantages of using computers with Early Years children and where the balance should be;
- be well-enough acquainted with the issues to support established members of staff who want to extend their practice in digital technologies.

A reluctant teacher's conversion: an example of changing practice in an Early Years setting

The authors of this chapter have been working together since the early 1990s in a professional organisation called the MirandaNet Fellowship[1] (free to join), where educators share experience and expertise in an e-community of practice. Christina Preston is the founder of the MirandaNet Fellowship. Marion Scott Baker is a head teacher who is now retiring.

The chapter provides a longitudinal reflection on how the role of computers in classrooms has altered over the years and how practice has changed, through tracking Marion's adoption of ICT in her classroom and school. She starts as a young teacher and a reluctant practitioner as far as computers were concerned. By 2000 Marion had become head of the Nursery and Pre-Prep departments of Cheam School (formerly Inhurst House), where she was in a position to set the direction of the department's computing strategy for 3–7 Foundation Stage and Key Stage 1 pupils. In the following sections Marion speaks in her own voice.

Support from home

Research indicates that a key factor in the successful integration of computers into the primary curriculum is not only the levels of professional development available, but also whether the teacher has her own computer at home and family to help (Preston, 2004: Davies, Preston and Sahin 2009 a/b: Pachler *et al.*, 2011). Marion's experience was that:

> Without my husband's 'deadly digits' and encouragement from my daughters I would have been permanently shut out of the digital world. My sister is also a teacher educator and researcher in this field and my mother who is 88 is managing to research and write her memoirs on her laptop. These family members have maintained my interest even though I do not find computers intuitive and would have been content to avoid them altogether from a professional point of view.
>
> Watching my family has persuaded me of the value of digital devices in terms of life skills as these tools become more pervasive. We use technology all the time at home from sharing calendars to emailing friends and family. I download films and e-books and enjoy computerised machine embroidery so have learned to program designs. In the craft context I belong to lots of online interest groups and even purchase online craft lessons. In addition I am addicted to eBay and regularly Skype family and grandchildren.
>
> I really cannot get through a day without computers in my personal life and recognize that technology is part of every pupil's everyday life. As they have become more accessible and easier to use I have seen how digital technologies can support our pedagogy rather than interfere with it and I have been persuaded that they have an important place in today's classroom.

Training issues

Computers did not figure in Marion's initial teacher training or for the next ten years. Few teachers had more than two days' training on the use of computers in classrooms in their career in the 1980s and 1990s (Preston, 2004). Marion had had none. Marion is, anyway, of the opinion that learning how to use a computer as a pedagogical tool is difficult to absorb formally. Time for learning is usually pressured and one-day courses can raise teachers' anxiety levels as they do not give time to practise and embed skills.

In addition the first software she was offered in her early career and the remoteness of the networked computer room threatened to disrupt her relationship with her pupils and the practical play-based curriculum that were central to her child-centred approach to learning. Shared learning is one element of her pedagogical approach where the children have talk-partners so that they can help and teach each other. She explains that what was offered in early computer programmes seemed divorced from important lessons, such as self-esteem and respect for others, apart from shared work around a screen.

Marion explains how her view of teaching primary children effectively requires a very practical, hands-on approach to learning that conflicted with computer use:

> In those early days when I was less confident I did not want the added complication of introducing computers that were hard to use and unreliable. This did not help with work-flow or discipline. Sharing computers meant that half our children were wasting time and available 'games' were often educationally unsound. I was particularly unenthused by discrete lessons in internet use by the ICT coordinator in the junior school who had not realized that small children would spend a whole lesson typing their names to log on. In my view the most important aspect of primary learning in those days was to learn how to learn, encompassing interpersonal skills, speaking and listening and fine and gross motor and organizational skills. I could not see how these aspects of learning could be done better on computers.

Technical problems also compounded her suspicions that computers were a distraction from learning. Despite the fact that, unlike in many schools, an ICT technician was on site all the time much went wrong and a lesson planned using technology frequently failed completely. However, significant government funding for the UK software industry during the early 2000s resulted in an international reputation for innovative packages that do more than drill and practise. Many of the most famous first titles, such as Mike Matson's Granny's Garden[2], were designed by teachers and provided a new kind of interactive learning. Marion comments on how she used these resources:

> We used the adventure game, Granny's Garden, as a bolt on activity that the children could play as a reward (and to keep them busy) if they completed their work. But I did not see these standalone packages as an essential part of their learning.

When Marion became head of the school she tried to encourage professional development in digital technologies for the staff by employing a company to teach the staff how to use the new interactive whiteboards – but the training was skills-based and the software suite provided was based on an information transmission model of learning. The sessions bore little relationship again to the pedagogical model for Early Years and KS1. The trainers did not even mention that the children might use the board to present to other children.

As an alternative to ineffective training, Marion and some of her staff joined the MirandaNet Fellowship – a free online community of practice where practitioners choose to share with other professionals. Educators share their experience in several ways, online and face-to-face, and this is important when there is neither the time nor the finance to attend formal courses.

Systemic change in practice and pedagogy

It was Marion's international exchange work that changed her views about the potential of digital technologies:

> My real awakening was when I realized the potential of the Internet for bringing learning to life. My exchanges with other countries started when I worked with an American teacher on a data collection project that broadened the children's learning in a very real way. Mainly by exchanging emails they researched topics on homes, food and Thanksgiving, fascinated by the lifestyle differences between the two countries. We ran parallel cookery classes and each class produced a cookery book for their friends across the Pond. We read to each other on cassette tapes and exchanged tapes of country dance and square dance music. We got to know each other. The excitement in learning was palpable. One incident I remember is when the children could not understand why they could not talk to their American friends on Skype in the morning: I tried to explain about time zones. The children retrieved an old and dusty globe from the cupboard and I used a torch to show them how the sun moves around the earth. I have since continued similar projects between the schools and the Podar schools in India (Kaur, Scott-Baker and Preston 2011). I would like to extend our international work because I believe in the value for the pupils.
>
> In administration there is no doubt about the difference the Internet has made to making the administration of software easier for the individual teacher who used to maintain their own library of programmes that they largely bought themselves.
>
> Our computer system is vital for my job of managing the learning and tracking our pupils. Our Learning Management System (LMS) is also essential to sharing our lesson planning, especially in literacy and maths. This is also where we collate and keep records of progress and scores. Now, as well as sending desktop-published letters and newsletters, we contact parents by email and text. In addition we have our own school app.
>
> What has also emerged from the international strategy is the enrichment of the school's pedagogical practices. Most important is our changed relationship with the children, who are using the interactive whiteboards all the time to present their work. They progress at their own pace in learning using numeracy and literacy packages: Junior Librarian[3] software allows children to borrow and return library books independently. It also takes over the tedious cataloguing of books and allows us to monitor reading; Bug Club[4] e-books enable us to encourage reluctant readers to practise reading and comprehension skills at home. Children regularly record their learning via video and 'talk tins' and these also enable the children to listen to facts that they are not yet able to read in displays and self-chosen activities. Teachers refer frequently to vast banks of relevant materials, ideas and lesson plans, using resource banks such as Twinkl[5]. These resources help us approach topic work in a really creative way by sharing hundreds of good materials that are topical, inexpensive and disposable: often made by other teachers.

The impact of new policies

What has made a significant contribution in our primary practice is the completely different style of learning that has become statutory in Early Years and Special Needs.

Research about children's development, government policy both before and after the change of UK government in 2010 has changed the nature of what teachers do, as well as the quality and presentation of personalized materials. It has been established that one third of children enter school with delay in social, language and listening and/or physical skills. For this reason, the Revised Statutory guidance[6] emphasises development of these three EYFS 'Prime Areas' in a curriculum that is based on 'Play to Learn', with much of the learning taking place in the outdoor environment. Key to this curriculum is the children being able to pursue their own interests and being given time to problem solve, facilitated and supported by the teachers, in contrast to the traditional situation where learning is being teacher led. In this context, technology plays a vital part in recording and planning next steps in the learning journey of each child's learning, but is less relevant as a teaching tool. It is used primarily in group teaching on the interactive whiteboard and also in a group social context by collaborating to problem solve on free-standing computerized tables.

With often a quarter of a lifetime's difference in learning experience compounding the differences in intelligences and learning styles, at the Foundation Stage children necessarily follow very individual curricula. We use the digital camera to observe the children's learning, recording it and understanding it in the place where each child is. We record when a child has learned something as well as what they do not yet know and use this to plot their next steps. Keeping a learning journey for each child has made the teachers' understanding of learning more explicit and more efficient. It has been easier to personalize each child's learning programme and support them make their own decisions about what they need to learn next. Children have greater ownership of their learning.

However, I have concerns about a new government policy. The Coalition has decreed that the word 'play' cannot be used any more in policy documents as children must be 'learning' at all times. The danger here is that computers could be used largely to isolate children in order to learn facts, preventing them from actively engaging in the learning processes. These processes involve learning how to learn, interacting with other children, working in groups, mastering literacy and numeracy and gaining a knowledge of the world. A child needs vocabulary, broad headings and definitions while mastering knowledge, in order to develop the ability to see the links between different areas and to be able to transfer skills learned in one place to another context. I would not have believed in the early days of computers that the ability to use technology would make transferable skills easier to learn.

Classrooms can be baffling places but the way in which we use technology helps to make the world clearer and more accessible to children who do not read, whether they are pre-readers or children with specific learning difficulties such as autism and dyspraxia. For such children digital photography enables them to anticipate transitions through visual timetables. Resources are easily found if boxes have pictures on them. Photo sequences provide instructions for toileting and issuing a library book for example. This makes pre-reading children and those with special needs more independent and more confident to negotiate their way through a demanding day.

Empowering young children

Using digital technologies, and in particular touch-screens, ensures that children without good reading and writing skills are able to interact effectively with multimodal text on the computer. They can respond to aural instructions by dragging and dropping instead of having to type words. So, for example, they can do number exercises even if they cannot write numbers very well. They can match and organize shapes without the need for good motor skills. The formation of a number becomes much more understandable on a screen when colour and animation and a spoken instruction are available to help.

Teachers also have such a bank of illustrations at their fingertips. They can immediately pull up a relevant picture from a resource bank when children are sharing their experiences, such as a trip with family, in 'show and tell'.

In addition some of our classes were well prepared for a trip to Windsor Castle by illustrations of what they should look out for, which were retrieved from the Internet. Once there, they were able to interview the soldiers following the Changing of the Guard. They tried on their bearskins, saw where the soldiers ate and slept, examined the musical instruments and saw an ariel view of the castle from the roof. Throughout the visit the teachers took videos and photos about what interested the children.

Back at school the teachers used these materials as a basis for maths, craft, writing and reading exercises that stemmed directly from the children's experience and interests. Relevant resources collected in this way are easy to store and retrieve online. Immediate, fresh and bright, they are better for learning than traditional resources, as well as being in the control of my team. We can work so much more from the experience of the children.

Our pupils are all engaged and excited by this kind of learning that they largely drive themselves. I worry about how they cope with the more desk-bound and subject-led learning post seven when they will have fewer opportunities to make their own choices, solve problems and work with others.

What is empowering for these very young children is that they can record their thoughts in so many ways, visually and in sound, that they can still be articulate even if their reading and writing are not yet very mature. They are encouraged to express thoughts and feelings in far more detail at a younger age than they could do before. The advantages for children with special needs are particularly impressive.

This is a double-edged sword, however, because there is less motivation to practise the very difficult skills of reading and writing. On the other hand children are decoding and encoding across a wider range of media and developing concepts and ideas that are way outside the realm of experience of the average child some years ago.

I am very excited about how children can now learn now. People who are successful are the ones who have transferable skills to use in context – you can always find out facts like the dates of kings and queens of England on the Internet so you do not need to learn that kind of fact anymore, so education needs to train children to see these facts in context and to have a vision of the history that lies behind them. It is more important to emphasise the broader picture – develop children who love themselves enough to be generous to others, who understand how to work co-operatively and to leave behind what they know in order to explore the new.

We need to embed these thinking skills before they are seven: making sense out of the world based on a good vocabulary, ability to classify thoughts and to model clear thinking.

What I am asking as I retire is: will reading and writing be seen as core skills in the future and what broader skills, such as teaming and tracking and fine motor skills will we lose if we do not practise reading and writing? But if methods of assessment do not change then many of the new skills we are nurturing in the early stage of primary education will be lost when children enter a more formal junior school setting. Is this what we want as a nation?

Our pupils live in a constantly changing world of colour and action and can no longer be motivated by last year's materials dragged out of the cupboard and used again. Materials need to be bright, professional and up to the minute.

There is more to do. We still have our adult-sized and vulnerable laptops in a charging cupboard, whereas I want to have them available in the classroom all the time. I would love to have touch-screen devices instead so that the children's activities are not limited by their ability to control a mouse. I would also like robust, child-friendly, digital devices that are permanently accessible. We need better training as well. Teachers try to keep up to date but lack of finance and lack of support at home puts them at a disadvantage.

Changing beliefs and attitudes

I am aware of the popular science writing of Baroness Susan Greenfield (2008 and 2011), who is concerned that games or other digital artefacts are having an impact on the way that children's brains develop. She is also worried about how much private information the government and big companies know about us. She argues convincingly that two huge new forces – technology and the rise in religious fundamentalism – are, in their different ways, combining to threaten the control of our minds and the way our society functions. Her book, *The quest for meaning in the twenty first century*, (2008), draws on the latest findings in neuroscience to show how far we are and can be in control of the development of our brains and minds. It explores the actions we need to take to safeguard our individuality and to find the fulfilment that our current unfettered materialism cannot provide. Of course we need to consider these issues, but if we do not teach children how to use digital technologies safely and fruitfully in school, who else will?

The world is a very different place now from when I first started teaching and school needs to reflect this in my opinion. We are no longer training children to be factory fodder, compliant and unheard and I no longer believe that children

---

Task 20.1 Your view – the place for ICT in the Early Years

Susan Greenfield is also expressing concerns shared by others that if children use digital technologies too much their brains will develop differently. Where do you stand on this? Do you have evidence for your point of view that you can utilise in your new school in discussions about strategy, pedagogy and resources? Use the information in this chapter to help you to express yourself about the advantages and disadvantages of using computers with primary-age children and where the balance should be.

should be trained to listen and to do as they are told. A good classroom today is not a silent one but where one where children are talking as well as listening. We make sure that they practise how to be selective, how to respect other people's points of view and how to be critical of information too. We are also asking them to present information in different ways, to be creative and to have confidence in themselves.

I do wonder, of course, how many traditional jobs will be replaced when computers are even more powerful. Without these jobs, all our pupils will need to see opportunities and to be inventive. It is frightening to think that we are educating them for jobs that we can scarcely envisage. However, it seems obvious to me that digital technologies are bound to be part of that mix.

Overcoming the barriers to change is essential for a school and for teachers themselves if pupils are to be prepared for their digital future.

Teachers who are reluctant to use digital technologies

In England, lack of adequate continuing professional development programmes (CPD) for teachers means the landscape for training provision looks ever more 'patchy' (Daly, Pachler and Pelletier 2009). In 2008, Becta, the UK government agency for computers in schools (disbanded 2010), commissioned an extensive study of the landscape of ICT and CPD in the UK from 2007–2009 (Pachler *et al.*, 2011). As a member of MirandaNet, Marion was invited to respond to the questionnaire about reluctant teachers. She was keen to do this because she had always been intrigued by the resistance of some senior management teams and individual teachers to digital technologies.

The sample was forty openly reluctant practitioners from new teachers to heads, representing both genders in the primary and secondary sector and a range of ages, specialist subjects, regions and pedagogical dispositions. They were recommended for this research by colleagues who considered them to be outstanding, high-achieving professionals despite their resistance to using computers in classrooms.

I found these teachers with reservations should not be classified as 'technophobes' or as 'professionals with limited computer skills'. They all had an email address that they checked daily and they were all able to use basic computer software and search the web efficiently. In particular, they all used computers to complete a variety of personal objectives: booking tickets, downloading music and audio books and engaging in social networking at home.

Their professional reservations, however, which were carefully considered and well articulated, covered a range of issues:

- threatening e-safety considerations;
- anger about the futility of much unused data collection coupled with security fears;
- poor quality of equipment and Internet support;
- unreliable administrative systems;
- lack of support when new systems are adopted;
- draconian and illogical filtering systems;
- lack of demonstrable pedagogical benefit;

<hr>

Task 20.2 Supporting changes of practice

One key point from the research we have quoted is that the teaching profession benefits from support from home and from new entrants to the profession. How will you be able to help established members of staff who want to extend their practice in digital technologies without making them feel that they are failures?

<hr>

- clashes between interoperable systems;
- the lack of explicit pedagogical principles that promote deep learning in educational software design;
- the lack of availability of time to experiment with new ICT tools;
- lack of appropriate formal or informal CPD;
- the sense that computers were not important for the very academic student;
- the difficulty of finding the networks of colleagues working on similar issues.

Summary and key points

Throughout, this longitudinal study points emerge about the potential for empowerment of children and independent and collaborative learning at an early age. This approach is very different from traditional styles of learning and some teachers and policymakers are suspicious of learning that is about doing rather than imbibing facts.

Governor, parent and staff debates about where they stand on this topic will be increasingly influential in each school. The views of well-informed recruits will add new insight by bringing in knowledge about the technological world beyond the classroom.

If you are a student teacher check which requirements for your course you have addressed through this chapter.

Notes

All websites in this section were accessed on 5 August 2013.

1 www.mirandanet.ac.uk
2 www.en.wikipedia.org/wiki/Granny%27s_Garden
3 www.microlib.co.uk/products/JuniorLibrarian.aspx
4 www.bugclub.co.uk/
5 www.twinkl.co.uk/
6 www.education.gov.uk

Further reading and additional resources and websites

Innovating pedagogy

Sharples, M. (2012) *Innovating pedagogy 2012*. The Open University. Available online at: www. open.ac.uk/blogs/innovating/. Accessed on 5 August 2013.
> Professor Mike Sharples has been working in the area of innovation in collaborative learning. His team explores, for example, seamless learning and rhizomatic learning.

Continuing professional development in computing

Daly, C., Pachler, N. and Pelletier, C. (2009a) *Continuing professional development in ICT for teachers: A literature review.*

Daly, C., Pachler, N. and Pelletier, C. (2009b) *Continuing professional development in ICT for teachers.*

Pachler, N., Preston, C., Cuthell, J., Allen, A. and Torres, Pinheiro (2011) *The ICT CPD landscape in England.*

The reports can be freely accessed on: www.wlecentre.ac.uk/cms/index.php?option=com_content &task=view&id=363&Itemid=87. Accessed on 5 August 2013.

These three studies cover all the information about the English provision at the time. The first report offers a literature review; the second looks at effective models; and the third report looks at what kind of CPD is available to teachers in an increasingly fragmented market.

A community sharing practice and theory

The MirandaNet Fellowship, established in 1992, is an international professional collaboration of policymakers, educators, developers and researchers.

MirandaNet case studies are a rich source of data for practitioners and for the researchers who collaborate with governments, government agencies, charities and large and small companies to understand more about the best ways of encouraging innovation in teaching and learning.

www.mirandanet.ac.uk. Accessed on 5 August 2013.

Case studies by members: www.mirandanet.ac.uk/casestudies/.

Teaching programming

Lawrence Williams, a teacher in South London, has published a case study about teaching programming. Called 'Literacy from Scratch', his project is a response to the UK government's initiative to develop computer programming skills in both the primary phase of education (pupils aged five to eleven) and the secondary phase (aged eleven to eighteen). See www.worldecitizens.net/literacy-from-scratch/. Accessed on 5 August 2013.

References

Daly, C., Pachler N. and Pelletier, C. (2009) *Continuing professional development in ICT for teachers: A literature review.* Becta. Available online at: http://eprints.ioe.ac.uk/3183/. Accessed on 23 May 2014.

Davies, N.E., Preston, C. and Sahin, I. (2009) 'Training teachers to use new technologies impacts multiple ecologies: Evidence from a national initiative'. *British Educational Research Journal (BJET)*, 40 (5 September 2009).

Greenfield, S. (2008) *The quest for meaning in the twenty first century.* Hodder and Stoughton Ltd. Available online at: www.susangreenfield.com. Accessed on 23 May 2014.

Greenfield, S. (2011) *You and me: The neuroscience of identity.* Notting Hill editions. Available online at: www.susangreenfield.com. Accessed on 23 May 2014.

Kaur, Scott Baker and Preston (2011) *Leading schools in policy and practice: The programme for continuing professional development with Podar principals.* MirandaNet Fellowship. Available online at: www.mirandanet.ac.uk/casestudies/271. Accessed on 23 May 2014.

Pachler, N., Preston, C., Cuthell, J., Allen, A. and Torres, Pinheiro (2011) *The ICT CPD landscape in England.* Becta. Available online at: www.wlecentre.ac.uk/cms/index.php?option=com_content&task=view&id=363&Itemid=87. Accessed on 23 May 2014.

Preston, C. (2004) *Learning to use ICT in classrooms: Teachers' and trainers' perspectives: An evaluation of the English NOF ICT teacher training programme (1999–2003). Summary, full evaluation report and emergent trends for teacher educators and staff-trainers.* London. Funded by the Teacher Training Agency. Available online at: www.mirandanet.ac.uk/tta. Accessed on 23 May 2014.

Index